UNDERSTANDING
ROBERT PENN WARREN

Understanding Contemporary American Literature
Matthew J. Bruccoli, Series Editor

Volumes on

Edward Albee • Nicholson Baker • John Barth • Donald Barthelme
The Beats • The Black Mountain Poets • Robert Bly
Raymond Carver • Fred Chappel • Chicano Literature
Contemporary American Drama
Contemporary American Horror Fiction
Contemporary American Literary Theory
Contemporary American Science Fiction
James Dickey • E. L. Doctorow • John Gardner • George Garrett
John Hawkes • Joseph Heller • Lillian Hellman • John Irving
Randall Jarrell • William Kennedy • Jack Kerouac
Ursula K. Le Guin • Denise Levertov • Bernard Malamud
Bobbie Ann Mason • Jill McCorkle • Carson McCullers
W. S. Merwin • Arthur Miller • Toni Morrison's Fiction
Vladimir Nabokov • Gloria Naylor • Joyce Carol Oates
Tim O'Brien • Flannery O'Connor • Cynthia Ozick
Walker Percy • Katherine Anne Porter • Reynolds Price
Thomas Pynchon • Theodore Roethke • Philip Roth
Hubert Selby, Jr. • Mary Lee Settle • Isaac Bashevis Singer
Jane Smiley • Gary Snyder • William Stafford • Anne Tyler
Kurt Vonnegut • Robert Penn Warren • James Welch
Eudora Welty • Tennessee Williams • August Wilson

UNDERSTANDING
ROBERT
PENN
WARREN

James A. Grimshaw, Jr.

University of South Carolina Press

UNIVERSITY OF SOUTH CAROLINA *BICENTENNIAL*

Published in Columbia, South Carolina, by the
University of South Carolina Press

Manufactured in the United States of America

05 04 03 02 01   5 4 3 2 1

Library of Congress Cataloging-in-Publication Data

Grimshaw, James A.
   Understanding Robert Penn Warren / James A. Grimshaw, Jr.
    p. cm. — (Understanding contemporary American literature)
   Includes bibliographical references and index.
   ISBN 1-57003-395-1 (alk. paper)
  1. Warren, Robert Penn, 1905-—Criticism and interpretation.
  2. Southern States—In literature. I. Title. II. Series.
PS3545.A748 Z677   2001
813'.52—dc21   00-011818

To Lewis and Mimi Simpson

CONTENTS

EDITOR'S PREFACE

The volumes of *Understanding Contemporary American Literature* have been planned as guides or companions for students as well as good nonacademic readers. The editor and publisher perceive a need for these volumes because much of the influential contemporary literature makes special demands. Uninitiated readers encounter difficulty in approaching works that depart from the traditional forms and techniques of prose and poetry. Literature relies on conventions, but the conventions keep evolving; new writers form their own conventions—which in time may become familiar. Put simply, *UCAL* provides instruction in how to read certain contemporary writers—identifying and explicating their material, themes, use of language, point of view, structures, symbolism, and responses to experience.

The word *understanding* in the titles was deliberately chosen. Many willing readers lack an adequate understanding of how contemporary literature works; that is, what the author is attempting to express and the means by which it is conveyed. Although the criticism and analysis in the series have been aimed at a level of general accessibility, these introductory volumes are meant to be applied in conjunction with the works they cover. They do not provide a substitute for the works and authors they introduce, but rather prepare the reader for more profitable literary experiences.

M. J. B.

ACKNOWLEDGMENTS

Grateful acknowledgment is made to the Estate of Robert Penn Warren and to the William Morris Agency for permission to reprint material from the copyrighted works of Robert Penn Warren. Special thanks are due to Rosanna Warren, Gabriel Warren, and John Burt, Warren's Literary Executor, for their many kindnesses and assistance with my several projects dealing with the writing of Robert Penn Warren. Jill Krementz graciously provided her marvelous photo of Warren. Dr. Patricia C. Willis, Curator, Yale Collection of American Literature, and her staff at the Beinecke Rare Book and Manuscript Library have provided efficient, courteous support over the years. Part of this project was funded by a Texas A&M University–Commerce Faculty Organized Research Grant. William Bedford Clark and James A. Perkins were kind to critique a portion of a much earlier version of the manuscript. Professor Matthew J. Bruccoli deserves special recognition for his patience and guidance on many endeavors over the years. My thanks also to Chris Copeland, Editor, University of South Carolina Press, for immense help in seeing this book through the process. And to my wife who has been supportive of all my work I say, once again, thank you.

UNDERSTANDING
ROBERT PENN WARREN

CHAPTER ONE

Understanding
Robert Penn Warren

The end of man is to know.
All the King's Men (1946)

Robert Penn Warren (1905–1989) earned every major literary award that this country bestows on its authors, published in every major literary genre, and in collaboration with his friend and colleague, Cleanth Brooks, helped change the way literature was taught in this country before mid-century. In his sixty-eight years of productivity, Warren wrote ten novels, sixteen short stories, seventeen volumes of poetry, seven plays and television dramas, five textbooks, eight books of nonfiction, two children's books, and more than one hundred essays. The underlying concern in all his creative work may be summed up in one word: love. Using its broad spectrum of meanings from lust to unconditional divine love and observing its dominance in social relations, Warren explored the influence people with power or position impose on others. He asserted a connection between love and knowledge, one that is perhaps best articulated in his long narrative poem, *Audubon: A Vision* (1969): "What is love? / One name for it is knowledge."[1] The relation between love and knowledge is evident in Warren's exploration of two of his major themes: the necessity of gaining self-knowledge and the relationship of humanity to the past. Those issues and others, set in historical contexts, developed from his background and from his intellectual curiosity, his need to know.

Warren was born 24 April 1905 in Guthrie, Kentucky, just across the state line from Tennessee. When he was six years old,

UNDERSTANDING ROBERT PENN WARREN

Warren made friends with Kent Greenfield, who was seven years Warren's senior and who later pitched for the New York Giants. From that lasting friendship emerged poems such as "Pondy Woods" and "American Portrait: Old Style" as well as a story "Goodwood Comes Back." He also spent some of his summers around Cerulean Springs with his grandfather, Gabriel Thomas Penn, who had fought in the Civil War as a captain and who would tell him stories about the War, which were recounted nostalgically in the poem "Court-martial." From those accounts, young Robert Penn's romantic view of war was changed to a realistic view that allowed no room for glamor nor for the old lie, "*dulce et decorum est pro patria mori*" ("it is sweet and honorable to die for one's country"). Warren's father, Robert Franklin Warren, worked at the bank in Guthrie and had published some poetry, which Warren discovered in a book, *The Poets of America,* in the family library. But after he mentioned those poems to his father, Robert Franklin hid the book and never mentioned it again. Nonetheless, those early influences led the young Robert Penn Warren to write his first poem, "Prophecy," for *The Mess Kit: (Food for Thought),* a Citizens' Military Training Camp publication at Camp Knox, Kentucky, in 1922. However, even earlier, in 1921, at Clarksville, a town just across the border in Tennessee, Warren had published a vignette titled "Munk," the senior play titled "Dr. Good English and His Patient," and other short pieces in the Clarksville High School literary magazine, *The Purple and Gold.*

Another influential event in his life was the loss of his left eye. One evening in 1921, he and his younger brother, William Thomas, were outside in their yard. Robert Penn was lying on his back behind a hedge looking up "in perfect silence at the stars," probably thinking about his future at the United State Naval Academy to which he had been accepted. Not knowing where his brother was, Thomas hurled a piece of coal over the hedge. The coal hit Robert Penn's eye, an injury that later resulted in his having a glass eye. Because of this eye injury, he was disqualified from his appointment to Annapolis and instead attended Vanderbilt University just down the road in Nashville.

At Vanderbilt, Warren entered as a chemistry major but was soon converted to an English major as a result of his experience in John Crowe Ransom's freshman composition class, his friendship with Allen Tate, and his joining the Fugitives, a group of people of diverse fields but with shared interests in good food, good conversation, and good literature. A precocious youth with much energy, Warren was writing poetry under the influence of the seventeenth-century metaphysical poets, of Thomas Hardy, and of the modernists Eliot, Pound, and Yeats. His structure was based on traditional verse forms, in metered and rhyming lines, and his subjects were primarily matters of the heart.

A particular matter of the heart was Warren's unsuccessful love affair with Chink Nichol, who may have been, at least in part, the cause of the depression that led to his attempted suicide in 1924. Discovered in time by a friend, Charlie Moss, he was revived and received a great deal of moral and emotional support from friends and family.[2] Notwithstanding that one egregious mistake, Warren's pursuit in life seemed set. His love of history is evident throughout his writing, and he had been introduced early to Thomas Buckle's *History of Civilization* and to the work of other historians. What geography was to Buckle's writing, history was to Warren's writing. Warren drew extensively from history, especially in his fiction.

The original Fugitive group members included John Crowe Ransom, Donald Davidson, Allen Tate, Alec Stevenson, Stanley Johnson, Walter Clyde Curry, and Sidney Hirsch. Later others joined, expanding the group to include Merrill Moore, James M. Frank (Hirsch's brother-in-law), Willaim Yandell Elliott, Jesse Wills and Ridley Wills (cousins), William Frierson, Robert Penn Warren, Andrew Lytle (not formally elected), Alfred Starr, and Laura Riding.[3] Their meetings were often held in the home of James Frank, but in-between meetings in Ransom's or Curry's office or elsewhere were not uncommon. Not sponsored by Vanderbilt University and thus unfettered by institutional restrictions, the group provided for then undergraduate Warren a safe haven for independent thought and unencumbered creativity. Their little magazine, *The Fugitive,* published twenty-three of Warren's poems in its three-and-one-half years of existence. Only one of those early poems, "To a Face in the Crowd," was republished in later volumes of Warren's poetry until John Burt edited *The Collected Poems of Robert Penn Warren* (1998). That poem serves as the last poem in *Thirty-Six Poems* and in each of Warren's four volumes of selected poems, and it seems to carry a special significance for Warren. The fact that it first appeared in 1925, the year after his eye accident, and that it is addressed to "Brother, my brother" might lead to the conjecture that it was written as a way of forgiving Thomas. The poem, however, suggests the hard life that each of them faces.

After Vanderbilt, Warren went to the University of California at Berkeley for his master's degree and then to Yale University to begin his doctoral program in 1927. He interrupted his graduate work at Yale to study as a Rhodes Scholar at New College, Oxford University, where he received his B.Litt. in 1930. In California he

UNDERSTANDING ROBERT PENN WARREN

met Emma Cinina Brescia, and they were secretly married before he graduated from Oxford. During this five-year period between Nashville and Oxford, Warren was writing some nonfiction, but mostly poetry. His poems were appearing in publications such as *Poetry, New Republic,* and *Saturday Review of Literature.* Five days after the stock market crash in 1929, Warren's biography of John Brown was published, and the following year his controversial essay "The Briar Patch" appeared in *I'll Take My Stand: The South and the Agrarian Tradition.* His first short story, "Prime Leaf," which was a forerunner of his first published novel, *Night Rider* (1939), was included in the anthology *American Caravan IV.*

Newly married, a Rhodes scholar, and a published author, Robert Penn Warren began his teaching career at Southwestern College in Memphis, Tennessee, before moving to Vanderbilt for three years, and then to Louisiana State University in 1934. In Baton Rouge his writing career took a turn that would influence his work for the rest of his life. Three events stand out: his teaching Shakespeare, an interest that manifests itself in his fiction, drama, and poetry; his joining up with Cleanth Brooks, whom he had met in 1924 at Vanderbilt, and their subsequent work as editors of *The Southern Review* (1935–1942) and authors of *An Approach to Literature* (1936), *Understanding Poetry* (1938), and three other textbooks; and his starting a play, *Proud Flesh,* that became his best-known, most widely acclaimed novel, *All the King's Men.*

By 1940 Warren's versatility as a writer was apparent. His concern with human relationships and power dynamics, set in the historical context of the South, predominated his early fiction. These issues are central in *Night Rider,* a novel set in the late nineteenth century during the tobacco wars in Kentucky, and in *At Heaven's*

Gate (1943), a novel that has finance and land speculation as the main catalysts for power grabbers. Although he denied all labels applied to his writing, he was definitely concerned with moral philosophy, especially the concepts of hope, love, and endurance. In those scenes in which hope gives way to despair or in which endurance yields to instant gratification, love usually abides; if not love, then the realization of love lost affects his characters profoundly. His first volume of poems, *Thirty-Six Poems* (1935), followed by *Eleven Poems on the Same Theme* (1942) and *Selected Poems: 1923–1943* (1944), constitute his early period during which he focused on traditional forms and themes.

Over a dispute regarding *The Southern Review* and his salary, Warren left Louisiana State University[4] and joined Joseph Warren Beach's Department of English at the University of Minnesota in 1942. In Minnesota, Warren wrote book reviews for the *Chicago Sun* for "whiskey money," mixed and mingled with well-established faculty members and other up-and-coming young writers of the time, taught classes of 150 students, and continued to write fiction, criticism, and textbooks. From 1944 to 1945, he held the chair of poetry at the Library of Congress, the second occupant of that newly established position that became in 1986 the U.S. poet laureate position to which Warren was the first appointee. However, from 1944 to 1953, Warren wrote no poetry. Marital problems, the move from Baton Rouge, and too many other writing commitments are three possible reasons for this ten-year hiatus. *Selected Poems: 1923–1943*, which includes "The Ballad of Billie Potts," was his last volume from the early period. *Brother to Dragons: A Tale of Verse and Voices* heralded his return to poetry in 1953. He also stopped writing short stories after his collection, *The Circus in the Attic and*

Other Stories, appeared in 1947. As he explained in an interview in 1969: "I discovered that the overlap between the short story and the poem was very hard for me. And once this sense of using such material [of fiction] for poems became clear, I said, 'I don't want to write another short story.'"[5] More important as far as his literary reputation was concerned, *All the King's Men* was published in 1946, received the Pulitzer Prize in 1947, and was made into an Academy Award–winning motion picture in 1949. The novel was a tour de force dealing with a southern politician, Willie Stark, who resembled Huey Long, and a reporter, Jack Burden, who becomes the governor's hatchet man. The reporter narrates the stories—Stark's and his own. This work demonstrated Warren's talent as a storyteller and as a master of the English language. As productive as he was during this period, his activity served as merely a harbinger of his increased output in the next three decades.

Through the encouragement of Brooks, who had left LSU to join the Yale University faculty in 1947, Warren moved to New Haven in 1950 and became professor of playwriting in 1951, the year of his divorce from Cinina. During that time the New Criticism, which "is associated less with a body of theoretical doctrine about the nature of language and poetry than with a method of critical exegesis and explication," was in full swing and yet already under siege. In the 1930s the New Criticism (a label taken from John Crowe Ransom's book *The New Criticism*) was a critical approach that required the reader to focus objectively on the literary elements of the work of art. Among its practitioners were R. P. Blackmur, Brooks, Ransom, Tate, and Warren. Their emphasis was on the text itself, not the biography of the author or the history of the times. Brooks and Warren demonstrated this approach in *Understanding Poetry.* As a result of the success of their textbooks, they were described by one of their Yale colleagues as the "Castor and Pollux of the New Criticism."[6]

In 1952 Warren married the writer Eleanor Clark and continued to travel abroad as he had done in the past. Critics have speculated that with this second marriage Warren found the emotional peace necessary to begin writing poetry again. They had two children, Rosanna and Gabriel, who are the subjects of several of his poems. Warren took a break from teaching at Yale between 1956 and 1962, but rejoined the faculty in the Department of English. By then his volume of poems, *Promises: Poems, 1954–1956,* had received the Pulitzer Prize, making him the only recipient of that prize to win for both fiction and poetry. His fifth novel, *Band of Angels* (1955), was not given a favorable critical reception, and the movie based on that book received mixed reviews. His play, *All the King's Men,* which was based on his famous novel of the same name, was produced off-Broadway in 1959.

With the publication of *Incarnations: Poems, 1966–1968* (1968), critics such as Harold Bloom praised Warren's poetry as exciting, venturesome, and experimental. Warren wrote his last two novels in the 1970s—*Meet Me in the Green Glen* (1971) and *A Place to Come To* (1977)—and concentrated on poetry and to a lesser degree on criticism. His textbooks were in their third and fourth editions, and an American literature anthology (1973), edited with Cleanth Brooks and R. W. B. Lewis, contains brilliant introductory essays that are still required reading in some graduate programs. Warren's work on those textbooks since 1936, his keen interest in literature, his breadth and depth of reading, and his openness in discussing the qualities of literature have prompted scholars to refer to him as one of the most engaging critics of the twentieth century. Some of his criticism was collected first in *Selected Essays* (1958) and later in *New and Selected Essays* (1989), the year of Warren's death.

Retirement from Yale in 1973 provided Warren more time for his writing and travels, time spent reconsidering some of his poetry. He also continued to grapple with dramatization of the Cass Mastern story, from chapter 4 in *All the King's Men*, a story-within-the-story about power, love, and betrayal. The stage version, *Listen to the Mockingbird*, remained unpublished and, like his other plays, was in a continuous state of revision. It premiered 7 October 1998 at Texas A&M University-Commerce.

In 1974 he delivered the Jefferson Lecture in the Humanities, which was subsequently published as *Democracy and Poetry*. In it he articulated his perspective on literature and society on an individual level: "What poetry most significantly celebrates is the capacity of man to face the deep, dark inwardness of his nature and his fate."[7] Warren's concern with human self-knowledge is addressed in *Ballad of a Sweet Dream of Peace: A Charade for Easter* (1975), a drama adapted from the poem sequence in *Promises*.

Warren succumbed to cancer on 15 September 1989 and was buried in Stratton, Vermont, near his summer home in West Wardsboro, Vermont.

While each individual piece of Warren's canon stands by itself, it also connects with his other writing that preceded or was contemporary to the work at hand. Knowing the interrelatedness of Warren's work gives reading his texts an added dimension of complexity without intimidating the reader. His fiction represents the most popular genre in which he wrote, but he considered poetry the heart of his writing. However, based on the amount of time he spent revising his plays, one might surmise that drama was a dream deferred for him. And the nonfiction and criticism that he continued to write throughout his career serve as underpinnings to the major literary genres. As Cleanth Brooks notes, "The poetry, the fiction, and even the critical essays of Robert Penn Warren form a highly unified and consistent body of work."[8]

Thematically, Warren's works deal with attempts to understand the past, with efforts to grasp *a* truth if not *the* truth, with quests to gain self-knowledge, with acceptance of responsibility, with redemption, and with the virtues of hope, love, and endurance. Looking to Dante, Shakespeare, Hardy, Conrad, Dostoyevsky, Coleridge, Eliot, Faulkner, among many other writers, one finds the literary influences on Warren's creative writing. Warren read vociferously in other disciplines, including psychology, history, political science, sociology, and philosophy. Consequently, each of the thematic tracks contains remnants, adaptations, and interpretations of the concepts that he assimilated from these disciplines through his extensive reading.

Following Shakespeare's lead in using history as the backdrop for human drama, Warren demonstrates his deep concern with the past by drawing heavily on historical events in the South, such as the tobacco wars, finance and land speculation, political power and intrigue, the Civil War, slavery, miscegenation, exploitation, government intervention, prejudice, education, and high society. In each of his ten novels, the protagonists are confronted with a moral dilemma and must seek the truth that is weighted by a past event. Ultimately, the characters gain knowledge through their experience. Wrapped in a well-told story with three-dimensional characters, the novels provide a stage on which readers can live through the events vicariously, enjoy their catharsis, and feel informed as well as entertained at the end. Warren's adroit use of language enables him to create a credible setting and to establish in convincing fashion the characters' emotional states.

Each protagonist is involved with a journey, a quest. Munn in *Night Rider* seeks justice for the tobacco growers who join the Association of Growers of Dark Fired Tobacco from Kentucky and Tennessee. Murdock in *At Heaven's Gate* fulfills his quest for financial gain and brings along with him Calhoun, a young idealist seeking truth. Stark's journey in *All the King's Men* is a political one as he works his way to the Capitol, while Burden's journey is one of maturation. Beaumont in *World Enough and Time* travels far for revenge. Starr in *Band of Angels* tries to escape her past only to confront it in the end. Jasper Harrick and Isaac Sumpter in *The Cave* descend into the earth and find something they were not necessarily seeking. They were seeking fame and fortune but discover the horror of the inner self. Old Jack Harrick's journey is out of his past. Rosenzweig in *Wilderness* crosses an ocean to win his freedom from self-imposed bondage. Tolliver in *Flood* returns to his home in Tennessee before the town is lost forever in the name of progress. Murray Guilfort and Cassie Spottwood in *Meet Me in the Green Glen* must deal with how their lives are affected by Angelo Passetto, a foreigner and ex-con. Jed Tewksbury in *A Place to Come To* travels internationally to gain recognition and learning. As a result of their experiences all of Warren's characters have an opportunity to gain self-knowledge, to learn a version of the truth, and to deal with their futures or else confront death.

Their journeys, moreover, are not without obstacles, some of which are self-imposed, while others are imposed by forces outside the self. Humanity must deal with original sin that "stands like an old horse cold in the pasture" (70) as Warren describes it in his poem "Original Sin: A Short Story," or, in Stark's words from *All the King's Men*, "Man is conceived in sin and born in corruption and he passeth from the stink of the didie to the stench of the shroud."[9] In an article, "Knowledge and the Image of Man," Warren made the following comments in connection with original sin and knowledge: "Man eats of the fruit of the Tree of Knowledge, and falls. But if he takes another bite, he may get at least a sort of redemption."[10] As if original sin were not itself a sufficient obstacle, other barriers, perhaps offsprings of original sin, bar the protagonists' way. Social institutions and cultural heritage are two such barriers. The political arenas in *All the King's Men* and *World Enough and Time* deal most explicitly with Machiavellian power plays and bring into focus the metaphor that one cannot make an omelet without breaking eggs— that is, one must be willing to use distasteful or even destructive means in order to achieve more considerable ends. And each character has his or her tragic flaw, the two strongest of which seem to be hubris and wrath. Warren draws on Aristotle's concept of the"golden mean,"which supports moderation in all things, since too little of a virtue can be a vice, just as too much of a virtue can also be a vice. Warren presents to us characters like Jack Burden, who errs on the side of showing too little virtue. Like Hamlet, Jack fails to act and displays too little courage as a younger man.

Classical allusions abound in Warren's writing. Although readers can enjoy a work without recognizing these references, knowledge of classical allusions enhances the reader's understanding of the story or poem and deepens one's admiration for Warren's broad base of knowledge. Recognizing, for example, the reference to Cicero's *De Senectute* (*Concerning Old Age*) in *Night Rider* creates a deeper appreciation of the contrasting roles of Willie Proudfit and Percy Munn.[11] Likewise, the translated quotation from Virgil's *Aeneid* (1.402–5) in *All the King's Men* provides insights into the young Cass Mastern's character upon his first meeting Annabelle Trice:

> She turned away, and as she turned, her neck
> Glowed to a rose-flesh, her crown of ambrosial hair
>   breathed out
> A heavenly fragrance, her robe flowed down, down to
>   her feet,
> And in gait she was all a goddess.
>
>   (165)

Warren's poetry is replete with classical allusions as well. Poems such as "Two Pieces after Suetonius," "Myth on Mediterranean Beach: Aphrodite as Logos," and "Platonic Drowse" announce classical connections in their titles. The reward of understanding these allusions is the discovery of more complex meanings and a more intense sense of the language in Warren's works.

Richness of language in Warren's writing provokes mixed responses from reviewers. Some have considered his writing overdone, labeling his fiction "purple prose," while others have praised his stories as the prose of a master. "The language does all the work," claimed Henry Rago in his review of *All the King's Men*. Randall Jarrell added a further description of Warren's language in his review of *Brother to Dragons* for the *New York Times Book Review*: "Warren's florid, massive, rather oratorical rhetoric, with its cold surprises, its accustomed accomplished continuations, its conscious echoes of Milton and Shakespeare, its unconscious echoes of Eliot and Arnold and Warren, is sometimes miraculous, often effective, and sometimes too noticeable to bear." In the *Saturday Review* John W. Aldridge suggested that *Meet Me in the Green Glen* shows that "the rhetorical fattiness that has always been characteristic of Warren's fiction has been replaced by a hard texture of language very like his poetry."[12] Warren's command of narrative in writing the biography *John Brown: The Making of a Martyr* reveals that even in his early years he understood the relationship of language to meaning. Warren emphasizes the "knowledge of form" with "the form [as] a vision of experience, but of experience fulfilled and redeemed in knowledge," from which man gains an image of himself.[13] Two examples, one from his fiction and the other from his poetry, illustrate this point. Early in chapter 1 of *All the King's Men*, Jack Burden, the upwardly mobile idealist, describes Stark's facial expression when Stark realizes he has been politically duped. Jack uses the "yellow envelope of the telegram" as a metaphor to describe Stark's reaction. Burden's lengthy paragraph concludes with the profound sentiment that "the end of man is to know" (9). In addition to allowing insight into Burden's character and Stark's character, the content, the language, and the form of that sentence provide an overall statement for the story. Furthermore, in his last published poem "John's Birches," Warren exhibits his supreme awareness of the close connection between form and meaning. Warren adeptly manipulates a controlled, but not strictly metered form in his reflection on life and one's "place in the great Chart of Being." He makes use of two nine-line stanzas (rhyming a-b-c-a-b-c-c-d-d) and one ten-line stanza (rhyming a-b-c-a-b-c-d-d-e-e) to express his theme of a return to nature and to humanity (623–24). In this reflection "is the discovery of love, and law" that Warren recounts in "Knowledge and the Image of Man" (58).

Another of Warren's primary themes is time. Warren expresses a Bergsonian concept of time, which centers on the idea of "concrete duration" and the specific feeling of duration that man's consciousness realizes when it returns to its natural attitude, away from the abstract time used in mathematics, physics, and language. Warren's fictional characters and his poetic personae must live according to the Bergsonian conception of psychological time, as opposed to mechanically measured time. Intuition was for Bergson superior to the scientific intellect.[14] Notwithstanding the line "Time is a dream" (136) in the poem "Ballad of a Sweet Dream of Peace," the fact that time exists is not the philosophical question that Warren raises. Instead, Warren suggests that time does exist and that it is the responsibility of those who pass through it to use it wisely, learning from the past and leaving for following generations the lessons gained from time. The past is very much part of the present and a key to the future as Jack Burden, a student of history and, therefore, of time, realizes toward the end of *All the King's Men* and as Jed Tewksbury discovers in *A Place to Come To*.

The interrelatedness of time is a major theme in Warren's poetry as well. His poetry may be separated into three periods: the early period, 1922–1944, the middle period, 1953–1966, and the late period, 1966–1985. Warren's early poetry was heavily influenced by a number of sources, including his teacher at Vanderbilt John Crowe Ransom, his friend Allen Tate, and other poets such as Samuel Taylor Coleridge, Thomas Hardy, T. S. Eliot, whose long narrative poem *The Waste Land* Warren is said to have memorized and recited at the slightest provocation in the late 1920s and early 1930s. Harold Bloom notes that "From the start, Warren's characteristic mode had been the dramatic lyric; but after the poet turned sixty he internalized drama, in a great contest with time, with cultural and family history, and above all, with himself,"[15] by shucking Eliot's pervasive influence. The transition might be seen as one from modernism to postmodernism. Postmodern is a term used as early as 1951 by Black Mountain poet Charles Olson. Postmodernism is a cultural movement associated with the historical period following World War II that was marked by a shift in literary style and philosophical orientation. In *Postmodern American Poetry* Paul Hoover offers a tentative definition of postmodernism as "an experimental approach in composition, as well as a worldview that sets itself apart from mainstream culture and the narcissism, sentimentality, and self-expressiveness of its life in writing."[16]

In the 1920s and 1930s T. S. Eliot's poetry and criticism reflected the remarkable change that was occurring in English literature and was also affecting American literature. One tenet that Warren was able to discover in Eliot and to assimilate into his own poetry is the ability to see reality and deal with it honestly and with conviction in his poetry. A brief summary of four essays by Warren on poetics helps to reveal his opinions about what makes good poetry. These four essays—"Pure and Impure Poetry" (1942), "A Poem of Pure Imagination: An Experiment in Reading" (1946), *A Plea in Mitigation: Modern Poetry and the End of an Era* (1966), and *Democracy and Poetry* (1974)—span from 1942 to 1974. Over those thirty-two years, Warren developed flexibility in his aesthetic opinions.

In "Pure and Impure Poetry" Warren argues that impure poetry represents the desirable qualities of poetry because it includes what various theories of pure poetry espoused by Sir Philip Sidney, Ben Jonson, John Dryden, Percy Shelley, and Edgar Allan Poe, among others, exclude:

1. ideas truths, generalizations, "meaning"
2. precise, complicated, "intellectual" images
3. unbeautiful, disagreeable, or neutral materials
4. situation, narrative, logical transition
5. realistic details, exact descriptions, realism in general
6. shifts in tone or mood
7. irony
8. metrical variation, dramatic adaptations of rhythm, cacophony, etc.
9. meter itself
10. subjective and personal elements

The pure poem, on the other hand, "tries to be pure by excluding, more or less rigidly, certain elements which might qualify or contradict its original impulse. In other words, the pure poems want to be, and desperately, all of a piece. . . . There is not one doctrine of 'pure poetry'—not one definition of what constitutes impurity in poems—but many."[17] Warren finds a common denominator among theories of purity that "seems to be the belief that poetry is an essence that is to be located at some particular place in a poem, or in some particular element" (20). But for Warren in 1942, anything in the human experience was fair game for poetry, which in structure involves tensions at many levels. "A poem, to be good," he asserts, "must earn itself" and must involve the reader (24–25). Warren squares off against other critics' theories of poetry because the elements of ideas, truths, generalizations, and meaning are, if handled properly, intrinsic parts of the poetic experience, even though some will contend that they contaminate and make a poem impure.

Using Warren's list of ten elements missing in pure poetry, one can more easily see how his poetry of the middle and late years takes on the aspects of impure poetry. An example of a pure poem is his poem "The Garden" (59), which appeared in the October 1935 *Poetry*. It is a traditionally structured poem of four eight-line stanzas in octameter rhythm and a couplet rhyme scheme, and displays a wit and intellectual tone reminiscent of the seventeenth-century metaphysical poets such as Andrew Marvell. The epigraph, "On prospect of a fine day in early autumn," sets the scene described in stanza 1 as that gentle transition in nature from summer to fall. The persona gives the laurels to nature whose beauty bests the sculptors' "marbles" present in many gardens but absent in this particular one. The gardener, the lovers, and others who betook of "The grace of this green empery" are now gone. Perhaps the use of the word empery, with its archaic meaning of the territory of an absolute ruler, enhances that sense of days past. Only the jays and the cardinals are now left to lay claim to "the ruined state"—that is, the change of seasons that makes the gardener put away his tools and the lovers retreat to a more suitable place. The fourth stanza shifts its focus from the gardener, who ate a peach in the garden to allay his thirst, and from the lovers, who kissed there, to the one who sought peace.

For him, poised between "summer's lusts and winter's harms," linger the thoughts ("precincts") of deep religious significance ("sacrament") that can give meaning to those sensual gratifications of appetite and love, here described as "innocence." Perhaps, then, in the last stanza the persona describes a reenactment of the eating of the fruit and the loss of innocence in the Garden of Eden. Somehow he must reconcile the act of original sin in order to establish the peace and redemption that he seeks. The poem might qualify as a pure poem, or very close to it, by striving to be "all of a piece" (15), to invoke Warren's words to describe a pure poem.

In the poetry from Warren's middle period, readers will find more formal impurities in his poems—the beginning of a break with his earlier influences—but still the same thematic concerns about self, original sin, knowledge, endurance, hope, and love. The poem version of "Ballad of a Sweet Dream of Peace" published in *Promises: Poems, 1954–1956* is for Warren a radical shift in his use of poetic elements as he creates a surreal scene. The persona's need for peace, self-knowledge, and redemption in order to reconcile himself with original sin—an uncertain attempt at reconciliation at best—is imbued with religious significance. The poems of this period take on other impure elements, such as a pattern of precise, complicated, intellectual images, like those found in "Fatal Interview: Penthesilea and Achilles" (1958). Drawing from Greek mythology unbeautified and even disagreeable material, Warren's narrator muses about the hero's flaws of sloth and vanity.

Much of the poetry in Warren's middle period flows from his idea of the poem as pure imagination. During this period he produced one of the best pieces of criticism on Coleridge's *The Rime of the Ancient Mariner*. In "A Poem of Pure Imagination" Warren demonstrates his astute critical skills and insights into imaginary literature. Moreover, it provides further understanding of Warren's development as a poet. Warren's purpose, he succinctly states, "is to establish that *The Ancient Mariner* does embody a statement, and to define the nature of that statement, the theme, as nearly as I can" (337–38). In other words, Warren attempts to refute the contention that Coleridge's poem is a pure poem, one that should not mean, but be. In addition to those two goals, Warren tries to show that the statement the poem makes is consistent with Coleridge's theological and philosophical views. The theory of the "imagination" for Coleridge, and for Warren as well, "was primarily the indication of a particular attitude to life and reality" (341). That Warren bases his refutation of earlier critics on his close reading of Coleridge's own prose works is a sound technique to use in interpreting and understanding Warren's own works.

Acknowledging that a poem may have different meanings when viewed from different perspectives, Warren distinguishes two basic themes in *The Rime of the Ancient Mariner*. The primary theme he defines as "the issue of the fable" (348), which is a "story of crime and punishment and repentance and reconciliation" (385). He labels it "the theme of sacramental vision, or the theme of the 'One Life'" (348). The secondary theme he calls "the theme of the imagination." In his analysis Warren examines the qualities of a symbol, which for Coleridge combined "the poet's heart and intellect" (352). The purpose here, however, is not to discuss Coleridge's powerful poem but to offer Warren's essay as yet another way to understand Warren's work. In *The Imaginary Library* Alvin Kernan perhaps is implying conceptually that Warren's critical texts as well as his poetry and fiction represent an effort to address the loss of

pure imagination in American culture at a time in which contemporary writers and critics were unable to maintain a literary vision for
a society that had come to deny their values and methods.[18] In terms
of argumentative discourse, "A Poem of Pure Imagination" is exemplary and the technique and the issues addressed are instructive.
Critics of Warren's poetry, such as Victor Strandberg, Randolph
Runyan, and Calvin Bedient, appear to have benefited from Warren's models.

Twenty years after the publication of "A Poem of Pure Imagination," at the start of Warren's later period in poetry, he delivered
the 1966 Eugenia Dorothy Blount Lamar Lecture at Wesleyan College in Macon, Georgia. In his lecture, titled *A Plea in Mitigation*,
he comments on the cultural transition from modernism to a new
era. Two years later *Incarnations: Poems, 1966–1968* was published, a volume that announced to the reading public a dramatic
change, at the age of sixty-three, in his poetry. The interrelation of
form and meaning is still prevalent, but his form is freer and his language is unfettered by conventional prohibitions. How perceptive
his opening remarks were at that lecture when he noted the
approaching end of modernism. He admitted that he was not yet certain what would take its place. "Only the new language," he contended, "can let us know the nature of the experience potential in the
new world around us—and know the nature of ourselves."[19] In Warren's fiction and poetry, however, knowledge of the past is a requisite to an understanding of the present and a clear-sighted
anticipation of the future. He began experimenting with his poetry,
in part because he was continuously aware that his identity was
shifting as were the times. Harold Bloom and R. W. B. Lewis
recorded strong praise for Warren's poetic shift in his late period,

especially for *Incarnations*. In a 3 November 1966 letter to Warren, Cleanth Brooks responded enthusiastically to the six-poem sequence "Ile de Port Cros" in *Incarnations*: "what really bowls me over is the impact of the whole group taken as one beautifully interlaced and very nice, massive long poem."[20]

To see the change in Warren's poetry, one might contrast the fourth poem from *Incarnations,* "Riddle in the Garden" (225–26), with the 1935 poem "The Garden," which is discussed above. In the postmodern era, critics typically refer to the poet rather than the persona or narrator because poetry has become more explicitly autobiographical, even confessional, as demonstrated in the work of poets from this period, such as Sylvia Plath, Theodore Roethke, and Robert Lowell. Warren opens "Riddle in the Garden" with a declaration and observation: "My mind is intact, but the shapes / of the world change." His focus then turns on an overripe peach lying on the ground, rotting, divulging its secrets and showing evidence of another fall in the garden. The poet tells his readers "it / Loves God" and warns them with the invocation of the second-person referent "you" not to violate the "Gray bulge of fruit-skin of blister." Pain will follow. "You" are part of the world, and the poet concludes, "The world means only itself." This garden seems similar to one described in "The Garden" since both are seen in a ruined state, but the perspective has indeed changed. It is less romantic, more naturalistic in that the world is indifferent to the poet and if someone touches the decaying fruit he or she will be burned. But the sacraments are still represented in the confession the peach makes, its unction as it dies, and its proclaimed love of God even in suffering. In a following poetic sequence, "The Leaf," garden imagery is again prevalent and contributes to the poet's realization that "Destiny is what you experience." As he commented later in his 1974 Jefferson lecture, the past, the durable past, was man's redemption from death and his redemption into the fulfilled self. He has heard his secular father call to him, but could it also be his divine father who is calling?

The later poems included in *Incarnations* (the sequence "Internal Injuries," "Driver, Driver," "The World Is a Parable") are not strictly metered and include more unrhymed lines. They are constructed in four five-line stanzas with a one-line conclusion, thus giving at first glance the appearance of a more traditional pattern but freeing itself from convention within the poem itself. The volume on the whole is more of a continuous poem in two parts, a structure that became more prevalent in Warren's late poetry and that is explicitly acknowledged in the title of another volume, *Or Else: Poem/Poems, 1968–1974*.

In *A Plea in Mitigation* Warren asserts that "Every age, as it produces its own poetry, needs to produce its own type of criticism" (12). The relationship between poetry, criticism, and society became his next focus. The articulation of anticipated changes in poetic expression that Warren discusses in *A Plea in Mitigation* found broader expression in the 1974 Thomas Jefferson Lecture in the Humanities, titled *Democracy and Poetry*. Warren suggests that the literary imagination is linked to society in a triangular fashion connecting democracy, poetry, and selfhood. Warren's "meditations," as he refers to them, are two: "America and the Diminished Self" and "Poetry and Selfhood." In the first lecture he reviews "our 'poetry' [meaning the arts in general] here as a criticism—often a corrosive criticism—of our actual achievements over the years in democracy" (3). His central point is that "a developing and fundamental theme of our

writers" has historically been "the decay of the concept of self."
In the second lecture he addresses "the decay of the concept of
self in relation to our present society and its ideals," and his
emphasis shifts from poetry as diagnostic tool to poetry as ther-
apeutic (3). Not surprisingly, because of his Fugitive roots, Warren finds industrialization and technology, now the Technetronic
Age (Warren's term), large factors in the decay of self, a point he
documents by analyzing the writings of Whitman, Henry
Adams, Oliver Wendell Holmes, Hawthorne, Melville, Twain,
and others. *I'll Take My Stand*, the Fugitives' manifesto to which
Warren had contributed an essay in 1930, had said as much some
forty-four years earlier. After Truman's use of the atomic bomb
to end World War II in 1945, cultural disillusionment and decay
were seen to advance almost exponentially. Since the arts and
humanities were under attack—as they still are—poetry went on
the offensive against the detractors who are more a part of the
problem than a part of the solution. In defending poetry against
a world gone mad with technology, Warren asserts that "poetry
may affirm and reinforce the notions of the self" (42) which are
tied to our past. Warren here repeats what has become almost a
refrain in this lecture, "a society with no sense of the past, with
no sense of the human role as significant not merely in experi-
encing history but in creating it can have no sense of destiny"
(56). Perhaps Audubon in Warren's long narrative poem
Audubon: A Vision had in the end this same sense of destiny. Or,
to invoke the last of twelve sections of "I Am Dreaming of a
White Christmas: The Natural History of a Vision" from *Or
Else: Poem/Poems, 1968–1974:*

All items listed above belong in the world
In which all things are continuous,
And are parts of the original dream which
I am now trying to discover the logic of. This
Is the process whereby pain of the past in its pastness
May be converted into the future tense

Of joy.

(281)

Drama seemed to hold for Warren a life-long dream of achieving the combination of literature into a single, all-encompassing genre, since drama displays the narrative of fiction, the language of poetry, and the added dimension of a visual art. Warren's composition of the senior play in his high school literary publication, his dramatic rendering of John Brown's biography in narrative prose, and his beginning of *All the King's Men* as a play *Proud Flesh* in 1937 give ample testimony to Warren's dramatic leanings. In fact, he never entirely quit striving for the proper stage version of *All the King's Men* or of the dramatization of chapter 4 from that novel, the Cass Mastern story. In the three stage versions of the Willie Stark story—*Proud Flesh, Willie Stark: His Rise and Fall*, and *All the King's Men (A Play)*—Warren's concern is on the effects of power on those in authoritative positions and the trickle-down effects on the lives of those around them. Manipulation, control, and betrayal are clearly motivations and consequences behind the actions of the characters. In the unpublished manuscript copy of *Listen to the Mockingbird*, Gilbert Mastern lays bare the power dynamics behind social institutions: "But I do not see any institution as sacred. An institution is—is sacred—just as long as it gets something done" (1.1.9).[21] Mastern's attitude reflects that of several characters who exercise power in Warren's plays.

Warren's concern with power politics is also evident in *Brother to Dragons: A Tale in Verse and Voices* (1953). The gruesome tale of Isham and Lilburn Lewis, nephews of Thomas Jefferson, who butcher a slave in their meat house because he broke a favorite water pitcher that belonged to their deceased mother, is merely historical backdrop for the dialogue the character "R. P. W." has with the spirit of Thomas Jefferson. *Brother to Dragons* suggests that people must look at their past to understand their present and to have hope for their future. Toward the end of the verse drama, the narrator, "R. P. W.," expresses the connection between understanding the past and achieving self-fulfillment:

> The recognition of complicity is the beginning of inno-
>   cence.
> The recognition of necessity is the beginning of freedom.
> The recognition of the direction of fulfillment is the
>   death of the self,
> And the death of the self is the beginning of selfhood.
> All else is surrogate of hope and destitution of spirit.[22]

In addition to his textbooks, his articles of criticism on literary figures such as Faulkner, Hemingway, Porter, Welty, Conrad, Melville, Whittier, and Hawthorne, and his biography of John Brown, Warren wrote nonfictional prose on social and historical matters that were portrayed in various degrees of prominence in his fiction and poetry. Among his forays into nonfiction are *Segregation* (1956), *Who Speaks for the Negro?* (1965), *The Legacy of the Civil War* (1961), *Jefferson Davis Gets His Citizenship Back* (1980), and *Portrait of a Father* (1988), the most autobiographical piece produced by Warren. These works are also an integral part of Warren's canon and can provide a fuller understanding of his writing as well as of the historical context that influenced him.

Warren exhibited a command over a diverse range of literary and nonfictional styles. He strove always to improve his writing by experimenting with new forms and by grappling continuously with matters significant to the human condition. He was a teacher at heart, a student in his pursuits, and a philosophical moralist in message. Warren has earned the title of secular moralist through his concern with and compassion for the virtues of hope, love, and endurance. His professional life was dedicated to literature in its broadest and deepest sense, a dedication that is evident in his correspondence and his life's pursuits. Perhaps, however, the most important legacy he left is that of a compelling storyteller because readers engage literature, because they like it, "and [they] like it because [literature], as an image of life, stimulates and gratifies [their] interest in life."[23]

CHAPTER TWO

Early Fiction (1939–1955)

> Fiction, like the essay, drama, poem, sermon, or
> philosophical treatise, is the presentation of an
> author's way of looking at life.
>
> *An Approach to Literature* (1939)

Novels

Warren showed an interest in writing fiction as early as 1921, when he published two very short vignettes in the Clarksville High School monthly student publication, *The Purple and Gold*. These pieces are titled "Munk" and "The Dream of a Driller."[1] Though they are an adolescent's tales, they represent in retrospect his early leanings toward historical fiction. He had listened to his Grandfather Penn's tales of the Civil War, had heard the folklore of the region, and had read widely in local history. By the time he graduated summa cum laude from Vanderbilt, Warren was a published poet and was working on a biography of John Brown.

His first attempts at novels were aborted. "The Apple Tree" (1930–1932), retitled as "God's Own Time" (1932–1933), and an untitled second novel (1933–1934), which he identifies as such on the first revised draft, went unfinished.[2] Of his ten published novels, most critics acknowledge only one, *All the King's Men*, as a classic, and it is still read today as part of political science, history, sociology, pre-law, and American literature courses. Generally, the negative criticism is leveled at Warren's plots, said to be melodramatic and even sententious, announcing outright a story's moral. Part of that negativism, however, derives from the backlash against the

EARLY FICTION (1939–1955)

New Criticism, with which Warren had been so strongly associated. Nonetheless, Warren does know how to tell a good story in his fiction, and his novels are ripe with multiple levels of meaning. His early fiction shows his interest in moral philosophy and his metaphysical concerns with causes that motivate humans to conduct their lives as they do.

Night Rider

Warren realized that the public does not read fiction primarily to improve its moral and metaphysical understanding of the world— people read fiction mainly to hear a good story and to learn about their own lives while living vicariously the exciting experiences of fictional protagonists. In *Night Rider* (1939), his first published novel, Warren fulfills both criteria, providing an action story that has deeper philosophical meaning as well. The novel is based on the historical adventures of the night riders who violently resisted losing control of their land and livelihood to big tobacco companies during the Kentucky tobacco wars at the turn of the century. Intertwined with the surface conflicts of the story's action are Warren's deeper concerns with individual responsibility, the nature of space and time, knowledge and self-knowledge, familial relationships and history, and redemptive love. Those themes also permeate his other fiction and are the center of his poetry as well.

Warren wrote *Night Rider* while teaching Shakespeare at LSU and while writing *An Approach to Literature* with Cleanth Brooks and John Thibaut Purser. Shakespeare's use of Holinshed's *Chronicles* as source material for his plays could not have gone unnoticed by Warren, who also drew from history for his fiction. He was, at this same time, selecting fiction for *An Approach to Literature*, and therefore encountering writers to whose work he would return over the years (for instance, Hawthorne, Melville, Conrad, and others) as well as budding young authors, such as Eudora Welty and Katherine Anne Porter, whose work he helped publish in the newly founded *Southern Review*.

Critics were kind to Warren's first novel, though they have not been equally kind to some of his later fiction. Scholarly discussions of *Night Rider* credit Warren's conception of the story, his handling of description and details, his use of history, and his use of language in spite of the chilling distance of the narrator. Leonard Casper, the first critic to publish a book-length study of Warren's work, in 1960, faults Warren's choice of point of view, suggesting that Percy Munn, the main character, has at best a limited view of himself and the world around him.[3] In his 1981 study James Justus finds Warren's telling of the story dispassionate and disinterested.[4] Yet, for a first novel, *Night Rider* indicates the author's capacity for issues of large proportions. Three studies form a useful introduction to understanding *Night Rider*: John Burt's discussion of naturalism in the novel, governed by three sets of propositions (politics, character types, and genre), Hugh Ruppersburg's sense of Warren's American vision in relating historical events and their participants, and William Bedford Clark's critique in terms of Warren's response to the drama and fiction of social protest of the 1930s.

The ethical issues posed in *Night Rider* are evident throughout Warren's writing. Warren's concern with the reaction to political power and what actions transpire in the absence of that power brings into focus the concept of justice and the just character. Drawing on Utilitarian philosophy at times, Warren asks the burning moral ques-

tion: Does the end justify the means? In examining the Machiavellian self-interest that drives power politics, Warren blazes into the
"dark-fired" heart of humanity and illuminates the horror that
Joseph Conrad's Marlow discovers in Mr. Kurtz. The discovery of
self may involve a recognition of that horror, but the quest is "an
education both as to the character of that which is sought and in self-
knowledge."[5] In their quests Warren's protagonists wrestle with the
concepts of good and evil, of virtue and vice within the context of
their social identity and historical place. In creating a narrative history that represents a character's life, Warren shows how each character's life is part of the other characters' lives; one character's
actions affect other lives, an interrelatedness suggested by the spiderweb theory that Jack Burden discovers in his research on Cass
Mastern in *All the King's Men*. The nonvirtuous character, then,
might try to use other individuals as means to an end, as Senator
Tolliver does in *Night Rider* and Willie Stark does in *All the King's
Men*. Warren clearly focuses on philosophical matters in exploring
self-worth in the human condition, a topic which he had already
examined in his biography of John Brown.

Night Rider's Percy Munn is one such protagonist who faces
moral decisions based on the temporal and causal narrative history
of his life. In the opening scene Munn, a lawyer, reflects on the interconnectedness of the lives of men who attend the meeting of the
Association of Growers of Dark Fired Tobacco from Kentucky and
Tennessee.[6] What follows in plot in relation to the fictional association is based on historical events that center on Warren's birthplace,
Guthrie, Kentucky. The historical basis for the novel, however, was
not limited to Warren's native state. Tobacco farmers experienced a
similar struggle in the Reelfoot Lake region of western Tennessee in

the first decade of the twentieth century. To protect what they believed to be their God-given rights to the land around the lake, these farmers violently opposed the land entrepreneurs who were trying to develop the area.

In the surface story of the novel, the commercial competition between buyer and seller rages. Beneath the surface, one man seeks an understanding of his identity and of the truth. Percy Munn is an alienated soul from the start. His arrival on the train in Bardsville alone, his desire to be by himself after Mr. Christian takes him to his hotel room, even his reflections on his wife, May, suggest his isolation. Somewhat doubtful about the meeting of the association, which he is in town to attend, Munn feels betrayed after he lets Mr. Christian, Captain Todd, and Senator Tolliver persuade him to join. It is self-betrayal, however, because he does not stand by what he believes as Captain Todd seems to do. As he begins to recruit new members for the association, his feeling of separateness is overshadowed by a sense of "throbless pleasure" (39). The dark and isolation comfort him, abate his deeper philosophical questions of discovery of "the true and unmoved center of being, the focus of his obligations" (41). Riding home alone after one of the meetings, Munn falsely believes that he will come closer to a definition of reality.

Munn's inability to explain himself to May eventually erodes (perhaps unwillingly) the love he had once felt for her and leads to acts of cruelty, small at first but culminating in his raping her. Before that ultimate act of cruelty and betrayal, they have attended a party hosted by Senator Tolliver, with whom they stayed as house guests. While undressing for bed, Munn realizes "that all he knew was the blackness into which he stared" and he wonders whether that effort was merely his "staring inward into himself" (109). The two images that conclude the paragraph, snow and darkness, stay with Munn throughout the story, representing the coldness of his character and his inability to communicate the secrecy of his inner self.[7]

Munn's introspection and feeling of failure in meaningless acts are heightened by his retrospective look at Senator Tolliver's flattery, a betrayal that played on Munn's vanity and made him Tolliver's "lackey-boy." As tension mounts over tobacco prices and independent growers continue to sell their leaf outside the association, more forceful measures are proposed. Professor Ball and Doctor MacDonald suggest a plan to ruin the anti-association growers' fields. After Tolliver resigns from the association, select members form an inner group, the Free Farmers' Brotherhood of Protection and Control. Munn initially objects but again lets himself be persuaded to participate. He rationalizes that Tolliver's betrayal is responsible for his own acquiescence in the plan. Warren makes further use of the light and dark imagery to reflect Munn's isolation and desperation as the action moves toward a climax.

May notices a change in Munn after he begins riding with the night riders. Although Munn cannot perceive any difference when he looks at himself in the mirror, he has changed. Munn is not the man he perceived himself to be. He is further isolated from others, especially from May whom he feels he does not know any longer, and cannot communicate his thoughts and feelings to others. As he moves further away from others, he also moves further away from himself and finds he cannot truly know himself. The stereopticon cards that he looked at in three-dimensional perspective as a child symbolize a distinction between appearance and reality, a distinction he now has difficulty making. As the violence of the night riders increases, Munn's ability to discern appearance from reality grows weaker. Standing up for his beliefs, Captain Todd resigns from the association in protest against the night riders. The acceleration of events and the further weakening of Munn's belief in the sense of justice he once embraced lead to his killing Bunk Trevelyan, who recognizes him as one of the night riders, and to his rape of May that same night. Moral decay begins slowly but spreads rapidly and ends violently in Warren's novel.

Even nature, which Munn has admired and in which he sought consolation, evades him, he feels. The perfection of grackles recalled from boyhood is beyond his grasp after he has given himself over to moral decay. The same images and message are later refined by Warren and included in his poem "Grackles, Goodbye," in which the persona realizes "that only, only, / In the name of Death do we learn the true name of Love" (391). Perhaps Munn learns that lesson at the novel's end. Before reaching it, though, he attempts to find meaning through a return to his past. Estranged from May, Munn has an affair with Sukie Christian, Mr. Christian's daughter. May's aunt intercedes for May and rejects Munn's offer of a divorce. As a result, Munn becomes trapped with no exit. Intermingled with his personal conflict is the moral isolation of the night riders. Barn burnings and murders continue. In desperation the night riders take on a bolder strategy and plan to destroy the buyers' warehouses, a raid that shares similarities with John Brown's ill-conceived raid on Harper's Ferry.

Munn's own house is burned by men wanting him to put white, not black, tenants on his land. His world is becoming smaller, and he has not found the answer to his question of self-identity. In Munn's reflection on death, Warren uses a leaf as symbol, which will become a primary symbol throughout his writing. The leaf represents an extended metaphor in the following passage: "Death grew in you like the leaves on the trees in spring, gentle and tender and unobtrusive, and then, in the moment of knowledge, was already luxuriant, full-blown, blotting out the familiar objects. If not the small pain in the side, some word you spoke, some careless gesture, some momentary concession to vanity, some burst of pity, or some trivial decision—that was the bud, the leaf swelling toward recognition" (350–51).

Arrests and trials begin, and Munn goes into hiding. Finally, he hides at Willie Proudfit's farm. Proudfit, with his story-within-the-story of the buffalo stand, the plight of the Kiowa, and his adventures before he settled down, observes that man seems to have an innate, senseless penchant for killing. Sukie visits Munn there, and Munn rejects the idea of their going west and marrying. He tells her, "Love, it's not anything, not when it's not a part of something else" (440). Later Munn leaves Proudfit's place and vows that he will kill Senator Tolliver. But when he confronts Tolliver, whom he sees as nothing, he cannot do the act. Tolliver comments that "A man never knows what he is" (456). Munn then runs with soldiers in pursuit. Finally, as an act of suicidal resignation and defeat after he trips and falls, he fires his revolver in the air, thus accepting the riddle of bullets bearing his death.

Warren's character escapes into death, escapes from his nothingness, his not knowing who he is. In the end he cannot kill Tolliver, the man who betrayed him and, through that betrayal, sent him down the loneliest road in unease and isolation. Munn may have avoided this destiny but for his vanity. The quest for self-knowledge is a primary theme of *Night Rider*. The temptations one faces in seeking self-knowledge test a person's character and convictions, the sincerity of which cannot be known until the time comes for action. Percy Munn acts out of selfishness and in vanity, failing to understand himself and, therefore, not understanding others, such as May, Sukie Christian, and Bunk Trevelyan and his wife. Munn's journey can be read as an allegory of the human condition, a symbolic movement that is mirrored in the quests of Warren's other protagonists, though each character faces a slightly different set of circumstances.

At Heaven's Gate

Warren's second novel, *At Heaven's Gate* (1943), brings together the artistic spirit of Slim Sarrett, the rebellious nature of Bogan Murdock's daughter Sue, and the vanity of former athlete turned businessman Gerald Calhoun who thinks he knows who he is. Warren uses the third-person omniscient point of view and focuses on Jerry Calhoun's life, although the other characters play significant roles in this novel. *At Heaven's Gate* has been given short shrift in critical discussions of Warren's oeuvre. Casper reads the novel as a precursor to *All the King's Men*, which, on one level, it is. Justus finds in it "flaws aplenty" with its uneven style and melodramatic scenes. Clark sees it as a challenge to "the American ethics of success" and to corporate capitalism and rightly gives credit for his analysis to John L. Longley, Jr.'s thorough essay, "*At Heaven's Gate*: The Major Themes."[8] Burt and Ruppersburg make only passing reference to the novel in their discussions of Warren's canon.

At Heaven's Gate is, indeed, a harbinger of novels to come by Warren, but such a claim seems unnecessary since several of Warren's early novels share the same central issues. *Night Rider* has its renegade tobacco association pitted against big tobacco companies,

At Heaven's Gate has its unethical entrepreneur, Bogan Murdock, destroying the land, and *All the King's Men* has its Machiavellian politician. These novels suggest that the corruption at any level of society breeds discontent, mistrust, and defeat. Warren's concern is with the effects of corruption on individual lives and whether people are strong enough to resist moral decay. In *At Heaven's Gate* Sue Murdock poses this question concerning individual morality and responsibility. The characters caught up in the moment tend to ignore or reject their past and to lose sight of who they are. They live a life of lies that, on the one hand, protect them, but, on the other hand, erode the essence of their being.

Bogan Murdock, who believes music is the only pure thing in the world, tells Jerry Calhoun, to whom he is offering a financial job, that finance's "only function is to answer the needs of the land itself and the life which is dictated by the nature of our land."[9] What underlies such seemingly high-flown rhetoric is a rationalization for the rape of the land through unrestrained timber harvests and strip-mining. The phrase "nature of our land" metaphorically implies the issue of selfhood, and, therefore, serves as an example of another self-deception that Murdock practices. Jerry Calhoun's success as a football star in school is exactly the image Murdock can sell in his financial ventures. He even stoops low enough to use his daughter Sue to recruit Jerry for his business. Sue, however, is not a willing participant in her father's charades.

Murdock's wife Dorothy came from a distinguished Georgia family. In her life with her husband, however, love eluded her, and at age forty she finds herself isolated from and unable to communicate with the world. At one point in the narrative she feels reborn and begins to move back into the world, a move of short duration.

When she confronts Murdock with a lie about her affair with the military "hero" Private Porsum, her attempt to deceive fails and she is reduced to nothing in the eyes of her husband.

Murdock's interview in front of cameras in the last scene of the novel is yet another lie. Murdock says he takes "responsibility" for the failure of his financial firm Meyers and Murdock. He gives falsely altruistic reasons for the firm's decline, claiming that the business suffered because he honors friendships over financial gain. His self-proclaimed courage and reliance on a new-found loyalty is almost amusing in its falseness; it is the reverse of Percy Munn's denial that his reading to Miss Sprague was an unselfish act because he did it for himself, an element of ethical egoism. Murdock's acceptance of an artificial responsibility and the vain courage found in family traditions are the basis of the lie he will continue to live.

Bogan Murdock does seem to love his daughter, but he fails to change even after her death casts doubts about the level of that love. Sue, whom critic Lucy Ferriss sees as the central figure in this novel, is a rebellious young woman, spoiled by her father's wealth and position in the community and jaded by her lack of identity. In the way she relates to men, she might be viewed as a southern version of Lady Brett Ashley in Hemingway's *The Sun Also Rises*, but with less experience. A femme fatale who treats Jerry Calhoun like dirt one day and invites him to take her out the next, Sue manipulates most of the men in her life. Early in Jerry's relationship with Sue, he believed that truth resided in the image of her face. He even plans to marry her, but his understanding of Sue is dependent on his faulty understanding of himself. Sue tries to manipulate Slim Sarrett and Jason Sweetwater in a similar fashion. However, Slim has homosexual leanings, and Sweetwater is already married to a "beautiful blond Polack girl." Although Sue may be carrying Sweetwater's baby, he tells her he cannot marry her. He believes marriage is a kind of prostitution in which love rather than the body is sold for personal gain. Sweetwater, however, does believe in love (312). Sue does not. Slim Sarrett explains to her the complexities of the word *want*, connecting it with Sue's overtipping the taxi driver. Slim suggests that overtipping gives Sue the sense of being loved and admired. Ironically, Slim also tells her that she does not understand herself and so she creates versions of her identity that she thinks she can understand. Sue and Slim drift apart, and Sue exiles herself to a low-rent apartment and lives in a timeless world without past or future. After her father tracks down Sue and confronts her about returning home, Sue has an affair with Slim. Although he appears to be something of a self-appointed spiritual guru, Slim cannot help Sue gain the self-knowledge she seeks. When Billie Constantidopeles, a painter who is Slim's friend, tells the truth about Slim's father and his past, Sue turns to Sweetwater and confesses she does not know what makes her the way she is. Sweetwater replies, "There's something horrible in everybody" (307). Sue's horror is not knowing what she believes in before Slim Sarrett kills her. Her earlier cry, "*Oh, what am I*" (155) becomes Amantha's cry in Warren's later novel *Band of Angels* (1955).

Two other characters are also on quests: Slim Sarrett and Jerry Calhoun. Sarrett and his "followers" might represent Warren's parody of the Lost Generation scene in Paris in the 1920s. A young poet who seems to have an inner serenity, Sarrett is perhaps the most confused character in the novel. His statement that he does not "want to play Hamlet" (102) provides an early clue. Hamlet is a complex, confused character whose inability to act culminates in the deaths of six persons by the end of the play. Sarrett has read Shakespeare. His diatribe on Shakespearean tragedy and how critics have misstated the underlying theme echoes Warren's unfulfilled desire to write a book on Shakespeare. Sarrett identifies "the necessity for self-knowledge" (196) as Shakespeare's fundamental theme—a theme that courses throughout Warren's fiction. In his long, extended lie to Sue about his background, Sarrett has already explained the difficulties in gaining self-knowledge. The falsities of formal education, the inability of all but the "intelligent" people to achieve sincerity, the hypocrisy of organized religion, and isolation from reality prevent most people from acquiring self-knowledge. After losing his fight with Sweetwater, Sarrett returns and strangles Sue. Befitting to his character, Sarrett is in a hotel room writing poetry, which he has said "is the impurity which an active being secretes to become pure" (196), after he has just murdered Sue.

Sarrett tells Sue that Jerry Calhoun is stupid. Jerry certainly lacks the outward facade of self-possession that Sarrett displays, but both characters lack the self-knowledge necessary to live meaningful lives. All of the major male characters in *At Heaven's Gate* have difficult relationships with their fathers. Jerry's conflict is expressed most clearly in the last chapter as he is in jail thinking, "*Did I ever want my father dead?*" (388). He did not know what he wanted in his college years, when he studied geology but was easily persuaded to go into finance, and is embarrassed about his relationship with Sue. Jerry is another Warren figure who has difficulty communicating with others and who stymies his own progress with his vanity.

Jerry is befriended by Duckfoot Blake, an accountant for Murdock. Duckfoot teaches him about Murdock's business. Later he serves as Jerry's confidant, although Jerry lies to him about not being in love with Sue. Jerry joins the other characters who are caught in their own webs of self-deception. He lies to himself about being afraid of Sue and to Murdock about understanding Sue. Even after Duckfoot tells Jerry about Murdock's shady business deals, Jerry is indecisive, a tell-tale characteristic of a person who lacks self-knowledge. Jerry does not know what he stands for, and this flaw is part of the reason he, Duckfoot, and Porsum all wind up in jail by the end of the novel. Jerry's father visits him while he is imprisoned. The visit causes Jerry to realize that his actions are not isolated from the world and do affect others. This realization anticipates Jack Burden's spiderweb theory in *All the King's Men*. Yet, even though he recognizes that larger consequences accompany his personal actions, Jerry still rebels against his father's kindness. Back in his parents' home, in his old bed, he wonders what he shares with the Jerry Calhoun of his youth, feeling "nothing had ever been all right" (386). After soul-searching and introspective questioning, Jerry finds that he cannot come home again, that he does not belong. However, he is unable to break free from the restrictive father-son relationship that has plagued his life.

Warren has structured *At Heaven's Gate* with intermediate sections included between the chapters. These sections are each titled "Statement of Ashby Wyndham." Wyndham seems to function as an interlocutor, a kind of peripheral Greek chorus to the main-stage action. The Wyndham-Murdock stories converge through the Jason Sweetwater-Duckfoot Blake connection with the sawmill. Wyndham is a second cousin to Private Porsum, who is believed to be a World War I hero, but who turns out to be a coward. Both Wyndam and his cousin are fake heroes living a lie. Wyndham is religious. In his dealings with the Massey Mountain Company and with Marie, he refers to lessons from the Bible. Those observations serve as backdrops to the story and also foreshadow some of Willie Stark's observations about human nature in *All the King's Men*. Wyndham says a human being "ain't nuthin but a handful of dust" and suggests that a human being has "nuthin in him but meanness" (35). Almost as if he is commenting on Jerry and Sue's relationship, he notes: "A man don't take no thought on what he was or is or what will come" (119). He puts on equally high-minded airs about love, asserting that "love ain't nuthin if it ain't in God's eye" (120, 170). The kind of redemptive love Wyndham here describes ultimately evades Percy Munn as well as the characters in *At Heaven's Gate*. Wyndham's character is colorful and is fraught with sin and atonement. In the end his "salvation" comes from Miss Pearl, the madam of a brothel.

The novel's title offers some insight into the thematic concerns of the narrative. *At Heaven's Gate* is taken from Shakespeare's "Sonnet 29":

Yet in these thoughts myself almost dispising,
Haply I think on thee, and then my state
(Like to the lark at break of day arising
From sullen earth) sings hymns at heaven's gate.

Like the speaker of Shakespeare's sonnet, the characters in Warren's novel seem to be lost in despair and self-denial. However, unlike Shakespeare's persona, Warren's characters seem unable to find any glimmer of transcendence; instead, they seem doomed to failure and self-deception, far from heaven's gate.[10] The novel that follows *At Heaven's Gate* has become Warren's most famous and critically well-received novel, *All the King's Men*, published in 1946, three years after *At Heaven's Gate*.

All the King's Men

In some subtle and some not-so-subtle ways, *At Heaven's Gate* has characters, aspects of plot, and dialogue that prepare readers for *All the King's Men*, just as Casper suggested in his critical interpretation of *At Heaven's Gate*. Those metaphors, as Slim Sarrett referred to character, situation and plot, statement, and language, are part of Warren's overarching theme of power politics, with its implications of the ends justifying the means; utilitarianism; pragmatism; and corruption, sin, guilt, and redemption. What distinguishes this third novel from the other nine novels in Warren's canon may remain somewhat subjective in readers' minds. The shortest, best answer is simply to note the novel's heightened consistency of style, characterization, and narrative integration. In *All the King's Men* Warren was able to maintain a high writing style, to develop the major characters more fully, and to integrate the two stories (Stark's and Burden's) so that they work toward the same end. These strengths enrich this novel and contribute to its recognition as an American literary classic.

Warren wrote to David M. Clay in 1941 that he was going to convert his play *Proud Flesh* into a novel based on Huey Long's political career in Louisiana. The characterization of Willie Stark does indeed suggest parallels with Huey Long, as Ladell Payne has aptly noted in his essay, "Willie Stark and Huey Long: Atmosphere, Myth, or Suggestion?"[11] But as Warren has repeated publicly and privately, any events in Louisiana politics that occurred while he was teaching at LSU in the 1930s was merely backdrop to those larger thematic issues mentioned above, the deeper moral and metaphysical issues that enable this novel to endure.

The ten chapters of *All the King's Men* can be divided into five acts like a Shakespearean drama. Chapters 1 and 2 serve as an introduction to the stories of Willie Stark and Jack Burden. Chapters 3 and 4 provide a sense of rising action and a story-within-the-story to emphasize themes of guilt, sin, and betrayal in the main story. Chapters 5 and 6 contain the climax of the narrative with the discovery of the truth about Judge Irwin, Adam Stanton's agreeing to direct the hospital that Stark was building, Anne Stanton's affair with Stark, and Stark's giving the hospital contract to his political rival Gummy Larsen. Chapters 7 and 8 provide the falling action with Burden's trip west and the beginning of his reconciliation with his past. Chapters 9 and 10 complete the narrative's dénouement with Stark's assassination and Burden's acceptance of his responsibility in the world.

Betrayals move the action forward under a Hegelian dialectic in which the thesis of pragmatism, represented by Stark, is opposed by the antithesis of idealism, represented by Adam Stanton. In the end, realism, represented by Burden, emerges as the synthesis of those polarities. Though "man is conceived in sin and born in corruption,"[12] as Stark frequently quotes from Psalm 51, Adam Stanton clings to an idealistic and unrealistic concept of moral goodness and is unable to accept such a dim view of human nature. Burden learns that the world is all of one piece and that an individual can survive if he accepts responsibility for his actions in it. The power of redemptive love enables one to do so. Looking back over Warren's canon, the reader sees that theme of love as salvation endures throughout his fiction, poetry, and drama. Munn in *Night Rider*, Calhoun in *At Heaven's Gate*, and Stark in *All the King's Men* come to realize the consoling power of love, even though they do not necessarily adhere to it. Such thematic insights are made more memorable by Warren's extraordinary command of language.

EARLY FICTION (1939–1955)

A notable example of Warren's prose style in *All the King's Men* appears in the opening paragraph. It contains the descriptions, the images, and the diction that set the tone of the novel. The passage describes the new highway, the danger of road hypnosis, and the fieldhand who looks up in time to "see the little column of black smoke standing up above the vitriolic, arsenical green of the cotton rows, and up against the violent, metallic throbbing blue of the sky," his hoe blade flashing "in the sun like a heliograph" (3). In this first paragraph Warren paints a portrait of the natural world that is not at all idyllic or comforting. He reverses the pastoral mode, making nature appear violent and threatening, even synthetic ("metallic") and potentially poisoning to human beings ("arsenical").

Warren's exceptional ability to weave together language and theme is further apparent in his mastery of Burden's narrative voice throughout the novel. Early in chapter 1 Burden uses "purple prose" to describe the anxiety of waiting for the telegram. He concludes this passage with the assertion that "the end of man is to know" (12). This segment illustrates his "brass-bound" rhetoric as a glib-tongued reporter with a chip on his shoulder. Toward the end of the novel, Burden's rhetoric mellows somewhat as he acquires a sense of who he is. In contrast to Burden's smooth and polished style of expression is Stark's very pragmatic rhetorical mode. Stark is, after all, a man of action, whereas Burden is more of a man of words. Like Huey Long, Stark is an orator of high caliber, but one who always uses language towards very definite pragmatic ends.

The action of the novel moves on two levels: Stark's rise and fall and Burden's fall and rise. Stark represents the rural life in what can be assumed to represent the state of Louisiana, since the name of the state is not explicitly provided in the novel, while Burden represents the urban life. Stark's beginnings were humble. He slopped the hogs on his father's farm, married a school teacher named Lucy, and as county treasurer was used by corrupt local politicians in a bond vote that enabled their favorites to build a new schoolhouse. The faulty construction caused the deaths of some school children during a fire drill. Willie had tried to tell the voters about the faulty construction, but no one would listen to him.

Stark's and Burden's paths cross when "Cousin" Willie meets Burden in Slade's back room in 1922 just before Stark's first bond election. Stark is used in the next election by the Harrison outfit to split the MacMurfee vote, but he does not become aware of his role until Sadie Burke, a member of the Stark campaign troop, and Jack Burden, a reporter covering the campaign, explain the setup to him. After a dramatic confessional speech, Stark withdraws from the election and gives his support to MacMurfee. That episode serves as the awakening of Willie Stark, who, Burden muses, is a man born outside of luck, for whom his life history "is a process of discovering what [he] really [is]" (67–68). As a result of his aborted campaign, Stark discovers his true political identity, but not without paying a high personal price for this discovery. After the fiasco at the political rally in Upton, Stark returns to Mason City and practices law while waiting to run for office again.

Because the narration shifts from present events to past events, readers are aware in chapter 1 that Stark is currently governor of the state. In chapter 2 Warren reveals Stark's political background and introduces the major characters, such as Tiny Duffy, the lieutenant governor, who was once Stark's political foe. On a psychological level he is Stark's other self, and Stark keeps him around to remind him of his past. Chapter 2 also brings into relief the novel's concern with the issue of betrayal and deception. Betrayal runs rampant throughout the novel, from the deceptions committed by Jack Burden's mother at Burden's Landing to the lies of the upright judge named Irwin. Burden's mother remains unnamed in the novel. She has had four husbands: Ellis Burden, the scholarly attorney whom she betrayed with infidelity; Daddy Ross, the tycoon; Covelli, the count; and Theodore Murrell, the young executive. Judge Irwin serves in Jack Burden's memory as a father figure who, Burden learns after the judge's suicide, is his biological father. Burden's memories of his youth reflect his unwillingness to act and his not knowing what his values are. His home life provided no stability in those formative years. Later, when he was a history student in college, Jack would argue in his best pseudo-philosophical way with the aging scholarly attorney, asserting that "Life is Motion toward Knowledge" and that God is Death, the Father (160). In addition to the earlier emotional betrayals Jack Burden has suffered, he endures intellectual betrayals in this period of his life.

Chapter 4 is interrupted by another political betrayal dealing with the state auditor Byrom B. White and MacMurfee's political gang calling for the impeachment of Stark. This chapter is sometimes referred to as the Cass Mastern story. It was omitted in the first English editions of *All the King's Men* because it seemed superfluous. However, William Faulkner said it was the best part of the novel. On a first reading, the Cass Mastern portion may seem to be a distraction from the business at hand. Yet it is connected to one of the novel's major themes since it represents another story of betrayal. Cass Mastern is one of Ellis Burden's maternal uncles. Mastern's diaries, letters, and photographs have come into Jack Burden's possession, and Jack was planning to write a dissertation based on them. The story of Cass Mastern that Burden relates is set in the late 1850s and early 1860s. Gilbert Mastern, Cass's older brother, takes on the responsibility of Cass's education. Gilbert sends Cass to Lexington, Kentucky, to live with a friend named Duncan Trice and his young wife, Annabelle. Cass is a naïve young man, soon corrupted by the faster life in Lexington. He and Annabelle have an affair. Duncan learns of it and commits suicide, leaving his wedding ring under his pillow as a symbol of his wife's betrayal. Phebe, Annabelle's servant, finds the ring and knows of the affair. Annabelle sells her, much to Cass's consternation, and the lovers break up. Cass seeks atonement for betraying his host by fighting bravely in battle. As a private in the Civil War, he is injured outside Atlanta and dies in a hospital just as the war ends. From Cass's experience with the "common guilt of man," Burden articulates the spiderweb theory (200), which posits the interconnectedness of all lives. He also suffers from depression as a result of dealing with Cass Mastern's diaries and slips into the Great Sleep (201), an escape from his responsibility in the world.

By focusing on the pattern of betrayals throughout the novel, readers can more easily follow the chains of motivating actions and reactions that lead to dire consequences. Chapters 5 and 6, the climactic segment of the novel, contain Stark's betrayal in his affair with Anne Stanton, who is Adam Stanton's sister, and Jack's betrayal of himself when he takes his trip west. Early in chapter 5 Jack journeys into Judge Irwin's past at Stark's request. At the end of his search, Jack learns that "nothing is lost" (228) and that Governor Stanton, Adam and Anne's father, had helped Irwin in an unethical way. The discovery of a tarnish on the otherwise seemingly perfect records of both Judge Irwin and Governor Stanton constituted a betrayal for Adam and also for Anne, who may have begun her affair with Stark as a result of the discovery of her father's ethical transgression. Another catalyst in the series of betrayals is the arrogance of Willie's pride and joy, Tom Stark, who is a star football player. Tom's rebellious pride creates for Stark's political opponents a toehold that enables them to persuade Stark to give the multimillion-dollar hospital contract to their political crony Gummy Larsen. Whether for the right reasons or not, Jack Burden helps Willie Stark persuade Adam Stanton to accept the directorship of the new hospital. All the plots are now set for the resolution of the story's action in the next two chapters.

Chapter 7 involves Burden's trip west after he learns of Anne and Willie's affair. Returning from California, Burden experiences a mystic vision. He picks up a hitchhiker who has a facial twitch that he does not seem to notice. Burden muses on that twitch, identifying with it and discovering that the twitch knows that the twitch is all. This discovery of "secret knowledge" makes him feel free and clean and "at one with the Great Twitch" (334). In chapter 8 Burden is back in Louisiana and learns of Tom Stark's betrayal of a young girl who claims she is carrying his baby. Stark and Burden pay a late-night visit to Judge Irwin with the information Burden has found on him—information that shows that Irwin "had cuckolded a friend, betrayed a wife, taken a bribe, driven a man, though unwittingly, to death" (353). In being loyal to his boss Stark, Jack Burden unknowingly betrays his real father. Yet Burden's life is starting to find direction as he learns that the price one pays for knowledge is blood.

In chapter 9 Tom Stark sustains a football injury that results in his death. Willie Stark reneges on the contract with Larsen, a political betrayal. Adam learns of Anne's affair and assassinates Stark, an act, as Burden learns in the last chapter, that was set in motion by the jilted Sadie Burke, one of Stark's mistresses. Before he dies, Stark seems to realize the importance of love and fidelity and tells Burden that things might have been all different. Though seeming to come apart, Burden's life actually takes on new dimensions. His theory of historical cost posits that all change costs something. His theory of the moral neutrality of history sees process as neutral, while only results are good or bad. This theory of historical process as neutral reflects a consequentialist perspective drawn from utilitarianism, which suggests that the act that produces the most favorable consequences is morally justified.

Chapter 10 has often been read by critics as an epilogue, but it also represents the dénouement of Burden's story. He learns the truth from Sadie, who is in a sanatorium after suffering a mental breakdown. He sees Tiny Duffy and realizes that they are alike, an important step in his gaining self-knowledge. Burden encounters Sugar Boy, one of Stark's henchmen, but he does not tell him the truth about Sadie's as well as Tiny Duffy's part in setting up Adam. He visits Lucy, who now must care for Tom's son and who still clings to the belief that Willie was a great man. He makes amends with his mother, though he does not tell her the truth about Judge Irwin. Finally, Burden can marry Anne, now that each of them has come to a greater understanding of personal responsibility and a deeper sense of self-knowledge.

In *All the King's Men* Warren draws on the entire spectrum of love from the lowest level of secular love to the highest level of sacred love. Love as lust plays a major role in the novel, since adultery is one of the most prevalent forms of betrayal in the narrative. Stark has sexual affairs after he gains his political power. Sadie

Burke is his first mistress, but a string of short-lived sexual affairs follow. Lucy represents the patience and loyalty that mark marital and familial love since she endures Stark's betrayals and does not become publicly involved in his career. Burden offers a contrast to the kind of love Lucy represents in a statement about Old Man Stark's view of love. Even though Willie's father asks him to stay with him overnight and sleep under the same roof, Willie refuses to do so. Burden observes that it is not familial love that makes Old Man Stark want his son to stay, but "it is just something in the blood" (35), which he calls the fate of a man. Not until the end of the novel does Jack realize that his mother might be capable of loving and of being loved. He and Anne care for the aging Ellis Burden as an act of love for his mother and for his step-father. Ellis Burden comes closest to exemplifying the practice of sacred love in his care for George, "an unfortunate" (196). Clearly, though, Jack Burden's reconciliation with own genuine identity enables him to love others more unselfishly. He discovers the power of redemptive love, a theme that carries over to Warren's fourth novel, *World Enough and Time: A Romantic Novel* (1950).

World Enough and Time: A Romantic Novel

In *World Enough and Time* Warren again draws on southern history as source material for his fiction. The story for this novel is based on the 1825 murder of Col. Solomon Sharp by Jereboam O. Beauchamp in Frankfort, Kentucky.[13] The novel has generated a good deal of critical interest. By 1963 no fewer than fifteen scholars had published articles about *World Enough and Time*, which is considered by many critics as his second-best novel. In it Warren once again invokes dramatic scenes of violence to drive his story, suggesting perhaps that the penchant for dominance is a basic human condition. In *World Enough and Time*, as in his previous three novels, the protagonists seek social power, not realizing that knowledge is power and that self-knowledge is an integral part of the formula for maintaining productive authority; if self-knowledge is absent, then political authority rings hollow. Love is the other integral part of productive experience since love resolves the internal division of selfhood and enables positive external interaction with the world.

The omniscient narrator of *World Enough and Time* tells the story of Jeremiah Beaumont in dramatic fashion. On one level, Jeremiah's story may be viewed as a revised, expanded version of the Cass Mastern story since the conflicts that both young men undergo share similar philosophical implications. *World Enough and Time* not only elaborates themes that are also evident in Warren's first three novels, such as the necessity of self-knowledge and the redemptive power of love, but it also invokes character names from Warren's other novels, such as Ball, Burnham, and Burden. Moreover, taken together, his novels create the sense of a southern community because they contain stories that are set in several southern states, including Kentucky, Tennessee, Louisiana, and Alabama, and deal with place, manners, customs, and values of the region. In *World Enough and Time* Warren describes the relationship between Jeremiah Beaumont, Rachel Jordan, Col. Cassius Fort, and Wilkie Barron. Their lives are complicated by lies and betrayals, so much so that the reader must wonder along with the narrator at the end of the story, "Was all for naught?"[14] The answer lies in one's interpretation of the ending.

To tell this tale full of sound and fury, the narrator draws on a

picture, letters, and diaries of Jeremiah Beaumont, which have been
saved by Jeremiah's sister Laetitia Beaumont Baxter. From those
documents, though, the narrator admits that "we do not know that
we have the Truth" (4). What we have is Jeremiah's vision, given to
us through rich descriptions that provide a means for determining
the credibility of the character and the events described. These
descriptions of Jeremiah's past are reminiscent of Warren's writing
in *John Brown*, though Warren shows himself to be more mature as
a writer in his approach to Jeremiah Beaumont's fictionalized story.
The plot involves a love triangle between Beaumont, Jordan, and
Fort, political intrigue instigated by Barron, and a murder. The
novel's subtitle, *A Romantic Novel*, prepares the reader for Jeremiah's romantic attitude and suggests the narrative's attention to
setting, atmosphere, and images. Indeed, the novel's depiction of
natural settings points up one of its chief thematic concerns: the violence inherent in nature and perhaps in human nature as well. The
violence of the land is underscored throughout the novel, and the
narrator, in keeping with the philosophical bent of the young Jeremiah, ponders a metaphysical question concerning the relation
between the human and the natural: Is the land the scene Jeremiah
devised? Or, did the land and the history devise Jeremiah? (7)

Col. Cassius Fort is Jeremiah's benefactor. He is well-read in
poetry and philosophy, especially in Voltaire and Hume, and plans
to hire Jeremiah into his law firm upon recommendation from Jeremiah's teacher, Dr. Burnham. During his apprenticeship Jeremiah
falls in love with Rachel Jordan and attempts to court her. Because
Wilkie Barron, Jeremiah's friend, convinces him that Colonel Fort
is the father of Rachel's still-born son, Jeremiah leaves Fort's law
practice. After Jeremiah's dogged pursuit of Rachel's affections, he

finally proposes marriage to her. She accepts his proposal, but only if Jeremiah will avenge her wrong and kill Fort. Jeremiah is so deeply in love with Rachel that he accepts the condition as a point of honor and challenges Fort to a duel. When Fort refuses to duel, Jeremiah finds that he cannot stab him and leaves, having been morally defeated and deflated. In a letter to Rachel, Fort acknowledges his foolishness for thinking that they could be together and asks her forgiveness without the necessity of the duel. Fort writes that he is not a coward and is not afraid to fight Jeremiah but sees no reason to agree to a duel. He expresses affection and admiration for Jeremiah and wishes him a happy, healthy life.

After Jeremiah and Rachel marry and she is expecting their first child, Rachel feels her life is different now and no longer wants Jeremiah, who is still planning to act, to kill Fort. From young Jeremiah's vantage point, Colonel Fort has betrayed him by defaming his wife and by rejecting the honorable act of a duel. Jeremiah feels that Fort commits a third betrayal against him when Fort turns against the Relief party, which Jeremiah has been supporting in order to fight legislation that would deny relief to farmers during lean years. After a court ruling in favor of those supporting the anti-relief legislation, the Relief party, sparked by Barron and others, calls for an overthrow of the court by violent means. Fort, a respected, solid member of the community, issues a public condemnation of the Relief party's revolutionary tactics and appeals to citizens to follow due process of law. He also announces his candidacy for the state legislature. Barron now urges Jeremiah to take action against Fort. Against Rachel's wishes, Jeremiah decides to enter the campaign race. The political campaign gets dirty, and, unknown to Jeremiah, a broadside appears denouncing Fort and making public Fort's affair with Rachel. Another broadside is issued with Fort's rebuttal and an accusation that Rachel had the affair with a slave, an accusation that fuels the fire of revenge in Jeremiah's soul. Jeremiah murders Fort in a clandestine plan without honor. In doing so, he creates an unexpected dilemma. The anti-Reliefers want him convicted because he killed Fort, who had denounced the Relief party. The Reliefers need a hero and a martyr and, therefore, want Jeremiah to claim the deed as a passionate defense of his political beliefs. Jeremiah is imprisoned for the wrongful death of Cassius Fort. Inside his cell he ponders the meaning of his life, and he learns that truth can only come at the expense of lies. The parallel here between Jeremiah Beaumont and Jack Burden cannot be overlooked. As a result of losing a father figure, they must make new meaning out of their lives, or else risk losing sight of any purpose in their existence.

The web of deception that leads to Fort's death and Jeremiah's imprisonment is primarily the work of Wilkie Barron, who seems to be motivated at times by political ambition and at other times by pure evil. His own mother jokingly refers to him as "the imp of Satan" (45). When Jeremiah is working for Fort, Wilkie accuses him of being Fort's creature. After he introduces Jeremiah to Rachel, Wilkie manipulates Jeremiah again when he tells him that Fort is the father of Rachel's still-born child. Whereas Wilkie lives in the practical world, Jeremiah is blinded by his idealistic faith and has an inexperienced understanding of human nature. Thus, Wilkie is able to achieve the results that he otherwise could not achieve were Jeremiah less romantic and more pragmatic. Wilkie also prompts Jeremiah to support the Relief party. When Jeremiah does not participate actively in the group while he is farming the Jordan land, Wilkie accuses him of using Rachel's pregnancy as an excuse to back out of his obligations to the party. Finally, the truth emerges that Wilkie is behind the broadside that ultimately drives Jeremiah to murder Fort. At the trial, Wilkie's testimony is detrimental to Jeremiah's defense and leads to his conviction. Although Wilkie does help Rachel, who is imprisoned with Jeremiah as an accomplice, and Jeremiah escape to the land of the Gran Boz, Jeremiah realizes that Wilkie has merely arranged for them to be relocated from one type of prison to another. Symbolically, the location fits Wilkie's character. La Grand' Bosse (Gran Boz, Ole Big Hump, Louis Cadeau, Louis Caddo) is a betrayer *extraordinaire*, a river pirate of mixed blood who controls a wilderness swamp area somewhere between Tennessee and Louisiana where "nobody keers what yore name is or what you done" (458). Wilkie has every reason to want Jeremiah dead now in order to keep his reputation in tact. He can afford to act "in piety to old friendship" (508) and return Rachel's body to Frankfort and to arrange for proper interment of Jeremiah's head after One-eye, brother of Wilkie's hired cutthroat Lilburn Jenkins, brings it in to collect the reward. Wilkie's secret, the truth about his involvement in past crimes, is safe after Rachel's and Jeremiah's deaths. Wilkie's luck holds out for a while, but, in the end, he commits suicide for complex psychological reasons. As the narrator says, "Nobody knew why he did it" (509).

The relationship between Jeremiah and Rachel provides the circumstances that enable Wilkie to influence Jeremiah's decisions. Alluding to Shakespeare's *Othello*, Warren uses Wilkie as Jeremiah's Iago. Wilkie is the one who fabricates the stories about Fort's liaison with Rachel and fills Jeremiah with jealousy. Rachel, however, is not an innocent Desdemona. Rachel is another kind of romantic character, who has a dark, manipulative side. Like Jeremiah, she is not part of the real world. She manipulates her eager suitor from the outset. Her character has been bent by her mother Maria, who distrusts men in general. She has poisoned her daughter's sense of innocence. During one of Jeremiah's early attempts to court Rachel, she allows him to read to her from Plato's *Symposium*, following Diotima's account "of how the soul may progress upward by love" (75). Jeremiah's reading represents a step forward in their relationship, since his earlier advances have been rebuked by Rachel. The passage selected from Plato pontificates about the contemplation of absolute Beauty. Because both lovers are uncertain about themselves and are not in touch with the realities of the world as Wilkie and Fort are, they can only think lofty thoughts without the self-awareness necessary to being free. Though Rachel agrees to act honorably, she does not accept Jeremiah's proposal of marriage until he agrees to kill Fort. After Fort's letter to her, Rachel's feeling of being lost is appeased by Jeremiah's offer of love. They consummate this unrealistic feint of love that night in the library of her house.

Their married life is filled with arguments and reconciliations. Jeremiah farms the Jordan place successfully and earns the respect of his neighbors. He seems to possess the potential to become a productive citizen of the community, except that he hangs on to his foolish promise to kill Fort, a point of honor in his mind. He wrongly believes that killing Fort is the way to perfect justice and self-definition. After Rachel becomes pregnant with their child, she decides that he need not keep his promise. However, Wilkie is there to stir up Jeremiah's emotions. After Jeremiah is jailed, Rachel takes an active part in trying to find witnesses for his defense. Jeremiah feels that at least she is free and again part of the world. But an incriminating letter instructing a witness named Marlowe about his appear-

ance in court falls into the wrong hands through Rachel's careless-
ness and Marlowe's guile. Jeremiah is convicted, his request for an
appeal denied, and he is sentenced to death. Rachel confesses her
role as an accomplice in the murder and joins Jeremiah in the prison
cell. In jail they discuss the meaning of love and seem to grow emo-
tionally closer. Jeremiah is able to realize that "only when life and
death shake hands do we know what is real, and in that acquaintance
find our being" (413).

After Wilkie helps them escape, their life in the land of the
Gran Boz is not ideal. Jeremiah makes an effort to enjoy living there.
He participates in hunting and fishing, drinks too much, and reads,
but these activities do not bring him contentment. Rachel attempts
to find fulfillment in her life there, but also fails. Her attempt to care
for another woman's baby brings her no comfort. Jeremiah contracts
syphilis from an old hag and makes a bitterly ironic reference to the
resulting canker as "a jewel fit for a royal diadem" (491). Neither
Rachel nor Jeremiah can discover happiness, and when they learn
that Wilkie and Skrogg, a journalist for the Relief Party, are responsible for the broadside that was falsely attributed to Fort, Rachel
accuses Jeremiah of using her. Then she stabs herself. Jeremiah
leaves the Gran Boz to seek revenge against Wilkie but is overtaken
by One-eye and beheaded. Before his death, Jeremiah takes on a
sense of personal responsibility for his fate, recognizing that "the
crime is I" (505).

Jeremiah Beaumont wrestles with metaphysical issues concerning identity, self-knowledge, morality, truth, and honor. His ini-
tials, J. B., might suggest a connection with the suffering of Job in
the Bible. Though Jeremiah does indeed suffer a great deal, unlike
Job, he is a vain young man who falls victim to numerous betrayals,

not the least of which is self-betrayal. He is certainly bright enough and seemingly gracious enough to be successful in life, as his brief stint at farming demonstrates, but his lack of direction and his lack of character enable his friends to manipulate his life's drama. In *Web of Being: The Novels of Robert Penn Warren* (1975), critic Barnett Guttenberg sees Jeremiah as being caught between the world of action and the world of idea, unable to achieve an adequate synthesis of the two polarities. Casper suggests that, in his search for absolute knowledge, Jeremiah is doomed to failure, while Justus focuses on Warren's choice of narrator to emphasize the urgency with which Warren regards the past. In this novel of complex ideas, readers once more find that Warren uses his fiction to explore profound moral and metaphysical questions.

Band of Angels

In his search for his authentic self, Jeremiah asks, "What am I?" The question is not new to characters in Warren's novels, and it is asked once again by Amantha Starr, the protagonist in his fifth novel, *Band of Angels* (1955). Warren left among his papers an untitled three-page typescript account of how this novel originated. From J. Winston Coleman, author of *Slavery Times in Kentucky* (1940), Warren learned of a judge named George Kinkead, whom Coleman had interviewed. The judge's recollections went back to the years before 1861 around Lexington, Kentucky. He remembered the story of two little girls, "practically white," who were uncertain of their origin. When their father died and they returned from Oberlin for the funeral, they were seized amid public indignation and sold to a "discriminating" buyer from New Orleans to pay the father's debts.

When Warren was writing the Cass Mastern story for *All the King's Men*, he recalled the judge's story. It stuck in his mind, he writes, because it raised questions that it did not answer. Why did the father not set them free legally while he was still alive? Why did the public indignation amount to nothing? What would their life be like after they were sold? What would happen to them after the fall of New Orleans? Would their past be eliminated by the "blue-clad deliverers" from the North?

To answer the questions raised by the judge's story, Warren wrote *Band of Angels* about Amantha Starr (whom he refers to as Manty) and her struggle for freedom even after her master sets her free. In his manuscript account Warren asks, "Can anybody ever set you free?" Invoking some of the same language that he and Brooks used to describe the New Criticism in *An Approach to Literature* and *Understanding Fiction*, Warren concludes his unpublished essay:

> A key idea is not, however, a book. It is merely the thing that makes a book possible, the atmosphere, the climate, in which the book may grow. It is not the people, the events. The people whose lives were to touch Little Manty's life . . . had to come out of the imagination, too—the dealer who took her downriver on a steamboat; the buyer in New Orleans . . . ; the Oberlin sweetheart who reappears in New Orleans in a Federal uniform; Miss Idell, the mistress of her dead father who, also, reappears; Rau-Ru, the black child snatched from a jungle massacre on the Congo to become Lt. Oliver Cromwell Jones, hero; the Harvard graduate, an

idealist to whom the butchery of war must be justified by "Truth."

Each one had to have his own story in relation to Manty's story, and since the book was about freedom, each one was groping out of his special kind of bondage toward whatever freedom might be possible for him.[15]

This quest for freedom is a recurrent theme from Warren's other novels as well.

Amantha Starr, who serves as the first-person narrator of her own story, expresses a feeling of being lost in the bigness of the world and of being crushed to nothingness, a feeling not unlike Jeremiah Beaumont's sentiments in *World Enough and Time*. Amantha asks herself questions about need, love, self-definition, happiness, and pain, believing that if she knew the answers she could possibly feel free. After the death of her mother, who was one of her father's slaves, she was reared by her Aunt Sukie. Her father Aaron Pendleton Starr gave her a life with some advantages. After her father's death in Cincinnati, Manty's first love, Seth Parton tells her of her father's fraudulent business dealings and of his adultery with Miss Idell, the wife of Herman Muller. At the funeral, Manty learns that she is chattel belonging to the estate and is no longer free on even a literal level. She reflects on a philosophy lesson at Oberlin College, recalling the teacher's assurance that if we have sensations and recollections then we must have a soul.[16] In horror she thinks, "*I am I*" (64).

Though she will deny her heritage when it is convenient to do so, Manty's inability to accept her identity fetters her, thereby preventing her freedom. Sold to Mr. Calloway, who takes her to New Orleans, Manty first tries to hang herself. Failing at that attempt to be freed by death, Manty has a dream on the *Kentucky Queen* that she is manacled with the other slaves on the main deck and she tries to tell them that if they hold their breath they could be free (82). It was just a dream—Manty's dream of freedom. In New Orleans at the slave market, Hamish Bond buys Manty for two thousand dollars. He is the discriminating buyer who once ran slaves from Africa, but who now treats them as individuals. In addressing Amantha Starr by her nickname, Manty, Bond restores to her a sense of identity. Manty, however, is still confused about how to discover genuine freedom. She contemplates escape, but is checked by Bond's kindness, not by any physical restraint against her. As Philip Hallie has pointed out, kindness can be a harsher form of cruelty;[17] however, Bond's kindness does not affect Manty as if it were a disguised form of cruelty or control. Rau-Ru, on the other hand, finds Bond's treatment overly oppressive. Through her struggles to be truly free, Manty learns that the unpredictable thing, the unknowable thing is the self. With this realization Manty begins to attain a provisional sense of self-knowledge. During the night of a ferocious storm, she and Bond sleep together. Soon after their night together, Bond arranges for Manty's passage to Cincinnati, but she does not go. She is learning that no one else can set her free. Bond's comment to her is, "We're just what we are, little Manty. That's all we are" (139).

At this point in the action, Jereboam Byrd brings Bond word of the raid on Harper's Ferry, and Louisiana secedes from the Union. Warren is clearly familiar with this period of history and deftly weaves the events of the outbreak of the Civil War and the fall of New Orleans into his story. This historical backdrop is perfect for the struggle that Manty faces, since the Civil War is being waged over freedom, albeit a more abstract definition of freedom than the personalized conflict Manty must confront. Even when Manty thinks of Bond in terms of love, she feels guilty and trapped. Former acquaintances reappear in her life. Seth Parton has married Hannah Schmidt from Oberlin College and reenters Manty's life. He and Miss Idell, now Mrs. Morton, bring back depressing memories of her past. For her safety, Bond sends Manty away. Again she is forced to assume another identity as she weds Capt. Tobias Sears with Bond's blessing. Her husband commands a company of black soldiers fighting for the North, and Manty becomes a schoolmarm with the possibility of a new life, since, according to Tobias, one must work in order to live with oneself. However, her hope of a better life ultimately ends in failure and disappointment.

Manty cannot confront her past and, consequently, cannot discover her true identity. She imagines that her fate has been predetermined, thus covering over her personal responsibility for forging her own past and her future: "It was as though your life had a shape, already totally designed, standing not in Time but in Space, already fulfilled, and you were waiting for it, in all its necessity, to be revealed to you, and all your living was merely the process whereby this already existing, fulfilled shape in Space would become an event in Time" (265). In denying her responsibility for her past, Manty unconsciously destroys her dream of freedom. Miss Idell exploits her knowledge of Manty's past to blackmail her. Seth Parton reveals that Tobias does not suspect that Manty is black. Although she tells Tobias about her past, Manty's fear of betrayal sends her to Rau-Ru, who is now commissioned in the Union army as Lt. Oliver Cromwell Jones.

The action accelerates as the 1866 New Orleans riots escalate. Bond is hanged for freeing his slaves, Rau-Ru flees out of anger and frustration, and Tobias moves to the Hartwell plantation. Once more, Manty tries to find freedom for herself. She and Tobias move to St. Louis, where Tobias writes poetry and becomes famous for his book, *The Great Betrayal*, which focuses on the betrayal of individual freedom by big industry—a theme that is taken up by Warren himself in *The Legacy of the Civil War* (1961). Manty again fails to fulfill her longing for self-knowledge and feels that her life has come to nothing. In Sill's Crossing, Kansas, she encounters Rau-Ru, who is now a street beggar. When he dies, she believes his death finally sets her free from "those months of apprehension, bribery, propitiation" (359) until she discovers that she will never know the essential question of human existence and, therefore, will never know the answer for life's enigmatic suffering. Manty does learn, however, that only she can set herself free by casting off the solace of self-deception and acknowledging the truth about her past, no matter how painful it may be. Her lack of self-knowledge is one reason Manty has hate-love relationships with Seth Parton, Miss Idell, Bond, Tobias, Rau-Ru, and even herself. She does not know what community she belongs in. She is able to adjust to life in the black community as well as the white community. Her dilemma is discovering which identity is really hers.

Short Fiction

Warren's canon of short stories is relatively small, containing only about sixteen texts if one excludes the vignettes written for his high school literary publication. Several of these short stories are incorporated into his longer fiction. For example, Warren's short story "Prime Leaf" (1931) was expanded into *Night Rider*. Recognizing that his talent lay in novels and poetry rather than short stories, Warren did not devote much of his creative energy to writing short fiction. Indeed, his last published short story, "Invitation to a Dance," appeared in February, 1949, two years after his only collection of short stories, *The Circus in the Attic and Other Stories*, appeared. In his biography of Warren, Joseph Blotner notes that Warren stopped writing short fiction because he felt the stories got in the way of his poems.

Critics are somewhat divided about the value of Warren's short stories. Justus rightly suggests that Warren's short stories demonstrate his ability to express abstract metaphysical concerns by creating compellingly distinct, historically specific narratives: "From the beginning his uniqueness as a writer of fiction has been the curious way in which Warren is driven both to propound abstract philosophical problems and to explore the concrete actualities of time and place" (262). Casper finds less to praise in *The Circus in the Attic and Other Stories* than does Randolph Runyon who goes to great length to establish links between Warren's short fiction and his poetry.

Most of Warren's short stories are set in Tennessee, and all of them deal with the concerns already discussed in his longer fiction. His stories include "Prime Leaf," "Unvexed Isles" (1934), "Testament of Flood" (1935), "Her Own People" (1935), "When the Light Gets Green" (1936), "Christmas Gift" (1937), "How Willie Proudfit Came Home" (1938), "Goodwood Comes Back" (1941), "The Life and Work of Professor Roy Millen" (1943), "A Christian Education" (1945), "The Love of Elsie Barton: A Chronicle" (1946), "The Confession of Brother Grimes" (1946), "Blackberry Winter"

(1946), "The Patented Gate and the Mean Hamburger" (1947), "The Circus in the Attic" (1947), and "Invitation to a Dance" (1949). Five of these stories should serve as adequate examples of Warren's experiments with short fiction: "The Circus in the Attic," "Blackberry Winter," "The Patented Gate and the Mean Hamburger," "Goodwood Comes Back," and "The Love of Elsie Barton: A Chronicle." Three of these five stories were based on events or memories from Warren's youth. These stories deal with dreams, goals, and the discoveries one makes when one's dreams are either fulfilled or frustrated.

"The Circus in the Attic" tells Bolton Lovehart's story of his unhappy relationship with his mother. Simon Lovehart, who is a major in the Confederate army, dies of a stroke before Bolton is able to attend college at Sewanee in Tennessee. On his deathbed Simon tells Bolton to be good to his mother since she always means well. Bolton decides not to attend college in order to take care of his mother. However, she insists that he attend college and he enrolls at Sewanee. He does not complete his first year there before his mother suffers a heart attack, and he returns home to care for her. Back at home, he begins dating Professor Darter's daughter Sara, and starts writing a history of Carruthers County. Sara seduces Bolton in her father's house, but leaves Bardsville for a more glamorous life. Bolton's mother nags him about doing something with his life, and he retreats to the attic ostensibly to work on the history of Carruthers County. Instead of working on the history, he spends his time building a miniature circus based on one that captured his imagination when he was a boy.

Bolton must grapple with a question posed by Simon Lovehart as he reflects on his wife and son: "Is the present the victim of the past, or the past the victim of the present?"[18] As he abandons writing to work on the miniature circus, he rationalizes that one "can only love perfectly in terms of a great betrayal" (44). Bolton eventually marries Mrs. Parton, a widow with a son Jasper. She, too, is from the Lovehart line and is in her late thirties when they marry, while Bolton is fifty-nine years old. In 1940 Jasper is drafted into military service for World War II. He is killed in action in Italy and is awarded posthumously the Congressional Medal of Honor. Jasper's heroic act of bravery on the battlefield changes Bolton's life. Bolton sells his circus to raise money for the Red Cross as an atonement for his past. His wife is killed in an automobile accident late one night with a man named Captain Cartwright at the wheel. Both had been drinking. World War II ends. Bolton finds his way back to the attic and starts rebuilding his imaginative world. For Bolton, the present seems to be the victim of the past, at least in terms of his decision to remain at home to care for his mother.

"Blackberry Winter" has a first-person narrator named Seth, who tells a retrospective story of his life. It is 1945 when Seth narrates his memories of events that took place June, 1910, in middle Tennessee after a flood. Time, the narrator reflects, is "a kind of element in which things are" (64). Time does not represent linear movement; instead, events are fixed in time. The story of Seth, who is nine years old in 1910, is one of initiation. The flood has brought disorder, destruction, and death to the community. A tramp of unidentified ethnic origin comes to Seth's door asking for work. He is arrogant and surly and has a knife. Seth's mother gives him some menial cleaning chores in exchange for a meal. Seth is curious about the tramp, but goes to the cook's cabin to play, where he is confronted by another discovery about life. He is surprised at how much trash washed out from under their cabin, a place he had always thought of as cleaner than most. Seth is friends with Jebb, who is the cook Dellie's son. Seth loves Jebb's father, who is thirty years older than Dellie and a good man. Seth loves his mother and father, too. When Seth joins his father at the swollen river, he is taken with the image of his father sitting straight in his saddle amid the destruction of the flood. A dead cow floats past while they are there. The crowd gathered at the river declares that the dead cow belongs to Milt Alley, who represents poor white trash in the opinion of the community. When Seth's father returns to the house, he tells the tramp he does not need him now and offers him a half-dollar for half a day's work. The tramp insults Seth's father and leaves. Seth follows the tramp down the lane and asks innocently, "Where are you going?" The tramp's response makes a lasting impression on him: "Stop following me. You don't stop following me and I cut yore throat, you little son-of-a-bitch" (86). Seth's ambiguous response thirty-five years after this encounter has puzzled some readers: "But I did follow him, all the years" (87). For Seth, the tramp represents movement. He seems not to know specifically where he is going but does know with certainty that he is moving on. In his willingness to uproot himself and move forward without holding on to any social ties, the tramp displays a kind of freedom that Seth admires.

In the second edition of *Understanding Fiction* (1959), Warren recollects how "Blackberry Winter" evolved. He recalls going barefoot as a child and his feeling of betrayal when the weather in early summer sets the season back temporarily. He remembers the appearance of a tramp, who was "suspicious, resentful, contemptuous of hick dumbness, bringing his own brand of violence into a world where he half-expected to find another kind, enough unlike his own to make him look over his shoulder down the empty lane as dusk came on, a creature altogether lost and pitiful, a dim image of what, in one perspective, our human condition is" (640). Warren suggests that Seth discovers that he "had really learned something of the meaning of life, he had been bound to follow the tramp all his life, in the imaginative recognition, with all the responsibility which such recognition entails, of this lost, mean, defeated, cowardly, worthless, bitter being as somehow a man" (642).

"The Patented Gate and the Mean Hamburger" comes from the same period in Warren's career, a very productive time when he had just completed *All the King's Men* and his essay on *The Rime of the Ancient Mariner*. In his recollection about "Blackberry Winter," Warren notes that he has just turned forty, is somewhat anxious about his two latest works, and has begun thinking about an earlier unpublished story about a sharecropper in Tennessee. After "Blackberry Winter," he returns to the sharecropper story about a character named Jeff York, who owns a sixty-acre farm in Cobb County, Tennessee.

The story is set in 1935, after Jeff York has worked thirty years to earn enough money to buy his place. The pride of his accomplishments is his white patented gate. He is married and has three children. His wife has a passion for hamburgers. When the family goes to town each Saturday, the last stop is always Slick Hardin's Dew Drop Inn Diner. When Slick announces that the diner is for sale, Mrs. York shows an interest in buying it. The asking price is $1,450. Todd Sullivan, president of the local bank, will not lend the money to Jeff outright but offers to buy Jeff's place for $1,700. Jeff sells his farm and works to clean up the diner. After he and his wife are settled, Jeff takes a walk by himself in the country one Sunday. Neighbors find his body hanging from the main crossbar of the patented gate. Mrs. York is hurt by her husband's death but manages to pick herself up and continue to "fling a mean hamburger."

Like "The Patented Gate and the Mean Hamburger," "Goodwood Comes Back" focuses on the search for authentic individual identity and the effects of that search on other people. "Goodwood Comes Back" is based on Warren's boyhood friend Kent Greenfield, who was spotted by a major league scout and recruited to pitch for the New York Giants in the 1920s. He was a good pitcher and perhaps could have become a great pitcher, but he was homesick. He needed his bird dogs and the open spaces that he left behind in Kentucky. The team manager did not understand his need, and Greenfield did not or would not express it. In Greenfield's dilemma Warren saw the tragic breakdown of a person with great talent and potential for life.[19] Greenfield might have proven a major success had he been able to communicate his problem so that his manager could understand his need. In Warren's fictionalized account of Greenfield's story, Luke Goodwood marries Martha Sheppard and moves to a farm, but bad blood develops between her brother and Luke. A quarrel ensues and her brother shoots and kills Luke with a shotgun. The narrator, who relays much of the story based on what his sister named Mrs. Hargreave tells him, comments on the tragedy with a wry sense of country wisdom: "I have noticed that people living way back in the county like that are apt to be different from ordinary people who see more varieties and kinds of people every day" (119).

"The Love of Elsie Barton: A Chronicle" details Elsie Barton's life from her parental history to her relationship with Benjamin Beaumont, a tobacco buyer who seduces her. They marry and Elsie leaves Charlestown, Tennessee, to have their daughter Helen. Elsie survives the pregnancy and their marriage, which she is never able to understand. Benjamin Beaumont dies of a stroke caused by his debauchery in Nashville. The community serves as a kind of character in this story, which is told by an omniscient narrator. Elsie Beaumont is an old woman at the start of the story. The narration moves backward in time. Her relationship with the community and her self-imposed isolation remind one of Faulkner's "A Rose for Emily," but Elsie hides no corpse in the attic. She suffers quietly her error of vanity, fostered by Benjamin Beaumont before they were married. The next story in the collection, "Testament of Flood," seems to flow out of "The Love of Elsie Barton, and is more of a partial story that continues with Helen's classmate Steve Adams's crush on her. This kind of interweaving of narrative strands between different Warren stories is a prevalent movement in his canon. In *The Taciturn Text* Randolph Runyon has done a detailed analysis of how Warren constructs intertextual links between his short stories and novels. Runyon also provides a cogent reading of intertextual connections between Warren's poetry in *The Braided Dream.*

CHAPTER THREE

Late Fiction (1955–1977)

"Fiction brings up from their dark oubliettes our
shadowy, deprived selves and gives them an airing
in, as it were, the prison yard."

"Why Do We Read Fiction?" (1962)

Novels

The Cave

Warren's sixth novel deals with unsuccessful relationships that are
centered privately on pride, greed, and lust. The cave itself serves as
a controlling symbol, not unlike Plato's allegorical cave, of appearance and reality. *The Cave*, too, has an historical event as backdrop
to the fictive lives Warren creates,[1] demonstrating once more Warren's deep concern with the narrative quality of history as well as
with the nature of time.

Critics have located a range of meanings in *The Cave*. Burt's
discussion of the cave image in *World Enough and Time* connects
with that image in *The Cave* as "a place of lonely exultation and sexual excess."[2] Clark's brief assessment of the novel notes Warren's
critique of the media's negative intervention into people's lives.
Warren criticizes the media for creating a technological form of illusion. Justus introduces his discussion of *The Cave* with a reference
to Warren's essay on *Nostromo* that shows the connection between
that essay and the novel's thematic interest in "the cost of awareness
and the difficulty of virtue" (272).

Jasper Harrick, whom the reader never officially meets in the

novel, but whose presence is the center of attention, and Isaac
Sumpter want to get rich quick. To do so, they hope to find a cave
in Tennessee that will prove as much of a tourist attraction as Kentucky's Mammoth Cave. While exploring a cave near Johntown,
Tennessee, Jasper becomes trapped inside.

The discovery of his plight sets in motion a search that is covered nationally by the media with all the commercialism associated
with an amusement park. The community becomes concerned with
its public image. Timothy Bingham of People's Security Bank and
Nicolas Papadoupalous, the Greek café owner, jump on the media
bandwagon once Isaac starts selling the news about Jasper's disappearance. Though the novel focuses on the negative effects of media
overkill, an underlying concern of the narrative is to show how people respond in times of crisis. For example, Nicholas Papadoupalous
(nicknamed Nick Pappy) has failed in three previous attempts in the
restaurant business. His life is mired in personal crisis. His adulter-
ous affair with Dorothy Cutlick, his former waitress who is now a
bookkeeper at People's Security Bank, is passionless. Events at the
cave finally offer Nick Pappy a chance to transcend his personal fail-
ures. Although the crisis surrounding Jasper's disappearance offers
him a brief hope of success, this hope proves purely illusionary.
Once more, one of Warren's characters falls prey to disappointment
and failure.

The Harrick family is in a depressing situation. The father Jack
is dying of cancer and is alienated from his sons. His relationship
with Monty, Jasper's brother, is similar to Jed Tewksbury's relationship with his father in *A Place to Come To*. Jack's image over-
powers his son, who must learn to live through it and beyond it in
order to find meaning in his life. Celia Hornby Harrick, Jack's wife

who is twenty-five years younger than he, is a loving, caring wife who tries to make her ailing husband comfortable. Jack, on the other hand, wishes her dead at times. His selfishness, fed by overwhelming pride, interferes with all his relationships. Jasper, a Korean War veteran, is the son more like his father and the family member Jack comes closest to loving. After Jasper's death is confirmed, Jack reflects back on all the people he has hurt, some of whose names he cannot even remember. About Celia, he confesses that "he hadn't cared what even she had wanted or needed, what emptiness she had to fill to be herself. All that had mattered was his own terror when, not knowing for a second whose hand he held in the dark, he had been caught in the vertigo of his own non-being."[3] In the end Jack Harrick comes to believe that only through confronting death can one learn how to live (403). He is perhaps the only character in the novel with a grasp on reality. Celia feels the despair, isolation, and hopelessness of the loss of Jasper. Though she suffers deeply, she is able to endure.

The carnival atmosphere created by Jasper's disappearance is like a meaningless Christmas that has all the tinsel, lights, and decorations but is devoid of conviction. Monty Harrick and Jo-Lea Bingham, who are involved together in a sad teenage relationship, discover Jasper's boots and guitar at the mouth of the cave. Monty blames his low self-esteem on Jo-Lea, and he bears a love-hate feeling toward her. Jo-Lea is pregnant, and Jasper is rumored to be the father. Her father wants her to have an abortion, a suggestion which causes further strain with his wife. When Jo-Lea's mother confronts Jo-Lea about the pregnancy, Mrs. Bingham assumes the voice of moral righteousness and plays the role well in what is clearly her finest hour. After all is said and done, the Binghams plan to divorce.

Monty feels doubly betrayed, by Jo-Lea's affair and by the belief that Jasper was her lover. As the pitch of the scene outside the cave reaches a crescendo, Monty leaves in guilt and disgust.

Brother MacCarland Sumpter hides the truth that his son Isaac is the father of Jo-Lea's baby. In fact, he protects his son throughout the rescue operation. Isaac enters the cave, finds Jasper, and designs the rescue. He and Jebb Holloway go back into the cave to take food and supplies to Jasper. Isaac decides not to announce that Jasper is dead. Instead, he fakes getting the food to Jasper in order to keep the attention focused on the event, the price he is willing to pay for a little ego satisfaction. Isaac will profit from this story with news releases and magazine features. Even sensing the paradox of "powerlessness in power" (285), Isaac feels as if this event is his destiny. He is relieved when he does not find Jasper on the ledge, and he has a sense of redemption, a sense that he can now afford to be good. Brother Sumpter goes into the cave, confirms Jasper's death, and removes some evidence that would otherwise prove that Isaac had lied and that might create suspicion that Isaac killed Jasper. Isaac plans to flee the area. When Brother Sumpter confesses to Jack Harrick what Isaac has done, Jack offers no forgiveness, no redemption. Sumpter has confessed his part in his son's elaborate deception in order to save Isaac. He believes that it is a sign of courage, but it is a false sign, and leads to an unrealized salvation.

Jasper Harrick is the key character in the various soap operas that are played out in Johntown. Justus claims that *The Cave* is Warren's most "severely stylized fiction" (274) and points to the character of Jasper Harrick as evidence of Warren's overplaying of conventional stereotypes in the novel. Although Justus's critique of Warren's style in *The Cave* has some validity, Warren's overly styl-

ized manner is appropriate for expressing the novel's thematic
issues, particularly for articulating the Johntown community's need
to define itself in response to the crisis. Warren's stylized prose
reflects the fact that the world of Johntown is an illusion, manifested
and promoted by the media, based on lies and betrayals. As Lieutenant Scrogg says, "Folks believe what they want to believe" (350),
even about themselves.

Wilderness

Wilderness contains an intertextual link with *The Cave* through a
relatively minor character named Rachel Goldstein, a Jewish girl
with whom Isaac Sumpter is associated for a brief period. In *Wilderness* (1961) Warren provides another narrative based on the Civil
War. The novel represents a publication of opportunity on two
counts. First, along with *The Legacy of the Civil War*, it appeared on
the centennial anniversary of the Civil War. Second, it returned
Warren to a topic of deep concern for him that dates back to the stories his Grandfather Penn told him. Including the Cass Mastern
episode in *All the King's Men*, *Wilderness* is Warren's fourth and
final novel to make use of the Civil War as historical background.

In a 1974 interview with Marshall Walker, Warren talks about
the problem of *Wilderness* as a technical problem. He started it as a
novelette, but when it grew into a full-scale novel, the protagonist
did not develop. In the interview Warren describes the experience of
reading the novel in the following way: "You have the strange effect
of a central *hollowness* with a rich context, with the central character as an observer . . . involved *intellectually*."[4]

Although critics were not impressed with the novel, *Wilderness*

is a necessary link in Warren's oeuvre. It focuses on a character of
foreign origin, a displaced person who is not accepted as an equal in
society. In this regard *Wilderness* is a precursor to another story
about an outsider, Angelo Pasetto, the Italian sojourner in *Meet Me
in the Green Glen*. Neither character has the sense of self-worth necessary for living a meaningful life.

The same basic questions are asked in *Wilderness* that are
asked throughout Warren's fiction. As the characters change, their
attempts to answer those questions vary. Some acquire the necessary
self-knowledge and gain a productive sense of their identity, while
others do not. Adam Rosenzweig belongs to the former group. He is
a Jewish immigrant from Bavaria who comes to America to fight for
a just cause, freedom, by enlisting in the Union army during the
Civil War. That cause enables Warren to deal at least tangentially
with the issue of Jewish-Christian relationships. Rosenzweig
endures the requisite suffering and realizes his purpose. He knows
that he must leave the Wilderness, the area known historically as the
Pizen Woods, "in the fullness of time and human effort" to confront
his own responsibility for his fate.[5] That ending is not too far
removed from Jack Burden's acceptance of responsibility at the end
of *All the King's Men*.

What readers may find of interest in this narrative are the
descriptions of Adam's travels and the cross-section of humanity
that he encounters. The descriptions of Adam's journey are loaded
with literary allusions and connections to other works that Warren
would have known, such as Tate's "Ode to the Confederate Dead,"
Theodore Dreiser's "Free," Ralph Ellison's *Invisible Man*, Hemingway's *A Farewell to Arms*, and Warren's own "Ballad of Billie
Potts." Adam's adventures include his travel from Bavaria to New

York City, his stay in New York, his trip south to join the Union army, his stay in Virginia, and his trip to the Wilderness. Each segment of his journey is filled with the overwhelming question of justice and Adam's role in the world.

The portrayal of Adam's quest is realistic and far from the romantic view of the Civil War held by the young Robert Penn when he visited his grandfather on the farm near Cerulean Springs. Concerning the relation of the novel to the tales his grandfather told him about the war, Warren has commented that his grandfather did not romanticize the Civil War. In addition to Wilderness, Warren's poem "Court-martial" shows the impact of that realistic view on his art.[6]

Not unlike Audubon, the title character of Warren's book-length poem, Adam is of the world in Bavaria and believes in the world that he sees in nature's beauty. If he had not beheld those wonders as he did, he might have fled into his interior self, "the ironies of history and knowledge," into the "wisdom which is resignation" (4). Adam's conflict is between Jewish law, the Talmud, and human law. Adam goes against his paternal uncle, who tells him the freedom of the world is really the "freedom to kill Jews" (13). Adam wants the world to know justice. Adam has a clubfoot, but he does not let that handicap limit him. His rebellious nature moves him to find his self-worth, to be worthy of someone's love. He petitions to go to America with the altruistic goal of fighting for freedom, a goal scorned by his shipmates en route to America.

Safely on shore in America, Adam sees a black man being hanged, the first black he has ever seen, and then witnesses mob violence. He hides in a dark basement that is filling with water. He is aware of other people there and passes out. That he awakens in Aaron Blaustein's house calls for a willing suspension of our disbelief, since Blaustein is his uncle's friend, the very person Adam is seeking in New York City. Blaustein speaks of the South as being ignorant of the world and therefore destined for defeat. He becomes Adam's teacher and guide into the real world. Blaustein makes the observation that, if one stops believing in God, he falls back on history (69). Adam learns from Blaustein the significance of both God and history. At Adam's request, Blaustein arranges for him to travel south and join the Union army. As he travels with the black man named Mose Talbutt who saved his life that night in the flooded basement, he wonders about his life and tries to define himself by saying, "*I am what I am*" (94).

In Virginia, Adam offers to teach Talbutt to read. Adam learns that prejudice exists in the North as well as the South when Talbutt tells him he can be put in jail for teaching a "nigger" to read (173). Adam, the idealist, asserts that all men should be free. Jed Hawksworth challenges Adam's concept of freedom. Jed's concept of freedom is similar to Manty's in *Band of Angels*—that is, no one can set another person free. When Adam learns that Aaron Blaustein is dead, he feels devalued as if no one cared who he is or even if he is. He is alone. Adam is further depressed when he learns that Mose Talbutt is really Mose Crawfurd, a deserter from the Union army. Mose kills Jed Hawksworth and steals his money belt.

Adam leaves camp and joins up with the caravan of troops after General Grant arrives. The images of the scene are dark. "Life was seething desperately forth," but Adam is struck by the formation of troops, the ones "elected to know the grandeur of truth," that moment of courage in the face of death (234). Having found what he came to find, having lost his pain of lostness, now able to discard the past, Adam feels free to leave the convoy and go his own way.

He stops at a cabin occupied by a man and woman and shares some of his supplies with them. The woman, grateful, warns Adam to beware for his life when her husband leads him to the edge of the Wilderness. This warning recalls a similar scene in Warren's poem "The Ballad of Billie Potts," except that this time the guest is not killed by his host.

When he enters the Wilderness, Adam moves with certainty though he does not know the way. His quest now is "to know if there is a truth in the world" (289). He encounters eight marauders who turn over his wagon and steal his remaining supplies and his boots, which were specially made for his deformed foot. The marauders are attacked by men in blue, and Adam kills a man. At that moment his purpose is realized, and he feels that the world is just, because he feels guilty. He suffers a feeling of betrayal by Aaron, Jed, Mose, his father, and begins to mistrust everything he thought he knew. Walking in the boots of one of the dead men, whose name he does not know, he hopes that he can be "worthy of their namelessness," of what they had endured (310). At the novel's end, Adam remains utterly alone in the world.

Flood: A Romance of Our Time

Whereas Adam at the end of *Wilderness* is left completely alone, the characters in Warren's eighth novel, *Flood* (1964), are psychologically incarcerated in their doomed community. Loneliness and alienation are the key components of this novel.

Warren published two other books within two years of this novel, and the research conducted for them may have had an influence on *Flood*. *Who Speaks for the Negro?* (1965) may, for example, have prompted Brad Tolliver's remark that the heart of the race problem is southerners' inability to cope with people who are not lonesome, especially blacks. Warren also edited the book, *Faulkner: A Collection of Critical Essays* (1966), during this period. Two of Warren's own essays are included in the collection, "Faulkner: Past and Future" and "Faulkner: The South, the Negro, and Time," as well as one essay by Brooks, "History and the Sense of the Tragic: *Absalom, Absalom!*" All three of these essays are concerned with the same concept of time that is expressed in *Flood*.

In *Flood* Warren again draws on historical events to use as a backdrop for the novel. Though he may not have a particular flood in mind, his novel clearly takes into account contemporary narratives of the several catastrophic floods that swamped Tennessee.[7] In using the Tennessee floods as a basis for his story, Warren examines how people respond when placed in desperate situations. Such times of crisis raised questions in Warren's mind, questions dealing with individuals involved in those circumstances and the concept of home.

In a 1969 interview Warren explained how the novel started:

> In April 1931, the anniversary of the Battle of Shiloh, I passed through southwest Tennessee. I saw the old house, hanging over the bluff of the river, which I think was Grant's headquarters during the battle—the second day of the battle, I think it was. Anyway, I forget the name of the house. I didn't go in; I just saw it, drove past it, and the village was the germ of Fiddlersburg and that house was the germ of the Fiddler house. I just caught a glimpse of it in passing, about a ninety-second glimpse. It stuck somehow. I couldn't describe the town now, only the impression I carried away from it.

The—now, my God, what is it?—thirty or thirty-two
years I've been writing that novel.[8]

Warren went on to say that he considered *Flood* one of his two
or three best novels.

In "Faulkner: Past and Future" Warren writes that "Faulkner,
like Antaeus, could fight only with his feet on the ground—on home
ground; he had to work toward meaning through the complexity and
specificity of a literal world in which he knew his way about, as a
man knows his way about his own house without thinking how he
gets from one room to another; only in that world could he find the
seminal images that would focus his deepest feelings into vision."[9]
Like Faulkner, Warren worked within the world he knew, and his
character Brad Tolliver, a writer, returns to Fiddlersburg, his home-
town, to finish his screenplay about the town before it is sacrificed
to a new reservoir and hydroelectric project. Tolliver is accompa-
nied by Yasha Jones, a well-known director who is not from the
South. The narrative is told from the omniscient point of view and
provides insights into the community of Fiddlersburg from the perspectives of an insider and an outsider.

In *The American Vision of Robert Penn Warren*, Clark writes
that *Flood* "presumes to present its readers with the unsettling, but
ultimately liberating, 'truth' about the underlying phenomenological
world of ambiguities and paradoxes they are destined—and privi-
leged—to inhabit" (124). Justus establishes from the novel's opening a dominant image of superficiality and artificial identities—what
Justus calls "the use of stage properties for carrying the burden of
the self"(285). Justus suggests that Tolliver has returned to recover
his authentic self, while the uprooted community will reinvent its

identity through the new possibilities inherent in resettling (294). In *The Blood-Marriage of Earth and Sky* Casper asserts that "the more profound center [of *Flood*] is the mortality of *all* people and intimations of a resurrection, a reason for having been born" (43). As a supplement to Clark's and Justus's readings, one might observe that at best Brad Tolliver learns that seeking truth is important and that one must choose his own way in life.

Characterization is one of Warren's strong suits in his fiction. Brad Tolliver believes "if everything is fake then nothing matters,"[10] but his encounter with Jingle Bells (Mortimer Sparlin, an honors graduate from the University of Chicago) at the Seven Dwarfs Motel, with its fairy-tale motif, bothers him. Brad is a screenwriter, a master of illusion. His return to Fiddlersburg is both professional and personal. His business there involves writing a screenplay based on the fate of Fiddlersburg. The town will be inundated and the resulting reservoir will provide water for a new industrial complex. Once again lending an anti-industrialist bent to his fiction, Warren suggests that destroying a town and its heritage is the price of progress in the early 1960s.

The personal part of his return brings Brad back to see his sister, Maggie Tolliver Fiddler, in order to regain part of himself from the past. His search for his past identity also leads him to revisit his memories of Old Izzie Goldfarb, a Jewish tailor on River Street. Goldfarb had been kind to Brad and was part of that past. Though Goldfarb is dead, Brad returns to give him a final goodbye. Brad is also reminded of his first wife Lettice Poindexter, since his memories of her are tied to Fiddlersburg. He has gone through two wives, Lettice and Suzie Martine, and recollections of them flood back to him. Although reopening one's past is potentially a deeply emotional experience, Brad remains stoical and restrained. Writers are not without egos, and Brad is no exception. His stoic return without sentimentality pleases him. He has, after all, learned something about his craft and takes pride in his awards and accomplishments.

Yasha Jones joins Brad to get a feel for the place before he directs the production. Yasha Jones, originally from Russia, serves as a foil to Brad Tolliver. A World War II veteran and a widower with a sense of responsibility, guilt, and loss, Jones reads poetry and thinks deeply about the purpose of life. His humane sensibility is something to hold on to in an age of depersonalization. He is sensitive and understanding toward other people. Thinking about the movie he will make, he ponders the slippery relation between appearance and reality, lies and the truth: "reality was the uncapturable. That was why we need illusion. *Truth through lie*" (50). He views the world as if he is looking through a camera and works in the evanescence of the motion picture which allows no immortality (57). Jones explains to Maggie and her mother-in-law why he chose Fiddlersburg. He read a newspaper article about Fiddlersburg and had a "vision" (102), prompted in part by Brad's first book, a collection of seven short stories titled *I'm Telling You Now*. From his own heritage as a Russian Georgian, Jones appreciates and respects history, something that Brad takes for granted. He has thought about truthfulness, too. He tells Maggie about his law of information and evidence, which suggests that a straight question always gets a crooked answer (186). As a result, in his movies Jones makes statements rather than asks questions. With his characterization of Jones, Warren is able to provide the irony needed to balance the quest for self-knowledge. Jones considers himself a would-be physicist, and yet he knows the joy of abstraction, the pleasure of observing "how light falls on a leaf" (264). Jones's scientific, objective view as a would-be physicist counters Brad's artistic, subjective view as a writer. The leaf image may be particularly meaningful, since it is a recurring image throughout Warren's poetry. One interpretation of the leaf image relates it to the life cycle and the connection between man and nature, elements that Warren suggests must be understood on the quest for self-knowledge. Maggie is attracted to Jones, and they go off together. Brad celebrates their union and Maggie's humanness.

Other characters play supporting roles in the unraveling of Brad's life. He apparently loved Lettice Poindexter at one time. Early in their relationship they lived for the moment, seeking instant gratification. Lettice has several affairs before they marry, one while Brad is in Spain fighting for the Loyalist cause. When he returns, they marry and settle in Fiddlersburg where she paints and he writes. Their fairly hedonistic lifestyle eventually creates problems for them. After Lettice loses their baby in a miscarriage, she divorces Brad. Her psychiatrist Dr. Sutton refers to her as a Puritan idealist. Whether or not his analysis is correct, Lettice changes her lifestyle. She becomes a nurse in World War II and is stationed in New Guinea. After the war she becomes a lay worker in a Catholic home for old people in Chicago. She writes Brad a letter to tell him about her life. At that moment Brad realizes that Lettice is no longer a superficial image, but has become real to him as she has taken on a separate, individual existence. Nevertheless, he is unable to fulfill the human necessity that is his past and its connection to his present being. He has at least learned that the past is what he must seek in order to understand his present experience. His visit teaches him another lesson as well: *There is no country but the heart*" (440).

Brad has a difficult relationship with his sister, whom Lettice befriends. Because the advice she gives Maggie, Lettice feels responsible for her sister-in-law's sad life. After Lettice encourages her to live more fully, Maggie marries Calvin Fiddler, who is completing his medical internship in Nashville. On a visit to Brad and Lettice's house in Fiddlersburg, Maggie has an affair with a young engineer named Alfred O. Tuttle. Once he learns of the affair, Calvin Fiddler murders Tuttle. Fiddler is convicted and sentenced to imprisonment in the Fiddlersburg penitentiary. During Brad's return to Fiddlersburg, Calvin escapes from prison and shoots Brad, but then saves Brad's life and is returned to prison. Maggie has isolated herself from the community by devoting her attention to the aging Mrs. Fiddler. When she meets Jones, his sensitivity and caring help Maggie break her self-imposed isolation. They fall in love and subsequently marry.

Frog-Eye is one of Brad's childhood friends, who provides an alternative example for Brad. Frog-Eye is independent, choosing to live outside of society as a swamp rat. He has helped Brad leave Fiddlersburg years before. Frog-Eye shows Brad what Brad's father does when he makes trips to the swamp. Lancaster (Lank) Tolliver and Brad do not have a warm father-son relationship. When Brad sees his father drunk in the swamp and weeping, he loses respect for him. His lack of respect for his father allows Brad to strike out for a new life away from the constraints of Fiddlersburg. In what another example of the common motif of father-son conflict in Warren's fiction, Brad eventually learns that self-knowledge is the key to his freedom from his father.

Brother Potts, the one-armed Baptist preacher who is dying of cancer, provides the community strength and hope for the future.

Brad, however, substitutes history for religion, and his lessons are not as easily learned. He finds no solace in religion and must seek meaning for his existence by confronting his past.

Warren's mastery of characterization is enriched by the atmosphere and the setting of his stories. Warren's novels all take place in the South, the region he knows best. As Justus points out, the real setting of Fiddlersburg is obscured by the artificial setting that has been moved in during Brad's absence. This contrast fits into the larger conflict in the story between appearance and reality. In his writing, which imbues his life with a temporary sense of value, Brad substitutes illusion for reality, whereas Jones knows that nothing can be substituted for reality in life: even if one arrives at truth through lies, one must still actively seek truth or life will be drained of purpose. For the setting of *Flood*, Warren focuses on providing detailed descriptions of a particular southern town. He emphasizes the ambiance of the natural surroundings as Brad and Yasha look down at the river and into the loneliness of the woods and shadow. Upon arriving in Fiddlersburg, Brad sees that the town is outside of history without losing the feel of history. The setting brings him in and out of the past. He fails to confront his past fully, just as Fiddlersburg as a town is about to fail, its heritage about to disappear, flooded over by the wave of industrial progress sweeping over the South.

Meet Me in the Green Glen

Meet Me in the Green Glen (1971) reveals the lives of three main characters—Cassie Spottwood, Angelo Passetto, and Murray Guilfort—as they move through their somnambulistic world of shades and shadows. Although the thematic thrust is familiar to Warren's readers, the larger implications of the novel, the complexity of its characterizations, and the harmonizing effect of its technique produce a compelling narrative.

Begun in 1964, *Meet Me in the Green Glen* has as its basis a murder mystery, but, of course, murders in Warren's fiction are not new. In synopsis form the plot might read much like a sophisticated detective story, complete with trial scene. The novel begins as a stranger drifts into town and takes work as a handyman on a quiet, secluded farm. The community is small, seething, and southern, as the novel is set in Parkerton, Tennessee, a town near Fiddlersburg. The time of the plot is mid-twentieth century. The wife (Cassie) of the owner of the farm and the stranger (Angelo) become involved sexually. Eventually, the farm owner (Sunderland), who is bedridden, is murdered. The stranger leaves town, but is captured, tried, convicted, and executed for the murder. The bereaved widow breaks down mentally and physically. Interspersed through the story is the personality of a "trusted friend" of the widow (Murray), ostensibly her benefactor and protector.

Readers who look only at the surface action may find fault with this novel in the same way that they may find fault with all of Warren's novels. On the surface the novels may appear melodramatic. However, Warren himself provides an answer to these attacks by suggesting that life in the South at mid-century was itself melodramatic: "Melodrama was the breath of life. There had been melodrama in the life I had known in Tennessee, . . . but in Louisiana people lived melodrama, seemed to live, in fact, for it, for this strange combination of philosophy, humor, and violence."[11]

Although it may be self-consciously melodramatic, the story is not simple, however. Warren weaves together an intricate web of time in which the characters' lives are inextricably bound. Chronologically, the present action of the story (discounting the epilogue) covers the time from Angelo Passetto's arrival in Spottwood Valley in late November 1957 to shortly after his execution 21 March 1959, a period of less than a year and a half. In this respect the story is Angelo's story, a character who serves as the narrative's antihero. In another respect the story is Cassie's because she is the moving force behind the other characters' actions. Yet, Murray Guilfort's story is too much a part of both narrative strands to be subordinated to them. Cassie's release from the loneliness of the past leads to a recognition, a heightened sense of self-awareness. Murray's guilt complex also leads to a partial recognition of this authentic being, while Angelo's locked-in ego prevents him from achieving self-recognition. In *Meet Me in the Green Glen* all three characters oscillate between appearance and reality, and each suffers a conflict which arises from an illusionary sense of the self.

Sicilian-born Angelo Passetto is a parolee who hides from his past, suppressing the knowledge of his three-year term in the Fiddlersburg penitentiary and the memories of Guido Altocchi and his trial. Angelo subsumes Cassie's world of shadows into his "dark inner nothingness" and submerges himself, literally, under "the feather ticking, under the quilts, into the unreality" of the situation.[12] When he does not surface, he tries to flee from the "something just discovered in himself that he did not know the name of" (49). That "something" is his locked-in ego which makes him overly proud of his black silky hair, creates feelings of vengeance in him, and provokes the illusion that he is "all at once, as tall as the house, as tall as a tree, and as strong as God" (179). Daily he flees into the "reality" of work, much in the same way that Brad Tolliver uses work as a means of self-definition in *Flood*. Each night, however, Angelo faces the unreality of the meals prepared by Cassie whom he does not and cannot understand. Ironically, Angelo discovers that he has exchanged one type of imprisonment for another type. Although Cassie tells him that she always wants him to feel free, Angelo feels trapped. He vents his frustration through violence: he rapes Cassie, an act to which she is unresponsive, he reads pulp magazines that evoke excitement "in the blur of violence and lust," and he becomes involved in a violent relationship with Charlene, the mulatto daughter of Arlita Benton and Sunderland Spottwood. Cassie's submission renders Angelo defenseless; he is enraged and afraid until, at last, Cassie releases him from her "world of changelessness, where nothing had ever happened and nothing would ever happen" (125). From his own narcissistic dream of himself, however, he is never released.

Cassandra Killigrew Spottwood (Cassie) represents Warren's most successful attempt at creating a female character. Lucy Ferriss compares her to Thomas Hardy's Tess.[13] Cassie is a many-faceted person. Though she is forty-three years old, she still maintains a girlhood love for Cy Grinder and the regret of lost joy. Cassie escapes from the pressures of present realities by receding into her memories of her high school days with Cy Grinder. When Cy went away from her, Cassie's emotion of "going-awayness" (98) began.

Her character is marked by a darker side. She harbors a vengeful instinct toward the bedridden Sunderland Spottwood, a pupil-lover attitude toward Angelo, and a lonely and empty obligation to Murray Guilfort. After Cy leaves her, her life is measured in part by "going-awayness." Sunderland figuratively goes away from her when he is paralyzed by a stroke. Angelo, too, goes away after the murder of Sunderland, while Murray mentally deserts Cassie in her time of need. Paradoxically, Cassie's substitute for this figurative desertion is a firmer sense of reality than that of the two other main characters, a fact that she acknowledges in one of her interior monologues (98).

Like Cassie, LeRoy Lancaster, Angelo's defense attorney, discovers that the secret to imbuing life with some sort of provisional value lies in confronting one's own responsibility for one's fate. After the Supreme Court of Tennessee sustains Angelo's conviction, LeRoy muses to himself "that this was the way the world was, and a man had to deal with that fact" (295). Cassie has already told Murray that "you have to lead your own kind of life" (40). Cassie's acceptance of this philosophy does not come easily, but is hard-fought. After Angelo arrives, she goes through a period in which the nights are her illusion of reality and the days seem unreal. Cassie alone achieves a rebirth, which is her temporary freedom from Sunderland and from her shadows (153). Upon recognizing the truth of her illusionary version of herself, she gains her freedom from the past and is able to live in the present. When she learns later of Angelo's betrayal, she realizes the painful truth that the present is never completely free from the past. In recognizing this second fundamental truth, she earns her right to self-knowledge.

Murray Guilfort's role is, perhaps, the most straightforward part in the novel. Murray is all appearance and no substance. Like Cassie, he is left alone to wander "the darkness of his own head." Within that darkness Murray deludes himself into believing that he can repudiate the past and be transformed and redeemed in the future (29). To Murray, life is "a cat asleep in a rocker" (43). The metaphor reveals a potential link to Dreiser's *Sister Carrie*. In

Homage to Theodore Dreiser Warren interprets the meaning of Sister Carrie's rocking chair. He suggests that it is "motion without progress, life spent in mere repetition, a hypnotic dream without content" and represents "a perfect image of the success that 'got nowhere'" (29). The comment is equally applicable to Murray Guilfort, who ritualistically takes money to Cassie in exchange for a meaningless signed receipt and whose material success fails to free him from his inner prison. Even in confronting death he does not recognize his true self (372). His motives for helping Cassie are self-righteous vindication for his early failings and his need to feel superior to Sunderland. In spite of his appearance of goodness, Murray takes selfish delight in Sunderland's plight. He is therefore guilty of being one of the *"beggars and buyers and stealers and pickers of remnants"* (146). Angelo, in effect, takes away one of Murray's moral crutches through his affair with Cassie. Neither Cassie nor Cy Grinder is fooled by Murray's appearance; their knowledge serves as a prick of conscience to Murray who knows the truth about Angelo's trial and about his own inability to love anyone. In the latter respect he is like Angelo. Murray cannot realize the connection between love and knowledge that is asserted in the famous line from Warren's *Audubon: A Vision*: "What is love? / One name for it is knowledge." Whereas Murray does not possess the knowledge necessary for love, Cassie and Cy are able to grasp, through self-awareness and love, the meaning of "The secret worth / Of all our human worthlessness."[14]

The past continues to haunt Murray. Ironically, he is the founder of the West Tennessee History Association, an organization designed to preserve rather than to repudiate the past. Angelo lives his life in the remote, artificial past of dance halls and women in red satin dresses; he does not achieve a sense of the present when he attempts to make Cassie a part of that past. Consequently, both Murray and Angelo fail to assert their identity in time. They are unable to strike a harmony between past and present, a balance that Warren considers necessary to a fulfilling life. "Each of us," he writes in "Knowledge and the Image of Man," "longs for full balance and responsibility in self-knowledge, in a recognition and harmonious acceptance of our destiny."[15] Both Cassie and Cy Grinder, in distinguishing between what they ought to be and what they are, gain self-knowledge and the identity they have been seeking—the end of the dream.

In addition to the successful characterizations in *Meet Me in the Green Glen*, Warren provides us with a successful murder mystery. The question of who committed the murder remains a mystery in spite of convictions, confessions, and contentions. In a 1974 personal discussion about the novel, Warren told me that Cassie was the murderer, clear and simple. With all due respect to his authorial intention, it seems that textual evidence permits other interpretations as well as reasonable doubt about Cassie's guilt. This sense of doubt is not a detriment to Warren's detective novel, but adds an extra dimension to the story.

Angelo, Cassie, and Murray all have motives for killing Sunderland. Angelo's character is prone to bouts of violent anger. He even claims that "Someday he would kill that man [Sunderland]" who called him "Puss-Face" (120). He is a previously convicted criminal. He feels trapped, and a natural reaction for a cornered, desperate person is violence. Although Cassie holds him back, she is also his means to escape, providing him with money and a car. By killing Sunderland, Angelo would have a reason to escape and, at the same time, would avenge himself on Cassie, whom he has grown to resent (129).

On the other hand, Cassie has equally convincing reasons for killing Sunderland. She has been nursing him for over twelve years—a trial in itself. Before his stroke, Sunderland was never a "loving husband"; at best, his love was "amiable bestiality." Another plausible motive for Cassie would be jealousy over Charlene and anger at Arlita's prodding. Even though Cassie said she would not hold Angelo back, she might have murdered Sunderland in order to be free to go *with* Angelo. The truth about Sunderland's infidelity with Arlita could have inflamed Cassie into action. Her courtroom confession is hardly convincing or binding. When she tells Cy Grinder the "truth," she also admits that the worst part is disbelief: "You have to look in the mirror—look at your own face and say, it was you did it—and keep saying it, until something happens to that face in the mirror, till it goes all white and sick-looking, then suddenly, you know that that face believes it" (318).

Finally, Murray Guilfort has motives for murdering Sunderland. At one point he even thinks in a flash of rage, "*why can't he* [Sunderland] *die!*" (134). Sunderland is both an unpleasant symbol of Murray's past and a burden to his conscience. In this sense Sunderland is Murray's ideal scapegoat. Murray does not like Angelo and suggests to Cassie that Angelo should leave. In an act of potential foreshadowing, Murray is seen holding the very knife with which Sunderland is stabbed when he makes the suggestion that Angelo should leave. Instead of taking the illegal switchblade with him, he lays it on the table in Angelo's room (215). The evidence is still no more than circumstantial. Warren was rather clandestine about the exact dates of narrative events until the murder trial, at which time he detailed the events surrounding Sunderland's death on Friday, 11 April 1958:

2:30 A.M.	Cassie is in her red dress (222)
5:00 A.M.	Cassie gets up to care for Sunderland's sheets (237)
6:40 A.M.	Cassie says she shaved Sunderland (238)
7:30 A.M.	Time at which coroner sets the death (234)
7:31–36 A.M.	Charlene departs her house for the spring to meet Angelo (244)
9:25 A.M.	Cassie gets to Spottwood Corners' Store three miles from her house (233)
10:36 A.M.	Sheriff, coroner, and Murray arrive at Corners' (234)
10:52 A.M.	Coroner examines the body (234)

Between 7:30 A.M. and 9:25 A.M. almost two hours are unaccounted for; therefore, it is conceivable that if Murray were at the Spottwood house at 7:30 A.M., he would have had time to return to Parkerton before receiving the call around 9:25 A.M. One reason for implicating Murray in the murder is his actions afterwards. He is obsessed with Cassie's burned clothing, which he discovers all by himself and unobserved. He also seems to have carefully rehearsed Cassie for the trial and places a great deal of emphasis on eye contact while Cassie is on the witness stand (237). Third, Cassie's reference to changing the sheets at 5:00 A.M. echoes Murray's remembrance

of how often his wife's sheets had to be changed while she lingered on her deathbed (232). For all of these reasons, Murray is a potential suspect in Sunderland's murder.

Arlita, Sunderland's black mistress, is not seriously considered as a suspect, in spite of the fact that she has the opportunity to murder him. Arlita does not kill him when the opportunity presents itself because she knows the way the world is.

The identity of the actual murderer is not crucial to an understanding of the story's value. To detail the evidence against particular characters becomes academic and tedious. Similar questions of guilt exist successfully without solution in other serious works of literature as well. Actually, the novel reads better with some doubt left, since its open-endedness parallels the ambiguity of life itself and provides a richer range of thematic interpretations for the novel. If Angelo is guilty, something can be said for the strength of Cassie's love for him. If Cassie is guilty, southern justice is indicted. If Murray is guilty, Warren has it both ways.

If one does not hastily reject the story, based on the melodramatic aspects of *Meet Me in the Green Glen* and is instead willing to engage the plot and characterization on a deeper level, Warren's technique becomes more meaningful. Warren structures his novel dramatically into three books and an epilogue. Book one establishes the atmosphere of mist and shadows, a mood which prevails throughout most of the novel. The murder occurs in book two, which concludes with Angelo's sentence and Cassie's confession. Book three is a working out of the complications caused by that confession. In this third section of the novel, Cassie, whose name suggests an allusion to the Trojan prophetess in the *Iliad,* is found in dire circumstances that are likely to evoke pity and fear even in modern audiences. The dénouement follows in the epilogue, the style of which is distinctly journalistic and different from the omniscient point of view in the first eleven chapters. The device stimulates the sterile environment in which the characters complete their preordained roles. Cassie is in Dr. Spurline's sanatorium and at the end is with Miss Edwina. Cy is with Gladys Peegrum. Murray is locked away in his dark mind. Warren heightens these dramatic effects with symbols such as light and darkness, water and land, the containing structure of the house and the openness of outdoors, animals, parts of the body (especially the eyes), and machines and agriculture. His style suggests a sense of each scene through various mechanical devices—for instance, indented block paragraphs and italics—as well as through more subtle means. An example of Warren's more subtle technique is seen in the following Faulknerian sentence: "If all you had out of living was the memories you couldn't remember the feelings of, did that mean that your living itself, even now while you lived it, was like that too, and everything you did, even in the instant of doing, was nothing more than the blank motions the shadow of your body made in those memories which now, without meaning, were all you had out of the living and working you had done before?" (123–24). All of the elements in *Meet Me in the Green Glen* harmonize and produce a literary effect that goes beyond the criticism of the novel as mere melodrama.[16]

A Place to Come To

Warren's tenth and final novel, *A Place to Come To* (1977), opens with dark scatological humor about the death of Jed Tewksbury's father, who is described as "standing up in front of his wagon to piss on the hindquarters of one of a span of mules and, being drunk, pitching forward on his head, still hanging on to his dong, and hitting the pike in such a position and condition that both the left front and the left rear wheels of the wagon rolled with perfect precision, over his unconscious neck"[17] This event is not without relevance to the first-person narrator's life. Jed Tewksbury lives with the shame of his father's death until he can reconcile himself to the past and learn to accept his own identity and responsibility for his own life.

Given Jed Tewksbury's deep skepticism and the narrative's concern with ways of perceiving, Warren's philosophical bent in *A Place to Come To* may be identified with the empiricism espoused by Locke, Berkeley, and Hume, which posits a profound skepticism concerning the human ability to determine reality and suggests the fallibility of human perception. In a more general way, Warren's metaphysical attitude may connect to analytical philosophy, which focuses on the analysis of concepts and emphasizes the function of language. Warren's explanation of the skepticism of the postmodern world and his continuing concern with moral knowledge are manifest in *A Place to Come To*. As Casper notes in *Blood Marriage*, "*A Place to Come To* enacts a postmodern insight: in the absence of certitude, one can succumb to the absurdist's intellectual despair . . . , or can convert doubt into uneasy faith" (59). For Jed Tewksbury, experience is what you are; and he can say in retrospect that we have only the past with which to work to find meaning in life.

The action moves from Dugton, Alabama, to Nashville, to Chicago, to Paris, and to Rome, only to return to Dugton. The story details numerous relationships and sexual experiences, before returning to the intellectual realm of experience. Perhaps Jed Tewksbury has an unidentified sexual rivalry with his dead father, Buck

Tewksbury, in a way comparable to Lettice Poindexter's sexual rivalry with her mother in *Flood*. Out of grief and anger Jed's mother, Elvira, throws Buck's sabre, which he bought at an auction one night when he was drunk, into Podmore Creek (13), thus ridding herself of the phallic symbol that her husband flaunted and prided himself on.

Jed's mother encourages Jed's study and helps create his dissatisfaction with Dugton, which is described as "a valley of humiliation and delusive vanities" (25). He studies Latin and finds a way to see the world: "if you found a new name for a thing, it became real" (26). Jed's discovery allows him to escape into medieval literature, particularly into the works of Dante. His curious, probing mind and his perseverance at Blackwell College in Alabama catch Professor Pillsbun's attention, and he recommends that Jed study at the University of Chicago under Dr. Heinrich Stahlmann, the teacher who had changed Pillsbun's life. Jed's initial rejection by the University of Chicago leads him into despondency and loneliness. In thinking of Odysseus who had a place to be lonely for, Jed laments the fact that he has no such place (55). Overcome by his feeling of abandonment and betrayal, Jed aggressively confronts Dr. Stahlmann with a five-minute recitation of *The Odyssey* and earns Dr. Stahlmann's kind-hearted support. Dr. Stahlmann's words "*imperium intellectus*" are words of joy and inspiration for Jed (63). He becomes a father-figure for Jed, advises Jed and his studies in Dante and the epic (Stahlmann's famous seminar), and has a profound effect on his life.

Jed's academic life, that part of his dream, is successful. Out of his dissertation, "Dante and the Metaphysics of Death," Jed publishes an essay in a leading professional journal, *The Mediaevalist* of

London, and is almost immediately heralded as the leading scholar on Dante. Because of outside intrusions, his vanity, and his intellectual need to know and be free from his past, Jed's career becomes somewhat lower in his priorities. He rides high on his early reputation, but his life disintegrates into a variety of interludes.

Among the females in Jed's life, besides his mother, are Rozelle Hardcastle (later Butler and then Carrington), Dauphine Finkel (later Phillips), Agnes Andresen, Mrs. Jones-Talbot (née Carrington), and Maria McInnis (later Beaufort). Rozelle Hardcastle is perhaps the main detraction in Jed's life. She, too, has roots in Dugton, a town too small and poor for her charm, beauty, and intelligence. Rozelle is from the affluent side of town and is popular in high school, while Jed is not well-liked. Rozelle uses Jed by inviting him to the senior prom and asking him to kiss her. The kiss is not passionate, but it provokes in Jed's mind the word *love* (42). A woman like Rozelle thrives on excitement and tends to live her life by escaping from reality. She lives for the moment. She graduates as valedictorian in the Dugton High School class of 1935 and attends the University of Alabama. While at the university, she meets and marries Michael X. Butler, a promoter from Chicago residing in Fort Lauderdale. The marriage is a rebound attraction after Charles Burton's parents shield their son from Rozelle's seductive ways. Eventually widowed, Rozelle marries Lawford Carrington, a Nashville sculptor. She renews her relationship with Jed in Nashville.

Dauphine Finkel, a Jewish graduate student at the University of Chicago, is Jed's first sexual success, though the relationship does not last at the time because of her political leanings. Dauphine is also in and out of Jed's life. Years later when Jed returns to Chicago, they marry and have a son, Ephraim. Their marriage dissolves after five

years, but toward retirement Jed writes Dauphine for reconciliation
and a chance to be with his son. In ways imperceptible at first,
Dauphine replaces the strength Jed found in his first wife, Agnes.

Agnes Andresen jilted her fiancé for Jed, who found her appropriate for marriage after he returned to Chicago from World War II.
She was from Ripley City, South Dakota, already had her Ph.D., and
seemed to Jed a perfect soul-mate. And she loved him, too. In Ripley
City, Jed witnesses a different kind of loneliness, a "bleeding away
of the self into distance" rather than the internalized loneliness of the
South (94). The Western experience was new for Jed. Back in
Chicago after the wedding, life becomes strained for Jed, who is writing his dissertation. Agnes's unexpected cancer leads to her death
and provides a new impetus in Jed, who finds meaning in and for his
work. He asserts "the idea that for Dante death defines the meaning
of life, that, indeed, the core drama of the *Divina Commedia* depends
on this idea" (106). The deaths of his father, Dr. Stahlmann, Agnes,
and his mother carry personal and philosophical significance for him
and add to his understanding of the meaning of life. The lesson, however, is not learned instantly or without suffering.

Maria McInnes and Mrs. Jones-Talbot are two women Jed
meets after Rozelle sucks him into Nashville's elite society. Maria is
an insecure woman who is a devoted friend to Rozelle. Her brief and
almost romantic relationship with Jed gives her strength of character
and allows her to get on with her life. Her relationship with Rozelle
may remind readers of the relationship between Lettice and Maggie
in *Flood*. Maria later marries Dr. Beaufort. Mrs. Jones-Talbot is
Rozelle's husband's paternal aunt, Aunt Dee-Dee, and Maria's step-
mother. Her complex sexual intrigues define her lifestyle. After Jed
begins tutoring her in Dante, they have a single liaison. She assumes

indirectly the role of matronly patron of the renown scholar. Her
love affair with David McInnis, Maria's father and financial adviser
of the Carrington estate, is finalized in marriage after Maria finds
herself.

From the romantic connections recounted thus far, *A Place to
Come To* may sound like another portrayal of southern decadence in
the mode of Erskine Caldwell, Tennessee Williams, or Willaim
Faulkner. As in Warren's other novels, however, the action is not the
only, or necessarily the primary, focus. Jed's inability to have endur-
ing relationships is part of his problem in learning who he is. Rozelle
tells him that he does not know who he is, a revelation not unlike
Anne Stanton's words to Jack Burden in their youth. Though Jed
and Rozelle have their affair, Rozelle continues to stalk Jed in Rome
and in Chicago. His inability to resist the "mystic promise" of
southern women gives Rozelle the advantage. What, then, is Warren's point? One idea is that education and intellect do not protect an
individual from the loneliness of despair. Jed's redemption cannot
occur until he frees himself from his past, of which Rozelle is an
unhappy part, and he gains control of his life. He can only do that if
he knows his purpose. The moment comes when Jed realizes that he
must live in the past and future, not just the present. Again invoking
prose reminiscient of Faulkner, Warren has Jed admit to himself
when Rozelle comes to him in Nashville that that "which I had not
known, on the instant, knew that, without knowing, I had known it"
(193). In this knowledge he senses that his identity flees from him.
This awareness is his ultimate turning point. It represents knowledge
from experience. In making the Rozelle-Jed affair so explicitly passionate, imbuing it with a kind of carpe diem attitude, Warren grap-

ples again with the sense of betrayal portrayed in the Cass Mastern-Annabelle Trice affair. For Cass, the result is escape by death. For Jed, the response to betrayal is escape by travel. He goes to Paris and returns to teach in Chicago. During this period he has been married five years to Dauphine Finkel. He learns, not without anguish, that "every man has to lead his own life and has little chance of knowing what it means, anyway" (356). Rozelle has married a swami in response to Jed's setting her free after Jed ends their liaison—a heavily ironic reversal since it is Jed who sets Rozelle free, not the other way around. One of Jed's friends, named Stephan, has his life together and speaks to Jed in a wise manner that might be more familiar to an older, more experienced person: "we know that love is the poetry of substance and that poetry is the only language of value" (382).

The death of Jed's mother, who has married Park Simms, brings Jed back to Dugton. That visit returns him to his past, to his father's grave, to his mother's grave. It also returns to him his freedom to live his own life. As Agnes's death brought to him a feeling of love, so his reconciliation with the death of his past brings redemption for Jed.

A Place to Come To shares the same structure as *Meet Me in the Green Glen,* since it also contains three books and an epilogue. Book one treats Jed's early life until Agnes's death, following him from his loneliness in Dugton to Ripley City where he finds another kind of loneliness. Book two begins his Nashville adventure and ends with the collapse of his affair with Rozelle. That affair provides the turning point in Jed's life, though it does not provide the resolution of his greatest concerns. Book three provides the dénouement, the resolution for Jed and the hope of reconciliation, forgiveness, and love. As Robert Koppelman acutely notes, *A Place to Come To* shows the presence of a modernist version of spirituality.[18]

After completing his final novel, Warren then turned his attention to his poetry which, by 1977, had moved into a more definite and personal voice about many of the same issues he had explored in his fiction. Warren's novels qualify as good literature because they address themes that have concerned people in the past and that will continue to be of interest in the future. Those themes involve individual responsibility, the importance of place and time, the quest for self-knowledge, the relevance of history, and redemptive love. He presents them through the action of characters who have depth and who are believable. And as in other works of good literature, the plots are complex. Beneath each surface story lies layers of meanings, the discovery of which enhances the enjoyment of his fiction.

CHAPTER FOUR

Early and Middle Poetry (1922–1966)

> The end of poetry is the experience of the poem.
> And the end of criticism is to return us to the poem.
> But with a fuller sense of its density as an expression
> of life.
>
> *Notes on an Approach to Literature* (1975)

By the time of his death in 1989, Warren had published seventeen volumes of poetry. And yet, until the 1980s only two book-length studies of Warren's poetry had been published, *A Colder Fire: The Poetry of Robert Penn Warren* (1965) and *The Poetic Vision of Robert Penn Warren* (1977), both of which were authored by Duke University professor Victor H. Strandberg. The former volume demonstrates through careful analysis Warren's continuous concern with "the ultimate meaning of existence" (14) and the problem of identity in a mechanistic universe, a question Warren approaches in relation to "the idea of an unconscious, undiscovered self" (2). The Jungian concept of an undiscovered self becomes a significant image throughout his poems. In the second volume Strandberg continues his study of three basic themes in Warren's poetry: passage, the undiscovered self, and mysticism.

Other studies, including those by Casper, Justus, Burt, Ruppersburg, and Clark, consider Warren's poetry in the context of his entire canon. Casper's pioneering book on Warren's writing, *The Dark and Bloody Ground,* devotes a chapter to the four volumes of Warren's poetry that had been published by 1960 and brings attention to his poetic technique and themes. Justus's *The Achievement of Robert Penn Warren,* published twenty-one years after Casper's text, focuses on some of the major influences on Warren's poetry, especially the impact of his mentor John Crowe Ransom and of two early modernists, T. S. Eliot and Ezra Pound. Justus asserts that Warren's participation in the Fugitive group while he was an undergraduate at Vanderbilt had profound influence on his early development as a poet. Grouping the poems into two periods, 1923–1953 and 1957–1980, Justus explores Warren's primary themes and analyzes his experimentation with different poetic techniques. Burt's, Ruppersburg's, and Clark's studies all focus on a particular thematic context for reading Warren's poetry. They demonstrate the diversity of Warren's interests and the artistic skill which he employs to submerse himself in those issues.

Two other book-length studies have appeared about Warren's later poetry, Calvin Bedient's *In the Heart's Last Kingdom* and Randolph Runyon's *The Braided Dream.* Bedient praises Warren as "a poet of tragic joy" (4) and picks up where *The Poetic Vision of Robert Penn Warren* leaves off by examining the psychological and metaphysical nuances in selected poems. He pays particular attention to Warren's use of language. Runyon gives close readings to the last four volumes of Warren's poetry, analyzing the rich texture of the poems and demonstrating the relevance of Freud's work on dreams and the unconscious. His analysis also pinpoints the significance of the meticulously arranged order for the poems. Once considered by some readers as too complex and distant, Warren's poems come alive in the variety of thorough analyses performed by these critics as well as by other scholars who have expressed their interpretations of Warren's poetry in critical essays.

For the purpose of this discussion, I have divided Warren's poetry into three time periods: early, middle, and late. The early period (1923–1943), characterized by traditional verse forms and the influence of metaphysical poetry, includes *Thirty Six Poems* (1935), *Eleven Poems on the Same Theme* (1942), *Selected Poems: 1923–1943* (1943), and the uncollected published poems. The middle period (1953–1966) is an experimental period that signifies a break from earlier influences. It includes *Brother to Dragons: A Tale in Verse and Voices* (1953), *Promises: Poems 1954–1956* (1957), *You, Emperors, and Others: Poems, 1957–1960* (1960), and *Tale of Time: New Poems, 1960–1966,* published in *Selected Poems: New and Old, 1923–1966* (1966). The late period (1966–1985) offers forays into less traditional verse forms, which show that Warren has adjusted to the postmodern period. The poetry of the late period includes *Incarnations: Poems, 1966–1968, Audubon: A Vision* (1969), *Or Else—Poem/Poems, 1968–1974* (1974), *Can I See Arcturus from Where I Stand?—Poems 1975,* published in *Selected Poems: 1923–1975* (1976), *Now and Then: Poems, 1976–1978* (1978), *Brother to Dragons: A Tale in Verse and Voices (A New Version)* (1979), *Being Here: Poetry 1977–1980* (1980), *Rumor Verified: Poems, 1979–1980* (1981), *Chief Joseph of the Nez Perce* (1983), *Altitudes and Extensions, 1980–1984,* published in *New and Selected Poems: 1923–1985* (1985), and the uncollected published poems between 1943–1989.[1]

Early Poems (1922–1943)

In 1985, the year his last volume of poetry was published, Warren wrote an essay for the *New York Times Book Review,* titled "Poetry

UNDERSTANDING ROBERT PENN WARREN

Is a Kind of Unconscious Autobiography."[2] In this article he discusses the autobiographical element in writing by addressing incidents in his life that had lasting effects, such as his discovery that his father had published some poems, the outdoor skills of his boyhood friend (Kent Greenfield), his early passion for the poetry of Thomas Hardy and William Blake, memories from his grandfather's farm, his college friends who shared a similar infatuation with poetry, and his preoccupation with American history. Warren concludes the essay by asserting the connection between autobiography and art: "For what is a poem but a hazardous attempt at self-understanding? It is the deepest part of autobiography" (10). Warren's comment also shows that one of Warren's chief thematic concerns in his poetry is to negotiate a deeper understanding of the self. From what other scholars have successfully demonstrated and from what Warren himself has told us through his own criticism about poetry, we may safely conclude that his poems address metaphysical, historical, psychological, philosophical, and theological issues. The basic concerns apparent in his fiction are in his poetry as well: the individual's place in the human condition, his relation to space and time, the search for truth and the possibility of ever discovering absolute Truth, the redemptive power of love, hope, and endurance, the central significance of history, the nature of God, and the human relation to nature.

Warren's early period of poetry (1922–1943) contains characteristics that Warren derived from his early readings and the poems he memorized in school. Much of his early poetry is structured around an iambic pentameter rhythm and a definite rhyme scheme. It conveys somewhat conventional themes, such as the romantic vision of "Vision" and "Crusade," the war-destruction-rebirth motif

in "After Teacups," the man-woman relationships in "Midnight,"
the use of metaphysical conceits in "The Fierce Horsemen," and a
Dickinsonian tone in "Wild Oats." Warren's poems show an early
penchant for metaphysical questions about life and love. His gratitude to his freshman English teacher at Vanderbilt and fellow member of the Fugitives, John Crowe Ransom, is expressed in the early
poem, "To Certain Old Masters." This poem is not directly indebted
to Ransom the poet, but is indirectly indebted to Ransom the
teacher, who influenced Warren's reading and understanding of
poetry at a most impressionable period in his life.

One of the dominant verse forms in this period of Warren's
poetry is the sonnet, especially the Petrarchan (or Italian) sonnet.
Another member of the Fugitives and a dedicated sonneteer, Donald
Davidson, probably influenced Warren in this form, though Warren
was also reading and absorbing Elizabethan literature. Poems such
as "Iron Beach," "Apocalypse," and the two-poem sequence titled
"Death Mask of a Young Man" provide examples of Warren's use
of the sonnet form. In the octave of that sequence's first poem, "The
Mouse," the persona hears the doctor leave after his house call on an
upper floor. The details of the dwelling—the gas jet, the cracked
plaster of what is most likely a run-down apartment—are telling
signs of the persona's frame of mind and offer a clue as to why he
will not hear the shuffle of feet the following night. The sestet provides a more specific statement of the speaker's perspective. That he
does not know the origin of the crack in the wall "to save his life"
(10) suggests his long residence, but he does remember seeing a
mouse enter the wall there to stay out of the way of danger or death.
We are left to ponder whether the young man will find a crack in the
wall in which he can hide safely. The second poem of the sequence,

"The Moon," has dark images as well. In the poem's first eight lines, the persona cannot sleep and watches the moon pass his dirty window on its deliberate schedule. In the last six lines, the persona hears the cathedral bell toll "the death of the expiring hour" (13) and sees the setting of the moon. The young man seems to be contemplating the meaning of life in general and of death in particular. The imagery in the sequence and the focus of the young man's attention on death are not surprising since these poems appeared in the June 1924 issue of the *Fugitive,* just one month after Warren's attempted suicide. Regardless of whether he wrote them before or after his failed attempt, the thought of a life ended prematurely seems clearly present. The thematic concerns and images of "Death Mask of a Young Man" are youthful indulgences, but the form and poetic technique are indicative of a young writer with potential.

The young writer was reading poetry as well. His 1924 poem, "Adieu Sentimentale," has a rhythm that echoes Wallace Stevens's poem, "The Emperor of Ice Cream" (1923). "Alf Burt, Tenant Farmer" (1924) shows a richness and complexity not unlike E. A. Robinson's "Richard Cory" (1897). "Admonition to Those Who Mourn" (1924) exhibits a metaphysical touch similar to John Donne's "Valediction: Forbidding Mourning" (1633). "Easter Morning: Crosby Junction" (1925) is Hardyesque in subject matter. "The Wrestling Match" (1925), with its heavy alliteration and couplet rhyme scheme, is reminiscent of Andrew Marvell's poetry. Such comparisons are not intended to suggest that Warren merely copied other poet's verse. Indeed, one might rather conclude about Warren's early poetry what Harold Bloom observed about great writers: that the great writers have read the great writers who preceded them, have absorbed the central issues into their very marrow, and have found their own voice with which to grapple with those forces.[3]

The poems mentioned thus far have been published but have not been collected in any of the volumes of poetry produced during his lifetime. Another one of the sequences contained in the "Uncollected Poems, 1923–1943" is "Sonnets of Two Summers" (1924), in which the young Warren already begins to show signs of maturing as a poet. The rhythm becomes tighter, more coherent, the diction more revealing ("slow hoofs / Plashing the mud" [13–14]), and the poetic lines more continuous. These early poems deal primarily with death and love, and they raise religious questions, such as those put forth in "August Revival: Crosby Junction" (1925). In this poem the persona dismisses the preacher's word about the crucifixion in favor of the more pragmatic issues of man's labor in the field and the need for rest. The image of the literal harvest not being completed flashes in the young man's mind and parallels the incomplete figurative harvest, about which the preacher sermonizes.

During this early period Warren experimented with his own poetry in a variety of styles. After his study at Oxford, he composed "The Owl" (1932), which has a more varied rhyme scheme and makes use of slant rhyme (for instance, he rhymes afternoon with sun). In subsequent poems his use of feminine rhymes (for instance, he rhymes word with unstirred) and his choice of diction are but two indications of the growth of his sensitivity to the art. His growth is also apparent in his use of classical allusions, which may have been invoked in rather unassuming fashion as a result of Warren's study of Greek at Vanderbilt, his interest in Shakespeare and other Elizabethan poets, and Ransom's influence. "Love's Voice" (ca. 1936–38) is a lyric poem of ninety-six lines in eight-line stanzas, with octameter meter, and an a-b-a-b rhyme scheme.[4] In it the speaker addresses his loved one and uses the metaphor of a fable to express an unimaginable joy felt through their being:

> us, the fable
> Then let us turn now—you to me
> And I to you—and hand to hand
> Clasp, even though our fable be
> Of strangers met in a strange land
> Who pause, perturbed, then speak and know
> That speech, half lost, can yet amaze
> Joy at the root; then suddenly grow
> Silent, and on each other gaze.

> (89–96)

Warren had planned a volume of poetry as early as 1929 with a collection he had titled "Pondy Woods and Other Poems." The next working title was "Kentucky Mountain Farm and Other Poems" (1930), followed by "Cold Colloquy" (1933). The published volume in this period is *Thirty-Six Poems* (1935). The influence of T. S. Eliot is readily apparent in the first poem of the volume, "The Return: An Elegy." In *A Colder Fire* Strandberg notes Warren's indebtedness to Eliot's work, especially to *The Waste Land*. Elements of "The Love Song of J. Alfred Prufrock" are also there. Warren's imagery is dark, and the persona's appeal is a desire to bring his mother comfort in her time of sorrow. One of the repeated lines, *"tell me its name,"* is evoked later in Warren's career in *Audubon*. This repetition of a single phrase and the return to his basic concerns remain features of his entire poetic corpus and establish evidence for the claim that all of his poetry is a continuum, is part of a single overarching poem.

"Kentucky Mountain Farm" is a seven-poem sequence written in the late 1920s. Some critics have identified this poem as an early part of Warren's "Kentucky period," during which a large portion of his writing stems from his Kentucky roots. This sequence has been judged as one of the best examples of his early work and, consequently, has had much critical attention. Strandberg sees the continued influence of Eliot on Warren's inward search for reality. Casper views the sequence as a commemoration of "the hardness of hill country life" (59) that is disavowed by the youthful persona. Justus find the structure of the sequence important to Warren because it gives him the means to explore the poem's issues in a variety of narrative voices. On a thematic level the poem ranges from an examination of the indifference of nature represented by animate and inanimate objects—an indifference evident in Warren's use of the image of stone—to a consideration of the mutability of human life even for the one "who had loved as well as most." In exploring these themes, Warren delves into a potential means of infusing life with purpose based on love. The poem suggests that the hope for humanity must lie in the fact that one can love at all. The human need to learn to understand nature, even in the face of nature's indifference toward human presence, and the capacity to love are essential to one's ability to experience life more fully.

Other poems in this first volume merit mention. "Pondy Woods" is one of many poems that Warren derived from stories he heard as a youth about his home region. The persona in this ballad tells of the escape of a black man who is being chased by a posse into the swampy area known as Pondy Woods. The rhythm at times recalls the drum-like rhythm of Vachel Lindsay's poem, "The Congo": "Fat black bucks in a wine-barrel room, / Barrel-house kings, with feet unstable" (1–2).[5] Emulating Lindsay's style, Warren writes: "Big Jim Todd was a slick black buck / Laying low in the mud and muck" (7–8). Warren's ballad is based on the real-life lynching of Primus Kirby in Guthrie, Kentucky. His poetic account of this tragic event concentrates on the victim's minimal chance of survival against the indifference of nature and the savagery of humanity. Even Christ, "The Jew-boy," died, the persona caustically observes. Big Jim Todd does not have a prayer. To show Big Jim Todd's perseverance in the face of impending death, Warren quotes the poet Horace: "*Non omnis moriar*" (52), "I shall not all die."[6] Warren returned to the lynching of Primus Kirby in a later poem, "Ballad of Mister Dutcher and the Last Lynching in Gupton."

Poems that focus on family interactions are also present in this first volume of poetry. "Letter of a Mother" (1928) offers a peek into Warren's relationship with his mother, a topic treated in other poems as well. This early reference would have been written during the time Warren was a Rhodes scholar at Oxford, divided by a great distance from his mother—a separateness that did not go unnoticed by her. The speaker of the poem is the mother who imagines that her son questions not his "debt of flesh" to her but the obligation of gratitude to her. At the end of those speculations, she contemplates the end of everyone's life, the grave, describing it metaphorically as another womb "more tender than her own / That builds not tissue or the little bone, / But dissolves them to itself in weariness" (30–32). Throughout his poetic career, Warren stayed interested in detailing the connectedness and separateness found in familial relations. Several poems in Warren's canon focus on family members, from his grandfather to his own children.

Friendship seems important to the young poet as well and is present in "To a Friend Parting" and "Letter to a Friend." In "To a Friend Parting," the friend who is parting is going off to war, and the persona reflects on the impersonal nature of war and the effect on those friends not being shipped off to battle. In "Letter to a Friend" the speaker could almost be writing the friend who has gone to fight. Some time after the friend's departure, both have experienced life more fully, and the composer of the letter suggests that their experience ("voyage") "had rendered / Courage superfluous, hope a burden" (8–9). Yet, the speaker cannot cast away the traditional values of courage and hope; instead, he recognizes that living by them is a necessity, especially for those who do not know their own heart. Even if the friend triumphs, that victory will not endure like stone. Perhaps the poet is warning the friend not to become, like Ozymandias in Shelley's sonnet of that name, trapped in the dangers of vanity. The next poem, "Aubade for Hope," does not offer much incentive for hope early in the day, not from one's late-night reading, from "The unaimed faceless appetite of dream" (8), from the boredom that he faces in the coming day. A recurring motif in Warren's poetry as well as his fiction, the light and darkness imagery dominates the poem and sets the tone.

Warren's poetic technique has intrigued readers of his poetry. His ability to manipulate the nuances of metaphysical conceits while setting his poems in his own time and place seems to raise the subjects of his poetry to a higher level. The opening stanza of "Croesus in Autumn" uses the archetypal symbol of changing seasons to relate the passing of one's life: "If the distrait verdure cleave not to the branch / More powerfully than flesh to the fervent bone, / Should then gruff Croesus on the village bench / Lament the absolute gold of summer gone?" (1–4). The poem preceding that one is "Man Coming of Age." The predominant metaphor is the metamorphosis of the trees, the leaf now gone. In "So Frost Astounds" the persona's thought, "*So frost astounds the summer calyxes*" (9), shows remorse that the subject of the painting portraying a girl sitting by a window in "a dull blue dress" remains only an object for his mind. Death has killed the bloom of life that once she offered. The speaker's regret puts us in mind of Robert Browning's "My Last Duchess." One further example will illustrate Warren's recurrent use of the leaf metaphor. In the poem titled "The Last Metaphor" he describes the blowing away of leaves as winter approaches: "The wind had blown the leaves away and left / The lonely hills and on the hills the trees; / One fellow came out with his mortal miseries / And said to himself: 'I go where brown leaves drift'" (1–4). The image of the disappearing leaves seems to express a warning to find one's inner self and to seek a reconciliation with nature and with God: "Thinking that when the leaves no more abide / The stiff trees rear not up in strength and pride / But lift unto the gradual dark in prayer" (42–44).

Warren's poetry from *Thirty-Six Poems* forward deals with questions of the meaning of life, time lost or wasted, and death. "Problem of Knowledge" suggests an issue related to these quintessential questions: that the problem of gaining knowledge is the arrogance it fosters in the desire for complete knowledge. Thus, this arrogant will to attain unattainable absolute knowledge does not represent a pride of success but an almost sinful pride in even thinking that it might be so.

In other words, self-deceptive vanity is one of the problems of gaining knowledge. Warren did not abandon hope on this point; he continued to seek ways for an individual to discover self-knowledge. He suggests that the way is different for each individual.

"To a Face in the Crowd" apparently holds particular significance for Warren because he includes it as the last poem in each volume of his selected poems. The speaker acknowledges his own ties with other human beings, asserting an archetypal relation of all humanity through common ancestors, "an ancient band" (10). He suggests that his must come to terms with this ancient past in order to find relevance in present relationships "Borne in the lost procession of these feet" (28).

Warren's second volume of poetry, a pamphlet in the Poet-of-the-Month series published by New Directions, is *Eleven Poems on the Same Theme* (1942), for which he received the Shelley Memorial Award. The "same theme" that unites the eleven poems is the theme of love, but not just the image of romantic love. The poems are also about fraternal love, maternal love, and divine love. "Bearded Oaks" has a carpe diem tone about it as the two lovers rest beneath the moss-covered oaks, submerged in time, outside of history. The appeal is similar to the appeal in Marvell's "To His Coy Mistress"; Warren's speaker concludes his persuasive argument:

> I do not love you less that now
> The caged heart makes iron stroke,
> Or less that all that light once gave
> The graduate dark should now revoke.
> We live in time so little time

And we learn all so painfully,
That we may spare this hour's term
To practice for eternity.

(33–40)

These poems reflect a greater maturity in Warren's poetic voice. They are more focused, and although the verse form remains traditional, it is tighter. By 1942 Warren and Brooks had published *An Approach to Literature* and *Understanding Poetry,* and their collaborations on describing the elements of good poetry seem to have strengthened Warren's own writing. "Picnic Remembered" concerns two lovers who loved unrestrained by thoughts of time and knowledge of reality. The deception over, they know now the curse of life's passing. The concluding image, perhaps the persona's desperate hope, asks, "Or is the soul a hawk that fled / On glimmering wing's past vision's path, / Reflects the last gleam to us here / Though sun is sunk and darkness near / —Uncharted Truth's high heliograph?" (45–49). "Original Sin: A Short Story" takes its speaker on an interior journey into the unidentified pronominal reference "it," which is the nightmare that fumbles at your door and follows you wherever you go. The confrontation with this archetypal dark presence is agonizing: "Hope is betrayed by / Disastrous glory of sea-capes, sun-torment of whitecaps / — There must be a new innocence for us to be stayed by" (31–33). "It" may try the lock, wander at night, or stand idle "like an old horse cold in the pasture" (45). Too many do not want to confront this nightmarish, primal "it" at all, which, though not explicitly named, represents original sin, humanity's burden in this life. The next poem in the volume, "End of Season," offers a more positive view as summer ends and the vacationer faces the reality of winter: "—you must think / On the true nature of Hope, whose eye is round and does not wink" (35–36). Taken together, these poems reinforce the importance of love, hope, and endurance in attaining one's identity and self-knowledge. "In separateness only does love learn definition" (25), the persona reflects in "Revelation" after speaking harshly to his mother who reacts more lovingly than does her son, whose thoughts well up in murderous imaginings. From his mother's forgiveness he learns "Something important about love, and about love's grace" (32).

The patient in "Pursuit" needs "A change of love" (29), while in "Question and Answer" the persona questions God's plan, the answers to which do not come from nature but "In truth the true / Answer of you" (45–46). In light of the flight from Egypt and the suffering that he perceives the Israelites endured, the speaker asks God the question in Job-like fashion. "Love's Parable" is also about divine love, though this poem has caused debate among several critics. In the poem human beings embroiled in civil conflicts finally arrive at "love's mystery" (22), only to lose it in their ignorance: "We did not know what worth we owned" (33). The poem takes a grim view of the possibility of rediscovering the value of love, since humanity harbors only contempt for love. The philosophical question at the heart of the poem is one that appears in Warren's fiction as well. The poem opens up the metaphysical question of the possibility of human beings ever knowing truth: "Are we but mirror to the world? / Or does the world our ruin reflect"? (65–66). A sense of optimism, albeit rather small, comes at the end of the poem: "That hope: for there are testaments / That men, by prayer, have mastered grace" (79–80).

Three new poems appear in Warren's last volume of poetry of this early period, a period that was followed by a ten-year hiatus from writing poems brought about by a number of factors. In *Selected Poems: 1923–1943* are "Variation: Ode to Fear," "Mexico Is a Foreign Country: Five Studies in Naturalism," and "The Ballad of Billie Potts." "Variation: Ode to Fear" is, indeed, a variation of William Dunbar's poem, "Lament for the Makaris [Poets]."[7] The repeated refrain, *"Timor mortis conturbat me"* ("Fear of death confounds me"), follows each of Warren's stanzas. The stanzas contain the speaker's playful laments over modern and somewhat frivolous annoyances, such as a visit to the dentist or the surgeon and an overdrawn bank notice, juxtaposed against the more serious concern about his own mortality.

"Mexico Is a Foreign Country: Five Studies in Naturalism" articulates a feature of Warren's poetry discussed by both Strandberg and Justus. Strandberg refers to Warren's first volume of poetry as the "dark night of naturalism" (9), while Justus views naturalism for Warren as "the secular counterpart of original sin" (4) but with a close connection to Warren's Christian view of man. Casper, on the other hand, reads the poetic sequence as a satire "on the inadequacy of naturalism as a philosophy" (72).[8] The first two poems in the sequence, "I. Butterflies over the Map" and "II. Siesta Time in Village Plaza by Ruined Bandstand and Banana Tree," portray the traveler insensitive to a different and poorer culture, in which the flies are not few and love of the local beauties is easy if not free. As he drinks down his last beer, he considers the creature comforts of staying cool, which is not easy to do in the Mexican heat. The tourists (plural now) observe an old man, "Old, and all his history hung from his severe face" (7) in "III. The World Comes Galloping: A True

Story." They observe him eating a peach and sarcastically observing that the world comes galloping when a youth gallops his horse through the street. The one eating is to the tourists just an old "fly-bit man" (29). The tourist (now singular) observes the soldiers in the Plaza in "IV. Small Soldiers with Drum in Large Landscape." The soldiers do not show a great deal of military demeanor. The tourist wonders why they march and notes that their presence changes nothing in nature. To him they have no purpose, but he takes momentary pleasure in the thought of sharing their freedom. Warren's playfulness with language, "From *what* to *what,* from *if* to *when*" (41), brings to mind e. e. cummings's nonstandard use of language. The last poem in the sequence, "V. The Mango on the Mango Tree," establishes the tourist's shared guilt with the fruit, God's plan to "Divide and rule, mango and man" (17). His atonement might come if he could only ask for and give forgiveness. Man's plight, like the mango's plight, is death and decay until that time comes.

The poem that drew the most attention in *Selected Poems: 1923–1943* is "The Ballad of Billie Potts." It is a spine-tingling story of a family's greed and the fatal end that results from avarice. Warren's headnote explains that he originally heard this story from one of his relatives. She placed the location in a section of Western Kentucky known as the land "Between the Rivers" (the Cumberland and Tennessee Rivers), which is now known as the Land Between the Lakes. The rhythm is musical, and the poem is best experienced when read aloud. The narrative is interrupted by parenthetical descriptions and philosophical insights somewhat in the manner of a Greek chorus. Big Billie Potts, his wife, and Little Billie Potts run an inn at "The place for a ferry" (40), where travelers can take their ease. Big Billie would assess the travelers' wealth, and when they left the inn, he would ambush them on the trail and rob and kill them. Little Billie is to try his hand at the ambush, but the stranger outdraws him and wounds him. Little Billie returns to the inn, suffers Big Billie's disapproval and anger, and heads west to seek his own fortune. The parenthetical comment reads: "For Time is always the new place, / And no-pace. / And Time is always the new name and the new face, / And no-name and no-face" (247–50). Eventually, Little Billie comes home, meets Joe Drew on the trail, and tells him he made his fortune in the West and is going to bring his folks some luck. But Little Billie has changed a great deal and knows his parents will not recognize him, so he plans to have some fun first. Little Billie plays the guest, teases them, and never tells them he is their son. Believing him to be just another guest, Big Billie murders him. They do not discover his true identity until after Joe Drew sees them the next day and tells them he saw Little Billie. That night they return to the body and find the birthmark, which was "shaped for luck" (471). The speaker adds a pointed reflection to the ballad: "And our innocence needs, perhaps, new definition" (495).

Warren's poetry during this period shows the maturity of a budding poet, but he stopped writing poetry for ten years. Possibly he simply had too many other projects to work on. During this ten-year hiatus from poetry, he produced three novels (*At Heaven's Gate, All the King's Men,* and *World Enough and Time*), two textbooks (*Understanding Fiction* and *Modern Rhetoric*), a collection of short stories (*The Circus in the Attic and Other Stories*), and his famous critical essay on *The Rime of the Ancient Mariner.* In addition to the time spent producing this impressive amount of writing, his time was also taken up by his move from LSU to the University of Minnesota, his extensive travel abroad, and his marital problems.

He did not resume his poetry career until 1953, when he published *Brother to Dragons: A Tale in Verse and Voices. Promises: Poems 1954–1956* received the Pulitzer Prize and marks the beginning of his middle period of poetry.

Middle Poems (1953–1966)

The years 1953 to 1966 show Warren moving more into his own voice in his poems. His poetry of this period exhibits an increased use of poetic sequences and a freer verse form, although he did not abandon traditional forms. He also places an emphasis on images introduced in the early period such as the wind, the leaf, mountains, the hawk, the sea (especially the sea glimmer), the woods, and darkness. Moreover, Warren's poetry of the middle period shows that he is concerned with the same themes that mark his earlier poems, with almost an obsessive interest in the rage of joy. Warren continues to examine the burning issues with a more personal touch, with an increased use of dream imagery, and, toward the end of this period, with more thoughts about God. Warren has said that he was not a conventionally religious man, but his poems from the end of the middle period and throughout the late period clearly indicate a strong faith in a higher being.

In an essay, "The Dramatic Version of *Ballad of a Sweet Dream of Peace: A Charade for Easter*," Warren discusses the origin of that ballad and its relationship to the sequence of poems in which it first appeared. The poems in *Promises: Poems, 1954–1956* are arranged thematically, with "Ballad" very near the end of the volume. By positioning it near the end, Warren implies that "it was a sort of summarizing commentary, a the-

matic focus." "Ballad" represents "certain key and typical situations of the pattern of life generally conceived."[9] Like a play in
the theater of the absurd, reality in "Ballad" is obscured by unexpected juxtapositions and unnatural behaviors. The dialogue in
the poem is distinguished by the use of italic and roman fonts to
mark different speakers. In the first poem, "1. And Don't Forget
Your Corset Cover, Either," the questioner asks why the "*ele-
gant bureau*" is left in the dark woods, "God's temple" (14). The
respondent gives two casual replies before saying it is for the
naked old lady who polishes and restores the wood in it. She is
the questioner's grandmother who searches the past for her own
identity, which is represented by the bureau (a symbolic altar).
She is alone in the dark as is everyone who has not found his or
her genuine identity. The next two poems also deal with Granny.
"2. Keepsakes" reveals the contents of the bureau: *The Book of
Common Prayer,* a lock of gold hair (from the grandmother's
youth), "A bundle of letters, some contraceptives, and an orris-
root sachet" (8), all left by previous owners. With the discovery
of an old-fashioned doll, the respondent reveals the grandmother's death at childbirth. She suffers from the betrayal of
promises made about the life she would live. Then, "3. Go It,
Granny—Go It, Hog!" picks up the image of hogs the questioner
slopped as a boy. Though the hogs are long dead, the respondent
explains that "all Time is a dream, and we're all one Flesh, at
last" (8), the ultimate climax to life. The hogs and death are the
horror of Granny's discovery. Other figures appear in those
woods in "4. Friends of the Family, or Bowling a Sticky
Cricket." These figures cry out, "Show me Thy Face!" (15), that

is, the voice in the dark. The respondent uses imagery of the crucifixion of Christ to identify the woman who came to the questioner's bed in the afternoon, "lip damp, the breath like myrrh" (15) in "5. You Never Knew Her Either, Though You Thought You Did, Inside Out." The "Two toads in coitu on the bare black ground" (6) symbolize the corruption of the flesh made one. In "6. I Guess You Ought to Know Who You Are," the birth-blind "*brat*" who astonishes the questioner was, but for the grace of God, to have been the questioner himself. The respondent suggests the position of prayer—eyes shut tight and bowing on one's knees—as "the quickest and easiest way" to make the discovery of self. And the last poem in the sequence, "7. Rumor Unverified Stop Can You Confirm Stop," the respondent repeats the "rumor" of the second coming:

> That the woods are sold, and the purchaser
> Soon comes, and if credulity's not now abused,
> Will, on this property, set
> White foot-arch familiar to violet,
> And heel that, smiting the stone, is not what is bruised,
> And subdues to sweetness the pathside garbage, or thing
>   body had refused.
>
>   (10–15)

Those seekers of the truth of the second coming search for reality, "For Reality's all, and to seek it, some welcome, at whatever cost, any change" (8), not suspecting the rumored change. Warren's chorus in the dramatic version expands on the idea of the desirability of confronting reality even if its exact nature remains unknown. Were one able to know fully the nature of reality, however, things would not be the same. The implication carries over into Warren's fictive characters, who believe in the individual's responsibility for confronting reality and that fate is not absolutely predetermined (for example, Percy Munn, Bogan Murdock, Willie Stark, Jeremiah Beaumont, Amantha Starr, Jack Harrick, Adam Rosenzweig, Brad Tolliver, Murray Guilfort, and Jed Tewksbury). For those characters who seek reality but cannot find it, things could not have been different.

The other poem that summarizes the broad thematic concerns of all the poems in *Promises* is "Dragon Country: To Jacob Boehme." Like "Ballad," "Dragon Country" is another example of the Southern grotesque tradition in *Promises* that offers similar commentary on the other poems in the volume. It focuses on a legend associated with an area of Kentucky that has experienced unexplained deaths and disappearances. These grim and mysterious events have brought national attention to this otherwise dull, routine locale. Although the cause of the deaths and disappearances is unknown, the persona speculates that the Beast, the embodiment of the land's evil, might be a needed replacement for "the ennui, the pleasure, and night sweat, known in the time before / Necessity of truth had trodden the land, and heart, to pain, / And left, in darkness, the fearful glimmer of joy, like a spoor" (50–52). Human need seems to be nothing more than an identity of reality through language without dependency "On desire, or need" (48).

R. W. B. Lewis has called *Promises* "the turning point in Warren's poetic career."[10] It represents his first volume of poems after a ten-year hiatus, though his longer verse drama, *Brother to Dragons,* had appeared in 1953. It also represents a legacy dedicated to his two young children, Rosanna and Gabriel. Leonard Casper observes that, by dedicating poems to his children, Warren "has now given them not only life but knowledge of that indebtedness which goes with the expense of memory and the course of blood: kinship."[11] But readers might want to join Victor Strandberg, Robert Koppelman, and others in exploring further Warren's legacy.

In his 1966 Eugenia Dorothy Blount Lamar Lecture, *A Plea in Mitigation,* Warren discusses the end of the era of modern poetry and notes that each age leaves its legacy, which fertilizes the new age's reaction to and growth out of its literature and its criticism. He further states that "every age, as it produces its own poetry, needs to produce its own type of criticism, its own type of exegesis and apology."[12] Not even in his latest poetry, *Altitudes and Extensions, 1980–1984* contained in *New and Selected Poems: 1923–1985,* did Warren embrace the postmodernism of the Black Mountain poets such as Charles Olson, or that of the New York School of poets such as Kenneth Koch. These poets claimed that their "open form" was a reaction against the New Critical mode—that is, against correct grammar, logic, regular meter, rhyme, stanzas, coherence, condensation, and control.[13] Warren said the San Francisco Beats "constitute a footnote to modernism, rather than a radical reaction against it. . . . For example, Ferlinghetti reminds one of Cummings with sauciness somewhat blunted and the language blurred."[14] Warren's dedication to poetry as an expression of life was unrelenting to the end. Furthermore, the negative responses to Brooks and Warren's approach to literature constitute another form of legacy, if not also a credit to it.

Warren knew what I. A. Richards had spotted in 1925: "Poetry, like life, is one thing. . . . Essentially a continuous substance or energy, poetry is historically a connected movement, a series of successive integrated manifestations."[15] And Brooks, as if to demonstrate this concept, later wrote that Eliot, Yeats, and the other modern poets built upon the Romantic tradition by incorporating structural devices from it.[16] Warren's first period of poetry, which culminated with *Selected Poems: 1923–1943,* clearly connected itself to the metaphysical tradition. Other influences on his later poetry are numerous. For example, Brooks, James Justus, and others have noted the influence of T. S. Eliot on Warren's work. R. W. B. Lewis has noted Warren's attraction to Thomas Hardy's notion of fate as well as what Monroe Spears called Warren's sense of "personal responsibility for older American literature."[17] Warren and Brooks found that students in the late 1930s did not know how to read poetry. The predicament was not new since Richards had indicated that students at Cambridge University in the 1920s did not know how to read literature.

In Brooks and Warren's 1936 edition of *An Approach to Literature* and their 1938 edition of *Understanding Poetry,* the influences of Richards and of Ransom are evident. Richards had boldly stated that "criticism . . . is the endeavor to discriminate between experiences and to evaluate them," and he asked the questions critics should seek to answer: "What gives the experience of reading a certain poem its value? How is this experience better than another?" The central question, one which Warren continued to address throughout his career, is basic: "What is the value of the arts?"[18] The New Criticism's critique of the state of the arts was partly influenced by the Agrarian reaction to industrialization, technology, and science—a reaction explicitly stated in *I'll Take My Stand.* When Ransom declared that "criticism must become more scientific," he was not abdicating to science; rather, he was trying to put the arts on a more rational level, detached and objective as scientific inquiry. If criticism is to be objective, he contended, it should not rely on historical studies, nor use linguistic studies as a pragmatic basis, nor confuse moral content with whole content. Instead, it should look at the work of art as a whole, not merely at abstracts of its complete, unified meaning.[19]

Acknowledging the influence of New Critical theory provides a better understanding of Warren's poetry. From those early concepts and considerations emerges a legacy initiated in part in *Promises* and developed further in the last half of Warren's poetic career, beginning with *Incarnations* and ending with *Altitudes and Extensions.* The focus for the moment turns to the second section of *Promises,* the Gabriel section, about which Koppelman observes: "[It] presents many of the poet's lifelong concerns such as the fusing of the personal and historical consciousness, acknowledgment of the human propensity for violence, humility before the larger forces of time and nature . . . and the necessary role that suffering and evil play in bringing about the human search for meaning and redemption."[20]

Adapting a statement Brooks and Warren make in *Understanding Poetry,* one can readily apply it to the first poem, "What Was the Promise That Smiled from the Maples at Evening?": "Even though the account of a [son's reminiscence of his youth and his deceased parents] seems almost as far removed as possible from poetry, it arouses the kind of interest which poetry attempts to satisfy, and, as we have already said, comprises the 'stuff of poetry.'"[21] "What Was the Promise" implies a story that lies behind the poem.

The story is based on the persona's reminiscence of his youth and its implications on his present being, on his self, as he revisits his child-hood home, which is now empty. In the first four of six seven-line stanzas, the narrator reflects on the promises implicit in maples at sunset, in bullbats at sunset, in the last light of day, in dying. In the last two stanzas the revenants of his parents provide the answer. Keying on other questions from *Understanding Poetry*—What feel-ing is Warren interested in giving the reader? What meaning does he want to convey? How has he used the elements of the poem?—one can explore further the legacy.

Putting New Critical theory into practice, Warren chooses the poem's details carefully in order to achieve a particular effect in the reader, thus making each detail an integral of the poem's overall meaning. The smile from the maples, though dim and recessed, away from the expectant youth, announces at the sound of clicking heels the fathers' return to their homes, each aware of his own unspecified burden. The awful responsibility of time and the burden of self-knowledge—that is to say, the burden of life culminating in death—are not specifically acknowledged, although the dark images and the white hydrangeas' "spectral" appearance, the appearance of the first firefly at dusk, and the evening star announce the end of day literally, the end of life symbolically.

The promise of death is further elaborated in the second stanza as the youth, "Too little to shoot" the bullbats this year, collects one that has spun down, wet with blood, with its eyes still open. He touches death with ambivalent feelings: "your heart in the throat swells like joy" (14). The language in stanza 3 builds emphasis on the lesson of death in subtle ways: "last light had died," "children *gravely, down* walks, in spring *dark, under* maples" (16), play with shoe-box trains that are empty except for candles inside as they blow "for crossings, lonely, *oo-oo*" (18). The images portend death. The youth flees impulsively from their calling and hides. The poem opens up a sense of ambiguity concerning the origin of the calling. Perhaps it represents the voices of the other children. Or perhaps it belongs to the parents who accept their responsibility by calling their children in for the night.

Stanza 4, transitional in effect, shows the youth's wonder "after the dying was done" (22). Gone are the years of his youth, "like burnt paper," the occupants of his parents' house, and the hydrangeas. Having returned to this silent house, the narrator, however, is aware of the night sounds of the creaking door, the nonhuman sounds of the house. The images remain dark and cold as the persona, who, long after his childhood, visits his parents' graves, both the landscape and his heart subdued by the prevailing gray light—the shade between white and black, evoking a spectral image. His vision, penetrating "deep down" through the glass-like ground, reveals for a moment his parents—Ruth and Robert—"agleam in a phosphorous of glory, bones bathed" (34) side by side. The illumination, both literal and symbolic, having been spent, the narrator gazes at the "heart's familiar," the landscape and the town, under the evening star. At this idyllic moment, his mother's voice calls, "Child," and his father explains the promise: "We died only that every promise might be fulfilled" (42). Biographer Joseph Blotner comments on the poem's unexpected movement from the natural to the supernatural, from the real to the surreal, suggesting that this shift in "What Was the Promise" foreshadows Warren's subjects in the poems that follow it in this section of "Promises": "This shift, from the literal and nostalgic to the surreal and visionary, served to prepare the reader for such poetic variations as a tale about a monster, a recollection of hanged bushwhackers, and a phantasmagoria about a skeletal grandmother attacked by wild hogs in a dark wood."[22]

Every promise becomes a metaphorical conduit from life to death, for the maturation process, for the memories of youth, and for the foreshadowing of one's own death, which, in turn, fulfills every promise and makes way for the next generation of life. The images introduced earlier—maples, flowers, bullbats, children, parents—all have come and gone. These natural entities have fulfilled the cycle of life, and their identities, their selves have emerged in the fulfillment of their natural destiny.[23] However, this prose paraphrase of Warren's poetic achievements cannot fully encompass the effect the poetry itself has on the reader. To invoke a relevant passage from *Understanding Poetry* and apply it to the analysis just presented, Warren's poetry "does not depend on the kind of general statement which we have given in our prose paraphrase. The material is arranged so that we feel the effect intended without the direct statement."[24]

Warren's form in this poem uses rhymed meter (one is tempted to say iambic heptameter, but that label would be inaccurate) in the pattern a-b-a-b-c-a-c. The dialectic light and dark imagery suggests alternatively the youth's lack of knowledge, the end of life, and the exposure to knowledge. The imagery helps create an inquisitive attitude for the persona. If nature is indifferent, it is so because man is indifferent and fails to see the relationship between nature and human life. This poem provides a means to explore the meaning of

life. One response might be to declare that the meaning of life is to
fulfill every promise responsibly and to complete one's existence by
accepting a natural death. Acceptance of the natural cycle allows the
individual a span of time that promises hope and joy. Strandberg
describes the poem's language as the "imagery of benediction":
"The ultimate 'promise' . . . is the promise entailing a willing sacrifice of self, ultimately meaning death, by which every generation
paves the way for its successor."[25]

This in-depth analysis of only the first of nineteen poems in the
Gabriel section opens up the question of what one can discern about
the legacy of promises. Calvin Bedient, for example, asserts that for
Warren "rhyme is an invitation to oversing. . . . The sensitive and
critical point in Warren's poetry was and still is tone."[26] Although
Bedient finds tone also to be a chief fault in Warren's early volumes,
others might claim that Warren's control over tone is precisely his
strength and part of his legacy. For example, poems and poem
sequences that follow "What Was the Promise" not only develop the
section's tone, they also make the entire volume a kind of complete,
unified poem rather than a collection of scattered, unrelated poems.
The thematic and tonal unity of the volume is apparent if one con-
ducts a brief survey of the poems included. In "Dragon Country" the
reader finds a "fearful glimmer of joy" (52), while in "Ballad of a
Sweet Dream of Peace" ("Keepsakes"), the reader discovers the
grandmother's bureau in the woods, "the life they had promised her
she would live" (28), and "that poor self she'd mislaid" (30). In
"Lullaby: A Motion Like Sleep" the reader once more makes a joy-
ous discovery, finding a sense of "Time's irremediable joy" (29).
This unified sequence of discoveries spills over into the last poem in
the volume, "The Necessity of Belief."

Depending on one's reading of "Ballad of a Sweet Dream of Peace" and "Dragon Country," the necessity for belief may represent human redemption through God's love. Clearly, the naturalistic approach, which suggests that humanity is utterly isolated in a mechanistic and ultimately purposeless universe, is here abandoned by Warren.

In addition to the poetic legacy Warren has left for Gabriel and Rosanna, Warren, along with Brooks, left a legacy of understanding what good poetry can be. If "most people are thoroughly satisfied to admit the value of any activity which satisfies a basic and healthy human interest," then perhaps they can comprehend that the value of poetry "springs from a basic human impulse and fulfils a basic human interest."[27] Brooks has written that "a number of Warren's poems . . . concern themselves with explorations of the problem of knowledge," poems which are obsessed with a consciousness of the past that drives us back upon history in search for meanings.[28] On a larger scale the following comment by Frank Kermode reinforces Brooks's observation about Warren's poetry: poems that deal with an historical event "make history strange and they are very private in their handling of the public themes. They can protect us from the familiar; they stand apart from opinion; they are a form of knowledge."[29] That Warren's legacy lives on is asserted by Norman Fruman: "The paradoxical effect of these catastrophic developments [backlashes to the New Criticism] . . . has been a sharply increased respect for what the first generation of New Critics achieved in displacing the ossified hegemony of historical studies: a refocusing of primary interest upon the poem and not the poet, the tale and not the teller, upon the centrality of language in literary studies."[30]

You, Emperors, and Others: Poems 1957–1960 was deemed a

failure by many critics. Strandberg, however, provides an excellent rebuttal to the critical consensus by emphasizing the volume's positive qualities. Indeed, this volume is not without merit. It contains eight poem sequences, the first of which is titled "Garland for You" and provides the reference for the "you" in the volume title. "I. Clearly about You" suggests that one cannot escape blood knowledge, knowledge of the heart, whether one accepts himself or not. The poem is structured as a quatrain with alternating rhymes (a-b-a-b). Some of the other poems in this sequence vary in meter and rhyme scheme, but all of them use rhyme. Each poem in the sequence addresses a phase of self-identity, of learning the lesson stated in the last poem of the sequence, "VIII. The Self That Stares": "To recognize / The human self naked in your own eyes" (19–20). The different sections of the poetic sequence resemble the phases in an individual's life. The poem examines the soft-spoken namelessness of innocence in "II. Lullaby: Exercise in Human Charity and Self-Knowledge," and then it considers the initiation of the Ivy leaguer in the "gray flannel suit and black knit tie" (22), the one whose identity is subsumed in the crowd in the following section, "III. Man in the Street."

Upon reaching middle age in "IV. Switzerland," the speaker makes an appeal for those travelers who have reached the same end of "pain, need, guilt, lip-biting, and spasm" (27) and need God to deliver them back to joy. Life at this point is only a dream, a dream of youth, as the speaker longs "For belief in the old delusion in which you have always believed" (4). The persona finds a solution to the real question in the fifth poem by advising the dreamer to avoid "the thought that, on your awakening, identity may be destroyed" (32). In "VI. The Letter about Money, Love, and Other

Comfort, If Any" the persona narrates his past mistake of trusting a deceptive person who left him in debt. Foolish enough to follow this trail of deceit, neglect, and abuse, the speaker eventually reconciles himself to the primal penchant for dominance in himself and sees the path of redemption, "by that new light I shall seek / The way, and my peace with God" (86–87). This discovery of the horror in the human heart is reiterated in "VIII. The Self That Stares," as is another lesson: "To recognize / The human self naked in your own eyes" (19–20).

The volume title's reference to "emperors" is most notable in the sequence, "Two Pieces after Suetonius," who was a Roman historian in the second century A.D. "I. Apology for Domitian" draws a parallel between the emperor and the "you" addressed in the poem, who is doomed to a similar fate because of his vanity, greed, and fear of impending death. The second poem, which comes in two parts, is "II. Tiberius on Capri." In the opening part, the persona reflects on the emperor's lusts, on the lusts of modern humanity, and on "the paradox of powers that would grind us like grain" (28). He throws a stone from the ruin into the sea to protest the ways of God to man, to invoke Milton's famous line from *Paradise Lost*.

In the sequences viewed thus far from *You, Emperors, and Others,* one readily perceives the intensity with which Warren treats his subject matter, an intensity that he implies belongs to Everyman. One of the most famous sequences of the volume is "Mortmain," a five-part series that examines the meaning of a father's death to a son, who struggles to remember what he knows of his father's life and to articulate what it all means. The sight of his dying father creates a sense of loss, of being out of control of the moment: "All things . . . / Were snatched from me, and I could not move, / Naked

in that black blast of his love" (27–32). In that moment of fear and
love, the speaker recalls an image of his father at age sixteen working on "the first railroad in the region" ("II. A Dead Language: Circa
1885," 5). He also imagines his father studying Greek, and remembers the grammar book he has found about seventy years later when
he cannot understand the father who studied that language "amid
History's vice and velleity" ("III. Fox-fire: 1956," 29). In "IV. In the
Turpitude of Time: n.d." the son recognizes that "In the heart's last
kingdom only the old are young" (25) who have become their own
song. From that acknowledgment comes a vision in "V. A Vision:
Circa 1880." The vision centers on the father in Trigg County, Kentucky, as a boy "With imperial calm" (33) entering "The shadow of
woods" (34). Warren's invocation of leaf imagery is once again evident as "one high oak leaf stirs gray" (35) with rain as an omen of
hope.

The "Some Quiet, Plain Poems" sequence provides the "and
Others" section of *You, Emperors, and Others.* These six poems
continue the search for joy stemming from the past, in the present,
and as hope for the future. The sequence records the isolation felt by
a traveler in a far land, a sense of aloneness magnified by the surrounding stillness and the noticeable absence of bird sounds. The
persona realizes the futility, if not the impossibility, of returning to
his past but finds hope in recalling the sound of his young aunt's and
her husband's voices singing in moonlight; they "aspire / Some life-
faith yet, by my years, unrepealed" ("IV. In Moonlight, Somewhere,
They Are Singing," 24–25). This sequence passes through a tender
moment, the persona's thought of an owl-call in Italy being
answered by a remembered owl-call in Kentucky. The sequence
ends with a debate in the last poem, "VI. Debate: Question, Quarry,

Dream," in which the speaker "considers more strictly the appalling logic of joy" (25) brought about by his sense of the past combining with his sense of the present and the image of his son sleeping, a symbolic representation of the future.

The other poems in this volume continue to record Warren's search for solutions to life's existential dilemma: if death is certain, what is the purpose of life? In "Ballad: Between the Boxcars (1923)" the speaker records the following response after he remembers the accidental death of a fifteen-year-old boy:

> For we are in the world and nothing is good enough, which is
>   to say that the world is here and we are not
>   good enough,
>
> And we live in the world, and in so far as we live, the world
>   continues to live in us,
>
> ("III. He Has Fled," 28–32)

Warren considers humanity's search for purpose in the past, which, according to "Two Studies in Idealism: Short Survey of American, and Human History," involves "killing and you-know-what" in the first of two Civil War poems set in the sequence. From killing animals to killing human beings, one has a right to die for the Right. The traveling salesman in "Nocturne: Traveling Salesman in Hotel Bedroom" has a need to remember that "vision is possible, and / Man's meed of glory not / Impossible" (29–31). Considering the cobbler's meager, God-fearing life, the persona challenges God's judgment as to whether Mr. Moody has been short-changed in "So You Agree with What I Say? Well, What Did I Say?" Toward the end of *You, Emperors, and Others,* Warren more obviously makes transitions between poems, carries over key ideas, repeats significant words, and refers back to a previously mentioned person or object, thus reminding his readers that the sequence and, moreover, the volume as a whole should be read as a unified poem rather than as a series of isolated poems. The penultimate sequence, titled "Nursery Rhymes," uses children's rhymes such as "Hickory-Dickory-Dock" as a platform for adult rhymes. It serves as preparation for the last sequence, "Short Thoughts for Long Nights." It contains nine individually titled quatrains, the last of which, "Grasshopper Tries to Break Solipsism," sings of God's love but for questionable reasons of self-serving motives and vanity.

If *Promises* and *You, Emperors, and Others* are transitions into Warren's middle period, *Tale of Time: Poems, 1960–1966* clearly marks a new voice emerging. This collection is a meditation on death as a means of imbuing life with purpose. The poems begin in free verse, without a rhyme pattern, and with dark images of war, of the world as adversary, and of grief. In the "Tale of Time" sequence the speaker makes clear the volume's deep interest in finding existential meaning: "Between the beginning and the end, we must learn / The nature of being, in order / In the end to be," ("IV. The Interim," 7–9). The volume implies that love has many different manifestations, ranging from the kind of love offered by a prostitute in Squigg-town to a mother's love. Ultimately, the volume is concerned with knowing how to love. It poses the question, what is love? It shocks readers who first encounter the answer it provides: "you / Must eat the dead" to find joy, perhaps even immortality ("The Interim," part 8, 1–2). Beyond the literal grotesqueness of this image, the persona asserts the need to move past the loss of a loved one and, therefore, to move past history, in order to find one's authentic self and love again. Continuing his line of thinking about death, the speaker wants to know about the afterlife—if such a realm even exists—and what the dead think about love in "VI. Insomnia." In part 4, after the truth settles in, new images, symbolized by stars, are reborn.

Human time is measured from birth to death. The time in between perplexes the persona in the "Homage to Emerson, on Night Flight to New York" sequence. It portrays his puzzlement over reality as a drunken allegory in which everything has significance, as Emerson thought, or a multiplication table to stay the fear of flying, or as experience and a way of living that can become truth. The juxtaposition of "Shoes in Rain Jungle" suggests an irony. It is an anti-Vietnam War poem that considers the larger perspective of history by including the caveat that "All wars are righteous. Except when / You lose them" (14–15). Wars, too, represent death—one of the four horsemen of the Apocalypse. In the context of the interplay between time and space with respect to life, death, love, and history, the persona stretches to know the true meaning of life. The "Fall Comes in Back-Country Vermont" sequence enforces that stance with the figure of the dead voter, "Deader they die," in the first of four poems. The female date in the second poem is afraid she will catch the death of the one who died on the mattress on which she makes love, though he died of cancer and will not spread it. The human fabric lives on unaffected by death's grim hand in poem three. The persona tries to envision the eagle he once saw diving into mountain shade, thus affirming life and courage and, for the speaker, a vision of love as he touches "the hand there on the pillow" beside him (14).

In a "Prefatory Note" to *Selected Poems: New and Old, 1923–1966,* Warren suggests the historical import of literary texts, "for poems are, in one perspective at least, always a life record, and live their own life by that fact."[31] Certainly Warren's observation rings true in the first poem in the sequence, "The Day Dr. Knox Did It." "I. Place and Time" is set in Cerulean Springs in 1914 when the persona is nine years old. The scene is white-hot, while "the leaf / of the oak tree curls at the edge like leather" (16–17). "II. The Event" describes a suicide, an unexplained death in the eyes of a nine-year-old, who asks his grandfather, a Confederate veteran, "What made him do it?" At a loss for words, the grandfather says, "For some folks the world gets too much" (41). The boy's curiosity takes them to the place where Dr. Knox committed suicide, a hayloft that is now mysteriously clean in spite of the fact that it marks the place where Dr. Knox put the twelve-gauge barrel in his mouth and ended his life. In "V. And All That Came Thereafter" the persona looks back in time and confuses his own sins and learns that "we must frame more firmly the idea of good" (64).

The "Holy Writ" sequence returns to the search for truth, for what must be believed in as truth. The speaker explores the conflict between flesh and faith, and prays that God not exist. The second poem in this sequence, in nine parts, is "II. Saul at Gilboa." In the fifth part the persona suggests the relation between knowledge and "the secret hope within" (9). In the seventh part he shudders in a "rage of joy" (30). Perhaps the persona finds joy arduous and somewhat frustrating as well, especially if the price of delight is unexpected self-knowledge. In the final sequence, "Delight," each of the seven poems presents various images of delight, figuring it as being independent of human grasp, as love and instant joy, as a calm

dawn, as a dream, as untrustworthy, and as a sunset. The archetypal
life cycle is completed as the sequence moves from dawn to dusk.
Some of the lines contain echoes of Warren's literary influences.
Warren's line "Delight comes on soundless foot" (I, 2) puts us in
mind of Carl Sandburg's famous description of fog creeping silently
in. "From nothing of *not* / Now all of *is*" (V, part 1, 2–3) is reminiscent of e. e. cummings's word play. "Delight knows its own reason"
(I, 9) echoes Paul's words about love in chapter 13 of his first letter
to the Corinthians that "Love bears all things, believes all things,
hopes all things, endures all things" (verse 7). Even "IV. Dream of
a Dream the Small Boy Had" takes one back to the dreams Warren
himself portrayed in *Promises*. The tone in this sequence is playful
and the leaf image continues to carry the symbolic weight of the season or stage of life it represents. New leaves suggest a promise of the
future, while the pine leaf emblematizes things eternal. Warren
again uses rhyme schemes to underscore the mood intended as in the
playful a-b-a-a pattern of "I. Into Broad Daylight." The a-b-a-b
scheme of "VII. Finisterre" is also significant, pointing to the golden
moment at day's end that may cause the heart to wonder, perhaps in
delight.

The poems in *Tale of Time* reflect Warren's never-ending quest
for poetic development and his transition into the last two decades
of his poetic endeavor. In the poems of Warren's later period, his
break with the modernist traditions becomes apparent as he expands
his exploration of poetry well into the latter decades of the twentieth
century.

CHAPTER FIVE

Late Poetry (1966–1985)

> the value of poetry . . . springs from a basic human
> impulse and fulfils a basic human interest.
>
> *Understanding Poetry* (1938)

Poems (1966–1975)

The first four volumes of this late period of Warren's poetry include *Incarnations, Audubon: A Vision, Or Else,* and *Can I See Arcturus from Where I Stand?* In these volumes Warren makes use of less traditional, more loosely structured verse forms. On a thematic level the images become more graphic (see the sexually explicit imagery in "Flaubert in Egypt," for example), the diction more erudite, and the memories and quest for self-knowledge more intense.

Harold Bloom, a relatively late convert to Warren's poetry, praises *Incarnations* as "an extraordinary book." He boldly pronounces that in the poem "The Leaf" he finds "a textual point of crossing, the place Warren's poetry turned about, on his quest for an ultimate strength."[1] From its title, one might wonder what kind of incarnations we are to anticipate in this volume. Looking up "incarnation" in a dictionary might suggest a range of possible subjects for Warren's book. Does *Incarnations* represent a bodily manifestation of a supernatural being, as in the incarnation of Jesus Christ? Perhaps it shows a personification of a particular abstract or intangible quality, or an instance of occupying a given condition as in hopes for a better life next time around? Or could the volume embody a combination of two or more of these choices?[2] *Incarnations* is divided into three sequences, a number charged with symbolic import in the Christian tradition, a detail that may suggest the first definition listed above, though it could be only a coincidence. The three parts of the volume are "Island of Summer," "Internal Injuries," and "Enclaves." They can be read as parts of a single, unified poem, just as Warren's entire poetic canon can be considered as a cohesive structure.

The three suggested definitions for the title of Warren's volume are present in the "Island of Summer," a fifteen-poem sequence. Also evident in this sequence are the three themes Strandberg discusses in *The Poetic Vision of Robert Penn Warren:* passage, mysticism, and the undiscovered self. "XIV. Masts at Dawn" touches on the bodily manifestation of God in nature: "we must try / To love so well the world that we may believe, in the end, in God" (21–22).[3] The ten-year-old son's discovery of a Nazi helmet in a dump triggers the persona's realization that "history / Like nature, may have mercy" (22–23) in "III. Natural History" (the quality of mercy being great). In "IX. Mistral at Night" the speaker's assertion that "this knowledge / Is the beginning of joy" (14–15) provides that instance of occupying a given condition. These three poems may serve as examples of the title's meaning, though this sequence supports a range of other interpretations.

The umbrella issue for the sequence seems to be the individual's role in the world and how one might discover what his or her role is. The persona meditates on "the / Nature of the soul" (2–3) in "II. Where the Slow Fig's Purple Sloth." The fig metaphor suggests that the discovery is within; and when it is reached, "It fills / The darkening room with light" (20–21). Warren toys with the original sin motif in his Edenic poem, "Riddle in the Garden," in which the speaker warns the reader not to expose the inwardness of the plum, an act which will cause more pain since the reader is "part of the world" and "The world means only itself" (18–19, 21). The persona then sees Aphrodite, goddess of love, beauty, and fertility, as the one who robs youths of their dreams, outwardly manifested by the old trying to appear young on the Mediterranean beach. In "IX. Mistral at Night" the speaker likens the world to wind and uses leaves metaphorically to represent one's life, the knowledge of which "Is the beginning of joy" (15).

Joy is the dream sought, the life to be lived but lived only to the fullest after the painful search for and discovery of self-knowledge. That self-knowledge may also represent the hope for a better life, if not now, then in the next incarnation, as in "XII. The Red Mullet." The persona's realization that nature forgives nothing prompts his attempt in the face of his own mortality (the great, red mullet) to develop as much immunity as possible and a familiarity "with the agony of will in the deep place" (14), that agony of will which many of Warren's fictional protagonists experience. The element of mystical connection between man and nature, which approaches a sense of almost Oriental oneness, is one path suggested by the persona of "Masts at Dawn" to gain the joy discovered in self-knowledge and, perhaps, in knowledge of God. The persona's identification with the past, evident in his father's voice calling to him in "XV. The Leaf," brings in the other part of the equation for the desired discovery: "The voice blesses me for the only / Gift I have given: *teeth set on edge*" (D, 1–2). The line "Teeth set on edge" creates an image of fear. For the persona, this fear might be a manifestation of his guilt, magnified through his self-knowledge of his sins and the sins of the whole world. Humanity is, indeed, insignificant when juxtaposed against the speed of light, which the persona says is "A sound like wind." This image represents another way of viewing eternity in contrast to transitory human life on the relative continuum of time.

The second sequence, "Internal Injuries," focuses on an inmate who is a convicted killer and is now on death row. The persona hopes that the inmate will receive a stay of execution, but this pardon does not come. The convict represents Everyman's life trials, "for we are all / One flesh" (6–7), as the narrator observes in "VI. Night Is Personal." Responding to the black woman being injured by the yellow Cadillac, the speaker admonishingly concludes, "we cannot love others unless / We learn how to love / Ourselves properly" (18–20) in "VI. Be Something Else." Extending a teleological view of human grief, he seems to reject Newton's view of absolute space and time and to side more with Einstein's view of relativity when he claims that "Truth lives / Only in relation" (13–14). This sense of metaphysical relativity is reiterated in the following poem, "VII. The World Is a Parable," in which the speaker claims that "Nothing is real, for only / Nothingness is real" (4–5). Stuck in traffic, he reacts with hope when the traffic begins to move, and realizes the time has come for him to begin a new life. His reaction to others provides him insight about himself.

The third sequence of *Incarnations,* "Enclaves," concludes with the two-poem sequence "In the Mountains," with the physical enclave in "Skiers" and the metaphorical enclave of being human in the boundaries of the world in "Fog." Though small and insignificant in the larger context, "The human / Face has its own beauty" (16–17). On an even smaller scale, then, the human heart, contextless, might be, though it is never explicitly stated, the locus of the soul in that vast whiteness of landscape.

LATE POETRY (1966–1985)

Warren's late period of poetry gives rise to two longer narrative poems, *Audubon: A Vision* and *Chief Joseph of the Nez Perce*. *Audubon* is preceded by a brief note on Jean Jacques Audubon and one of the most famous legends about him concerning his possible identity as the lost Dauphin of France, son of Louis XVI and Marie Antoinette. Overall, the poem phrases some psychological concerns of the famous ornithologist who paradoxically kills the very creatures he preserves in his paintings. Rather than a continuous narrative, Warren provides a "series of 'snapshots' of Audubon at various ages." John Burt further conjectures that Warren's repeated concerns with birds, hunting, nature, and exploration are bound by discovering "a character who can look upon the truth and not be silenced by it" and by reconciling the poetic power of the ballad and the "intelligibility of the commentary," a combination seen earlier in "The Ballad of Billie Potts."[4] In the opening poem, "I. Was Not the Lost Dauphin," the narrator explores Audubon's passion for ornithology, for knowledge of the world, and for self-knowledge, asking, "What / Is man but his passion?" (4–5). Audubon's ethical quandary involves the necessity of killing birds so that he can study and paint them. His moral sentiments against destroying the birds are pitted against his aesthetic impulse to represent their beauty through art. In an effort to extricate himself from this moral dilemma, Audubon takes a rather Darwinian view of the natural world, reasoning that the name of the world is survival. The scene at the cabin in which he spends a night and the subsequent hanging of the mother and three sons who stole from other travelers staying with them causes Audubon to reflect on his own mortality and identity. His courage in facing the truth of life and death enables him to continue to walk in the world. Truth cannot be spoken, only enacted, the omniscient narrator asserts in "IV. The Sign Whereby He Knew," as Audubon experiences his lack of identity. His killing was for love: "What is love? / One name for it is knowledge" (16–17) and is explained in "VI. Love and Knowledge." For the narrator, the story of time will be of deep delight. It is a story of living in time and removing life from time in order that it can be preserved in time. If that delight is a feeling of freedom in discovery of self, its price is rendered in blood.

In *Or Else: Poem/Poems, 1968–1974* Warren develops and refines his technique of forging parallels between the different poems in a volume by making dramatic interconnections and references in a poem toward the end of the work to a poem at the beginning, thereby keeping readers aware of the volume's unity. This volume uses "interjections" as links that are similar to Warren's use of interchapters in some of his novels. Warren focuses sharply on time in this volume, starting with "I. The Nature of a Mirror," in which "Time / Is the mirror into which you stare" (16–17). In "*Interjection #1: The Need for Re-evaluation*" the persona denies the image in the mirror as really representing himself because "Time / Is only a mirror in the fun-house" (1–2), a distorted view of reality at best. The surreal scene found in "II. Natural History" shows time stopped and the narrator's remanding the dead (the past) back to their graves. "III. Time as Hypnosis," represents a dream world in which self is nothing but "what / The snow dreamed all night" (10–11). The "Caveat" ("*Interjection #2*") warns that though the world must be perceived as continuous, only in discontinuity "do we / know that we exist" (9–10). The persona's dream of a white Christmas ("The Natural History of a Vision") is a return to his past, to the house which is now inhabited by ghosts of his relatives. The ghosts of the speaker's relatives show that time does not stop at the grave; instead, the past is never lost and remains continuous with the present.

In the process of exploring the nature of time, the persona realizes "the pain of the past in its pastness / May be converted into the future tense / Of joy" (part 12, 5–7). "*Interjection #3: I Know a Place Where All Is Real*" suggests a flaw in utilitarianism. Not everyone can accept the cost of that joy, which entails a rejection of the past; therefore, some are unwilling to reject the pastness of the past and, consequently, they walk away from the potential joy of the future. The poem is supposedly set "northwest of Mania and beyond Delight" (7). Few travelers who visit this realm return, but those who do remain do not stay long since many of them die, unable to face the savage reality in the human heart. "VII. Chain Saw at Dawn in Vermont in Time of Drouth" poses the question: "what man / Has learned how to live?" (19–20). Self-knowledge is important, and, in another invocation of a common theme in Warren's work, the price is the shedding of blood, an act portrayed in "*Interjection #4: Bad Year, Bad War: A New Year's Card, 1969.*" Time is forever in one dimension of "Forever O'Clock" but not in "X. Rattlesnake Country," though time continues to be treated almost as a character in the experience of the persona's life. He plays with the concept of time: "What was *is* is now *was*" (part 5, 1). The persona reminisces about a visit to a ranch in Montana. One of the two girls he recalls reminds one of Mrs. Jones-Talbot in *A Place to Come To* and might have been her prototype. If meaning escapes him, experience of his past does not, and the forever clock does not chime.

Two poems in *Or Else* deal more directly with sexual images than any others in Warren's canon. In "XI. Homage to Theodore Dreiser" the narrator portrays a character more to be pitied than envied, one who might "learn, in his self-contemptive distress, / The secret worth / Of all our human worthlessness" ("3. Moral Assessment," 16–18). "XII. Flaubert in Egypt," perhaps Warren's most sexually graphic poem, is about a character who pays the price for his sexual exploits and wears like a bright jeweled trophy the chancre of his dream. He has contracted syphilis. Back home and near death, he recalls "the palm fronds— / how black against a bright sky!" that constitute his most vivid memories of Egypt. "*Interjection #5: Solipsism and Theology*" bridges a gap between these two poems, with their focus on self as the only reality, and the following two poems that extend reality beyond self. The persona at least reflects submissively on the true nature of time ("XIII. The True Nature of Time") and on the barriers that prevent him from knowing it. But his attention turns outward to nature, to the human place in nature. In "XIV. Vision under the October Mountain: A Love Poem" he feels closer to reality, the "un-self which was self" (14), with his companion. But his companion, his beloved or God, remains unidentified. The dilemma continues in "XV. Stargazing" as he tries to imbue stars (a symbol of reality) with a love of God. The autobiographical element also becomes more pronounced in this phase of Warren's writing. This poem may be a poetic reconstruction of Warren's experience the night the piece of coal hit him in the eye while he was stargazing in his backyard in Guthrie. The speaker responds mentally to the girl's observation that he does not look at the stars: I know "That if I look at the stars, I / Will have to live over again all I have lived / In the years I looked at stars and / Cried out, 'O reality!'" (17–20). In the narrator's mind God and nature (the stars) are separated, reflecting nature's indifference to God. Clearly, autobiographical elements appear in "XX. Reading Late at Night, Thermometer Falling," in which the persona finds his father's poems and recalls his words of wisdom about finding happiness in his obligations rather than in his artistic leanings. Those memories Warren recaptured in part years later in *Portrait of a Father.*

The poems toward the end of *Or Else* seem to jump around in time, from the murder recounted in "XVI. News Photo" to a more current event inspired by Warren's son Gabriel, in "XVII. Little Boy and Lost Shoe," which has shades of imagery, diction, and rhythm of John Crowe Ransom's "Bells for John Whiteside's Daughter." Warren's "little boy" is "dilatory" in looking for his lost shoe, and his parents are exasperated by his seemingly impervious regard for time. Time is running out literally; "the sun will be down" (8) before he finds that shoe. On a metaphoric level the boy's life is passing quickly. He does not realize how rapidly his time is passing, but his parents are aware of it. To them, "time is money." The narrator knows, too, the indifference of nature: "The mountains lean. They watch. They know" (16); of course, they offer no solace to the parents nor encouragement to the little boy. "XIX. There's a Grandfather's Clock in the Hall" counters the escape from real time into eternity suggested by "Forever O'Clock," instead asserting that "Time thrusts through the time of no-Time" (18). Just as quickly in life, time passes through the death of a loved one to death of self. Warren also continues to address the question of the existence of a just and merciful God. His poetic narrators strive to believe in a divine presence but often are left with doubt, perhaps because they have not yet earned authentic self-knowledge, as in "XXI. Folly on Royal Street before the Raw Face of God." Humanity is left with the experience he has fashioned out of life in war, fishing, or art, symbolic allusions of conflict, leisure or survival, and intelligence. The persona, who is after all the same, concludes the next poem, "XXII. Sunset Walk in Thaw-Time in Vermont," with: "For what blessing may a man hope for but / An immortality in / The loving vigilance of death?" (part 4, 13–15). His immortality is his children.

Can I See Arcturus from Where I Stand? consists of Warren's 1975 poems in *Selected Poems: 1923–1975* and serves as the pivotal point in his late period. The idea of God seems to weigh heavily on Warren's mind at the age of seventy. His poems are structured into less traditional forms with longer lines. The persona of the lead poem, "A Way to Love God," recalls images of grotesque events, such as mountains disintegrating, Mussolini's legionaries preparing for war, the beheading of Mary of Scots, and the spiritual isolation of "a scholar who has lost faith in his calling" (32). He observes ironically that thinking "nothing would ever again happen. / That is a way to love God" (36–37). The question lingers concerning why God allows suffering to occur. The speaker feels the weight of human error in Time in "Evening Hawk." Nature, represented by the hawk, is unforgiving. The natural world is marked by the grim and violent struggle for survival. In this respect Warren returns to a naturalistic model for the indifferent physical world. He hears earth grind, history drip as humanity struggles for a tenuous survival, alone in an utterly detached universe. Unlike human beings, the hawk "Who knows neither Time nor error" (12) climbs at last light, a symbol of the timelessness and relative permanence of the natural cycle.

In these and his later poems love becomes a more predominant factor in the solution for humanity's existential dilemma. The persona wants to identify the " it" (love, perhaps joy) in "Loss, of Perhaps Love, in Our World of Contingency" and recognizes that "We must learn to live in the world" (30). Learning to live in the world is easier said than done. His memory of a lover long past provides momentary happiness in "Answer to Prayer," a poem in which Warren returns to quatrains with a-b-a-b rhyme. The next poem, "Paradox," plays on Zeno's paradox which suggests that motion is nonexistent. In the poem the speaker cannot quite catch up with the pursued (a loved one? his self?) seen by him as a more complex version of that paradox. The pain associated with love follows in "Midnight Outcry"; the uncertainty of consequences when one listens to nature's "truths" is offset by the need to know something in "Trying to Tell You Something"; and "Brotherhood in Pain" connects the "obscene moment of birth" (16) with the person one becomes after the harrowing experience of birth. The poem laments the fact that we all forget the experience of our birth as we enter into our lonely existence "in the delirious illusion of language."

In a letter to Warren on 2 April 1975, Brooks provides the following comments on the first poem of this section of new poems: "I like very much indeed 'Old Nigger [on One-Mule Cart Encountered Late at Night When Driving Home from Party in the Back Country].' I think the final section is superb. It repeats one of your big themes but does so in its own way and with a special richness of tonality. Indeed, this section represents you at your very best."[5] The persona, who is drunk, is driving too fast down a narrow road in Louisiana in July and barely misses a mule-drawn cart. He is obviously frightened, even haunted by the experience, and soberly acknowledges that life is pure fantasy and that his existence is insignificant in the world. The big theme of the poem centers on the ability of an individual to discover his genuine self, to gain self-knowledge through experience in the world as part of the human condition.

Poems (1976–1985)

In the last stages of his poetic career, Warren seemed to be approaching the summit of his creative powers in poetry, as Brooks, Harold Bloom, and other critics suggest in dealing with his poetry from 1976–1985. This period begins with the publication of *Now and Then: Poems 1976–1978,* which is divided into two sections. "I. Nostalgic" and "II. Speculative" reverse the temporal order suggested by the title, moving from then to now. "I. Nostalgic" provides a retrospective look at youth, touching on such themes as young love, and youth's ability to communicate with others, nature, and the self. "II. Speculative" then reveals the poet's focus on dreams, abstractions, and spiritual awareness in the autumn years of his life.

As in his earlier poems, Warren continues to question his purpose in life and his relation to both God and nature. The strength of this late poetry may, in fact, be in his bulldog determination not to accept any convenient answer in his quest for truth and knowledge. This determination may be found in the recurrence of Warren's exploration of love, hope, and endurance as positive values for imbuing human existence with meaning.

In the first poem, "American Portrait: Old Style," he returns to memories of Kent Greenfield, his friend from youth about whom he wrote in the short story "Goodwood Comes Back." Growing up in a time when the Civil War was not that far removed in history, the poet looks back nostalgically at his summers with his friend, "K," and the hard lesson that imagination is "The lie we must learn to live by, if ever / We mean to live at all" (part III, 52–53). The poet grapples with K's tragic fall and with old dreams that at one time seemed life's truths. He struggles with the thought of knowing that death is inevitable, but resists this thought because of his desire to experience a world yet unknown to him. His youthful endurance prevails as he concludes that "love is a hard thing to outgrow" (129).

In "Amazing Grace in the Back Country" the poet recounts attending a revival in an old carnival tent when he was twelve years old. Remembering the revival recalls to him the hypocrisy of professed grace under a "mania of joy" (29). His repulsion of the falseness of this kind of religious display and his fear of his own guilt cause him to run outside to vomit "On the scaly bark of a hickory tree" (55), an image harkening back to the ominous carnival-like atmosphere and its effects in *The Cave*. The poet's experience creates a sense of wonderment at it all and a more serious realization of his own mortality and his need for meaningful grace.

The concern with death is prominent in these poems. "Boy Wandering in Simms' Valley" tells the story of a farmer who commits suicide after his wife died of a sickness. The narrator imagines that "A dirt-farmer needs a good wife to keep a place trim, / So the place must have gone to wrack with his old lady sick" (13–14). Thus, the young boy, who has wandered into Simms' house years after the occupants are dead, wonders "what life is, and love, and what they may be" (29). In a following poem, "Evening Hour," the setting is a graveyard overlooking a town. The narrator speaks of a young boy who goes to that graveyard to look for arrowheads. He stays until the lights in town come on, lost in his own thoughts, and feels the impulse "To lay ear to earth for what voices beneath might say" (24). Perhaps, although the speaker does not explicitly say it, one learns from the past. Again, in "Orphanage Boy" a death affects a boy. The poem's narrator tells the story of Al, an orphan who works on a farm and has bonded with "Bob, the big white farm bulldog" (14). After a copperhead bites Bob, the persona's uncle tells Al to shoot Bob. Al does as he is told, then leaves home and is never heard from again. Six months later the narrator returns and finds a cross marking Bob's grave. The persona's matter-of-fact acceptance of Bob's fate and his puzzlement over Al's actions are apparent in his concluding speculation that "It must have taken nigh moonset" (45) for Al to bury Bob. The poet in "Red-Tail Hawk and Pyre of Youth" looks back on killing with more sensitivity. In his youth he kills "at that miraculous range" (56) a hawk that he stuffs the next day. The golden eyes stare without blinking at him now, "Gold eyes, unforgiving" (25) as they appeared just before he squeezed the trigger. Years later when the poet returns to his parents' house, he thinks about the hawk and wonders, "Could Nature forgive, like God?" (84). He finds the disheveled hawk in the lumber room, with one eye gone and responds with sympathy: "and I reckoned / I knew how it felt with one gone" (88–89). He builds a pyre and burns the remains of the hawk. In doing so, he hopes to expunge his guilt of youth's ignorance and to find redemption when his time has come through "the truth in blood-marriage of earth and air— / And all will be as it was / In that paradox of unjoyful joyousness" (120–22). The truth, of course, does not come, as Bloom has also noted in "Sunset Hawk: Warren's Poetry and Tradition," because the youthful killing of the hawk—an image of truth—does not ironically make truth. In his preface to *The Blood-Marriage of Earth and Sky: Robert Penn Warren's Later Novels,* Leonard Casper explains that his choice of title "is meant to suggest the way in which [Warren's] works may be considered meditations on a general communion, co-being, especially through collaborative narration in the case of his novels."[6]

Warren's obsession with the human inability to communicate is explicitly stated in "Mountain Plateau." The poet hears a crow utter "Its cry to the immense distance" but he "can make no answer" and says: "I have lived / Long without being able / To make adequate communication" (16–18). In the following poem, "Star-Fall," the persona and his loved one lie without need for communication beneath the stars: "each alone / Is sunk and absorbed into / The mass and matrix of Being that defines / Identity of all" (15–18). In that moment they commune through nature. The youth in the following poem, "Youth Stares at Minoan Sunset," has the ability to commune with nature, an ability that his observers, perhaps his parents, "do not yet have. Or have forgotten" (26).

In moving from the first section of *Now and Then* to the second section, Warren shifts from the backward look at *then* to the speculative look at *now*. In "II. Speculative" the poet conjectures further about death. As he ages he worries about memories fading, losing time with family and friends, being out of touch with nature, and not knowing himself. Perhaps the ultimate concern, which he avoids at times through denial, pertains to the existence of God and the human relationship to God. These poems are troublesome for the poet because they do not provide the answers he seeks. Perhaps as a refuge, then, he couches those inquiries in seemingly traditional verse forms, using unrhymed couplets for some of these poems and invoking rhyming four- and five-line stanzas for others. However, the poet continues to probe the difficult metaphysical questions and seeks the appropriate blend of sound and sense.

"II. Speculative" begins with two poems about dreams as dreams relate to time. The first, "Dream," posits the idea that "dream is the mother of memory" (6). It suggests that memory and time are inextricably commingled, for, without memory, "where—oh, what—is

Time?" (7). Like Jacob who wrestled an angel, the poet must grapple with his dream, "For the dream is only a self of yourself" (19); perhaps he too can gain something, truth or knowledge, by dawn. In the second dream-poem, "Dream of a Dream," "Time and water interflow" (9) in the poet's dream-search for definition of self. What follows in "First Dawn Light" after the last dream "is the true emptiness of night" (4) before the loneliness of day descends. The persona in the poem finds reality in dreams. He returns to the subject of dreams in the fourth from last poem, "Rather Like a Dream." On a walk alone in the mountain woods at sunset in autumn, the poet feels his mortality. His memories and thoughts gather "Each under a brooding leaf" (19), and "years / Are darkening under each leaf" (23–24). He feels "Another summer is now truly a dream" (16) and wonders whether like Wordsworth he should reach out "To touch stone or tree to confirm / His own reality" (2–3). The poems in this section are linked by various recurring images, such as the leaf and the natural seasons, as they relate to the poet's inner self.[7]

"Ah, Anima!" expresses the similarities between a natural disaster and the human soul "in the hurricane of Time" (3). He wonders whether he might be closer to that truth if instead of passive resistance, laying "In the shards of Time and the un-roar of the wind of being" (19), he should act and "leap / Into the blind and antiseptic anger of air" (127–28). He moves from a natural disaster to the abstractness of truth in "Unless" and believes happiness is becoming one with nature—that is, standing motionless and breathing "with the rhythm of stars" (22). In "Not Quite Like a Top" the poet takes his search to the highest level. He wants God to exist in order to deny Him. In recalling the prayer he prayed in youth and the belief that the earth "Spins on an axis that sways, and swings, from its middle" (2), he acknowledges his own ignorance about so much. The above poems represent three of nine unrhymed-couplet poems in this volume; they seem to represent the religious questioning side of the poet. For example, in the next poem, "Waiting," the persona tries to laugh off humanity's plight only to admit that whatever man has done he has done because God has allowed him "the grandeur of certain utterances. / True or not. But sometimes true" (26–27).

The other five poems in that form follow suit in their harsh questioning of humanity's role on earth, another way of looking at the meaning of life. "Code Book Lost" expresses the frustration of the persona's not being able to communicate with nature, to understand how the world and humankind might communicate. In "Sister Water" the persona asks, "But is there a *now* or a *then*?" (16). The thought that God "loves us all" is "a stab of joy," of hope, though the persona cannot pray: "You can wash your face in cold water" (26). "Memory Forgotten" stirs the persona's memory into a realization that the "liquid note" that he hears in the thicket "is only a memory / Without a name" (8–9). The poem ends with the following question: "What is it you cannot remember that is so true?" A few poems later, in "Heat Lightning," memory serves as a simile for heat lightning, but memory purged of emotion and meaning, as in the act of making love but not genuinely loving. He finally reaches a level of silence when the question is beyond answer yet is still lurking somewhere in his mind. After this point, the "Inevitable Frontier" finds the aging persona amid shadows and facing "Without warning, by day or night, the appalling / White blaze of God's Great Eye" (33–34) sweeping the sky and History "back to its burrow" (35). All that is left is memory, which fades as do the names once taught: "Plato, St. Paul, Spinoza, Pascal, and Freud" (32).

In contrast to the persona's questions posed in the unrhymed couplet poems, his attempts at answers are put forth in the four- and five-line stanza poems. "The Mission" reduces the persona's mission "to try to understand / The possibility of joy in the world's tangled and hieroglyphic beauty" (36–37). Redemption, he finds in old age, might be in learning to live with forgotten memories and "to pray to God to help us live with" (36) truth ("When the Tooth Cracks—Zing!"). He can be reminded of the marvel of the nature of passion, a memory evoked by his son's building a schooner in "Waking to Tap of Hammer." That optimism is followed in "Love Recognized," which describes the love that blankets like snow the world's hideousness into silence. Nonetheless, the poet realizes his dilemma in "How to Tell a Love Story," which relies so much on history that he cannot say the first word until he knows what it means. Perhaps he cannot even do that until the doctor examines the pain in his chest. He has already identified reality with pain in "When the Tooth Cracks—Zing!" Technology, represented in "Little Black Heart of the Telephone," is a constant intruder in his life; he fears the message from the other end in his dream. That message could be one of death or one the listener cannot remember. In "Last Laugh" the persona's loss of faith and of his belief in God is expressed through his analogy of "little Sam Clemens's," age twelve, seeing through the keyhole the mystery of life in his father's autopsy and the joke Clemens imagined until his wife, Livy, who loved God, died too and left him alone "with his joke, God dead, till he died" (41).

Toward the end of *Now and Then,* the persona begins to accept old age and the prospects of death. In "Heart of the Backlog" the persona considers the meaning of the past and of life and asks, "Is God's love but the last and most mysterious word for death?" (50). He has a fleeting thought to go forth toward death, or God's love, without looking back, a feat that is apparently easier said than done. In the following poem, "Identity and Argument for Prayer," the persona finds "Space and Time our arbitrary illusions" (12) and discovers his lack of self-knowledge. He accepts an existential model of identity, redefining himself at each particular moment of experience; he is who he is at this moment, now, and takes that realization as "an argument for prayer." The diver in the next poem, "Diver," goes under the geometric circles of the water and into a "timeless peace" beneath the surface while the onlookers know "An unsuspected depth and calm / Of identity we had never dreamed" (15–16). This momentary reprieve is replaced during a Christmas season, a time "when cards are exchanged" ("Departure") and people travel, with the recognition that all must go somewhere soon, that all must die. In a Christian context the realization of one's mortality at Christmas season is ironic. Juxtaposed to the Christmas season is a summer heat wave in "Heat Wave Breaks." Invoking Wordsworthian images of nature, the persona asks what his own life has meant (10) and "For what should we pray to our God in the rumble and flare? / That the world stab anew to our hearts in the lightning-stricken air?" (19–20). In "Heart of Autumn" the seasons pass from winter to summer to fall, that archetypal point in life at which the persona again questions his own purpose in relation to the migrating geese that seem to know "when the hour comes" to fly "The path of pathlessness, with all the joy / Of destiny fulfilling its own name" (14–15). The poet's heart grasps this realization of the innate pattern of the natural cycle "Toward sunset, at a great height" (24). This combination of theme and setting is reminiscent of the depiction of an essential natural process found in William Cullen Bryant's "Thanatopsis" and "To a Waterfowl." In Bryant's poems the force that guides the waterfowl permits "an unfaltering trust" that enables the persona to approach his grave and to lie down to pleasant dreams.[8]

The intensity of the poet's questioning of life in *Now and Then* is ameliorated somewhat by a stricter focus on time in Warren's next volume, *Being Here: Poetry 1977–1980*. Unique to this volume is the author's "Afterthought," a brief statement regarding apparent aberrations of some of the poems. As Warren tells his readers, he is still concerned with "reviewing life from the standpoint of age" and with the thematic structure of the arrangement of the poems that plays against "an autobiography which represents a fusion of fiction and fact in varying degrees and perspectives" (441). The poems are divided into five numbered but untitled sections bracketed, Warren explains, by the preliminary poem, "October Picnic Long Ago" and a coda, "Passers-by on Snowy Night." Both poems are printed in italic type, suggesting perhaps the poet's internal thoughts.

"October Picnic Long Ago" is a seven-year-old's reminiscence of a Sunday picnic that took place about 1912. The picnic is "all predictable," as the speaker recounts his mother's overwhelming joy of the moment and the beauty she beholds in nature around her. The end is undercut somewhat by the thought of the future, unknown, but leashed "*like a hound with a slavering fang*" (34). The coda then shifts from autumn to a moonlit winter night, a scene of nature's indifference to the two travelers who pass one another going in opposite directions. The persona, who is sensitive to the scene, wonders about the other traveler, his point of departure and his destination, with calm understanding that each must go his own way, the way he has chosen. The poet passes in this volume along the continuum of time from childhood innocence to a mature acceptance of life's road through the future. What was *is* is *was* now, and what will be is now, then was. From one perspective, time is a fickle femme fatale.

The first section addresses the beginning of life. The child of six first discovers the cave, symbolic perhaps of a womb, in which he later descends and knows "darkness and depth and no Time" (16) as he lays beneath the earth, in the earth's womb, thinking, past dreaming, *"Who am I?"* The transition into "When Life Begins" returns us to a boy listening to his grandfather's tales of the Civil War and the boy's wondering "when life would begin" (53), unaware of "Time crouched, like a great cat, motionless / But for tail's twitch" (55–56). Time itself is not death but is deeply interrelated to death in a manner similar to Shakespeare's sentiments in *Hamlet:* "this fell sergeant, Death, / Is strict in his arrest" (5.2.336–37). The thought of death, however dim, has been planted in Warren's text. Warren takes us to unnamed tobacco country in the poem "Boyhood in Tobacco Country," at a time when the poet tries to forget his own name and "be part of the world" (13). Unsure of what the years have wrought, he finds solace and safety indoors, out of sight of the harvest moon's gaze. His ambivalent feelings invoke grief and joy as do the feelings of Mr. Cinch that night, after his wife's funeral, when he tries "to write to his boy, / Far away" (22–23) in "Filling Night with the Name: Funeral in Local Color."

In rapid secession the first section concentrates on seeking reality, or knowledge of reality, through dreams and then moves on to reminiscences about a real or imagined death by train in Upper Ontario. The section concludes with the erosion of past reality by modern technology experienced by the persona's grandfather, who dreams of his Civil War exploits. The poet journeys through feelings of unworthiness, a guilt-trip evoked by remembering his middle-aged mother, with whom he had spent too little time, and by recalling his mother's funeral. He discovers that "In the name of Death do we learn the true name of Love" (20) in "Grackles, Goodbye." With that positive lesson learned, though not without sacrifice, the poet looks at youth in the second section.

In "Youthful Truth-Seeker, Half-Naked, at Night, Running down Beach South of San Francisco," the speaker wonders some-what confusedly whether truth lies in that which he experiences, "the grind of breath and of sand" (31), and whether he is fleeing to or from that truth. He lies on the beach, his ear pressed to sand, "cold as cement" (38), to hear what the world has to say. No word and no sign comes (45), and he feels foolish and speculates uncertainly about the future, wondering: "if years later, I'll drive again forth under stars, on tottering bones" (52). The assumption or fear is, of course, that he will not live to do so. The setting shifts from the warm beach to a colder country in the following poem, "Snowshoeing Back to Camp in Gloaming," in which the persona stands in awe of the magnificent scene and notes that "Time died in [his] heart" (17). The view on which the speaker reflects symbolizes the future ahead of him, the past behind him. The crow's voice, a voice of nature, speaks the truth for him as he finds his way back to camp, overwhelmed by the "unnamed void where Space and God / Flinch to come" (48–49). In his moment of anguish he cries out the question: "Oh, Pascal! / What does a man need to forget?" (52–53). If he is referring to "Pascal's

wager"—the idea that believing God exists has more potential benefit (salvation) and less risk than not believing, which has greater risk
(damnation) and little benefit—then his answer seems to be found in
the solace he takes in returning to human companionship and the
smile that awaits him. He cannot dodge the question, however. In
"Why Have I Wandered the Asphalt of Midnight?" he asks, "Why,
all the years, and places, and nights, have I / Wandered and not
known the questions I carried? / And carry?" (28–30). He knows
only his own heartbeat, an emblem of his authentic self, but perhaps
not well enough to answer his question about the direction of his life:
Is Truth to be found in the North Star? The persona, in the end, must
return to those people he has seen, the farmer plowing at dawn, the
trapper "on his dawn-rounds" (33) or the "old workman" (30) lean-
ing over his lunch box, yawning.

The questions continue about time and self and truth. He asks,
"What kind of world is this we walk in?" (10) in "August Moon," as
he seeks a way to decipher communication with the world. In a final
assessment he decides that one lives to be of use to a loved one. His
advice, then, is for the lovers to be silent in the darkness of the night.
Again, confounded by the lack of answers, he finds comfort in
silence. Silence, though, can create the atmosphere for introspection.
"Dreaming in Daylight" yields a persona who realizes that he is a
stranger unto himself, lacking self-knowledge. The poem concludes:
"you are less strange to them [the dream of eyes peering at him] /
Than to yourself" (40–41). "Preternaturally Early Snowfall in Mating Season" traps the narrator in a snowy wilderness. He hears the
mating struggle of a doe and a buck, verified the next morning by
"the marks / Of plunge, stamp, trample, heave, and ecstasy of storm"
(45–46). He finds "one name for happiness: the act" (32), the doing.

The poem "Sila" follows. The persona imagines a boy upon finding a human skeleton on the tundra, thinking that "*Two hundred years back—and it might / Have been me*" (10–11). The boy discovers a dying doe, husky bitten, and cuts the doe's throat to prevent her suffering. The act is not without emotion for the boy; sixty years later when the boy will be propped on "death's pillow" (112), the persona imagines that the boy will relive that act but will not be able to cry out because of shortness of breath. His discovery is what Jack London termed the law of life. The law of life is death. The persona tries to confront that end but does not do so satisfactorily for his own understanding.

The third section of poems deals with the relationship of the persona to nature. In "Empty White Blotch on Map of Universe: A Possible View," the speaker's own existence seems nothing more than the result of his father's lust, a bestial act of survival. He finds that truth is an abstraction, "only a shout, or clapped hand" (29), and he sees "no hope of change of condition" (40). In "Function of Blizzard" the speaker is somewhat critical of divine intervention, saying "God does the best / He can" (17–18) and sometimes lets snow brighten rather than just cover mistakes, unhappiness, and ruin in the world. The image created in "Dream, Dump-heap, and Civilization" permits the persona to assess his guilt by association with the human condition and civilization's complicity. The dump-heap of human trash in his dream is a metaphor for the indiscretions of his life, such as lying to his mother and hating her, and witnessing six kittens beheaded. The narrator, however, wonders whether civilization is possible without complicity. That thought is compounded in "Vision" when the persona, awaiting the vision that will reveal the truth, detects the possibility that it has come and he "just didn't recognize it" (44).

The persona marvels at the globe of gneiss, the hugeness and structure of that rock. After seeing natural beauty and the bear in "Part of What Might Have Been a Short Story, Almost Forgotten," he perceives that the lovers' hearts concealed the fatal truth in a charade of love. The communication sought is not found in "Cocktail Party" at which hypocrisy and the games people play prohibit even "normal communication" (24) "Deep—Deeper Down" allows an artificial escape for the persona and his friend Jim as they hunted and killed cottonmouths in the bayou in their younger days. The experience is translated later in life as the speaker's feeling pain in his old age and sickness. He tries counting "All those ever known who are dead now" (3) in "Better Than Counting Sheep" only to discover in a dream that he cannot remember their names; this discovery forces him to confront the fact that his name, too, will be gone. To all these human thoughts and reactions, nature is indifferent; it goes about its regular pattern of life and death, impervious to human rituals in "The Cross," the last poem of this section. Consequently, the narrator will not find nature's helping hand in revealing the truth he so desperately seeks.

The fourth section opens with the poem "Truth." Among other things, "Truth / Is the curse laid upon us in the Garden. / Truth is the Serpent's joke" (13–15). Truth is also the accumulated and immense wisdom of the dead, if only they could communicate it to us. The dead are outside of time, and "Time's metaphysic" in "On into the Night," what happens and does not happen at night, like nature's voices, is "in undecipherable metaphor" (37). The persona's stage in life now is beyond middle age. He escapes from the bustle of youth, and this escape to "Bowl-hollow of woodland" (1) becomes his solitude, his "grave" before he dies in "No Bird Does Call." In

"Weather Report," on a rainy day the persona spots one of the warblers that "yesterday / Fluttered outside" (7–8) his screen and is today still, offering "no promise of joy for tomorrow" (18). Though no bird calls, life goes on. On another occasion, in "Tires on Wet Asphalt at Night," the sound of automobiles leaves the persona wondering "what is left" (9). He goes back in time to his past and considers his need to listen to the sea as did the youthful truth-seeker. However, he cannot discover the link between then and now, between the tires on wet asphalt and the sound of wavelets. He clings "To our single existence, timeless, twinned" (16) in the next poem, "Timeless, Twinned," in which the future and the past lay bare that anxiety in his soul. In "What is the Voice that Speaks?" the narrator suggests that "All we can do is strive to learn the cost of experience" (24). Truth is related to the lesson of experience. The persona feels he could learn from the world but he cannot communicate with it or hear it. The point is made apparent when he hears "the creatures of gardens and lowlands" (20) and inquiringly declares that God may love them, too ("Language Barrier"). In "Lesson in History" he returns to question what historical figures did, saw, and thought at the moment of their death, and the hope lives that he will somehow, someway be able to communicate with the world, with nature. Again, however, a section of his life closes without his being able to "devise / An adequate definition of self" (15–16) in "Prairie Harvest."

In the fifth and final section of *Being Here,* the persona views life in old age. Section 5 opens with Warren's poem to Allen Tate, "Eagle Descending," in which the descent is not failure but "truth fulfilled." "Ballad of Your Puzzlement" has a headnote: *"(How not to recognize yourself as what you think you are, when old and*

reviewing your life before death comes)." Certainly the speaker recognizes the various roles he has played in the celluloid metaphor of
life, as tight-wire walker, like a fly stuck on flypaper, or as King
Lear shaking his fist at the sky. All of them are facades, mirror
images of what he was or might have been. "Antinomy: Time and
Identity" returns readers to the same questions asked in the previous
sections, and the persona moves through hope and despair to
become part of the natural scene. He cannot even have the identity
equivalent to the crow whose sun-purple gleams in magnificence. In
"Trips to California" the persona questions the reality of the past and
seeks the future as he looks toward California, "mother of dreams,"
with the thought that "Reality past may be only / A dream, too"
(40–41). "Auto-da-fé" allows the persona to find beauty in the flesh
of the body, but he cannot escape its transitory nature and the threat
of eternal damnation, when the body will be abused in flame and tor-
ture. If the speaker cannot communicate with nature and if nature's
images—linked to humanity only insofar as the changing seasons
symbolize the phases of human life—are indifferent to man's moods
and predicament, then who is left for him to blame for his fleeting
youth? In "Acquaintance with Time in Early Autumn" the persona's
hostile response to God for taking his youth and his joy culminates
in a profound hatred. Hatred, though, is not the opposite of love;
instead, apathy is love's antinomy. Thus, by expressing his hatred
for God in his moment of frustration, the persona perhaps unknowingly affirms his feelings for God, nature, and life. "Safe in Shade"
is a return in memory to the cedar tree under which the persona and
his grandfather sat in relative safety to time's passing and "man's
maniacal / Rage" (40–41) over the future, which brings with it old
age and death. The seven-part "Synonyms" ends with the last line:

"beauty is one word for reality" (117). This conclusion is hard to remember after the persona has experienced or imagined a series of scenes, some pastoral, others grittily urban, of cruelty to animals and salvation from the least expected "in the world's tangled variety" (116). When the persona returns to the beach, "Swimming in the Pacific," he counts the years before and after that he has visited that spot and still wonders "What answer, at last, / Could I give my old question?" (38–39). He seems to submit himself to the realization that reality is "a dream all years had moved to" (44). Then in the last poem, "Night Walking," before the coda, the persona thinks he hears his first bear of the season only to discover his son has awakened and has gone forth into the night. The persona follows his son, feeling a "Mixture of shame, guilt, and joy" (43) as part of his love and admiration for his son, who "lifted bare arms to that icy / Blaze and redeeming white light of the world" (58–59), of which the persona has longed to be a part.

Rumor Verified, Poems 1979–1980 has eight titled sections including the prologue and the coda. Its focus is similar to the poems in *Being Here*. The divisions of the volumes of poetry as well as the sequences and subsequences of the poems suggest the volume's structure, ordered by the author with quiet deliberation. *Rumor Verified,* for example, looks at the "Paradox of Time," "Events," "A Point North," "If This Is the Way It Is," "But Also," and "Fear and Trembling"—six distinct sections moving not according to chronological sequence but according to kinds of philosophical questioning. Warren did not let go of these questions of nature, God, love, memory, time, and self-knowledge because they are timeless questions without specific answers. Warren believed in Socrates' credo that the unexamined life was not worth living.

LATE POETRY (1966–1985)

The preliminary poem, "Mediterranean Basin," is a two-poem
sequence that stands as prologue to this volume. The first poem, "I.
Chthonian Revelation: A Myth," is a meeting of two lovers, almost
a fantasy in the setting of a cave a kilometer off the headland to
which they swim in starlight. The symbol of the drops of water
hanging on their fingers at the arch of each stroke suggests "each a
perfect universe defined / By its single, minuscule, radiant,
enshrined star" (66–67). The moment seems outside the threat of
time as the swimmers revel in existence without the weight of
responsibility. In "II. Looking Northward, Aegeanward: Nestlings
on Seacliff," the speakers (perhaps the two lovers again) climb a
seacliff and at the top imagine the historical events that might have
transpired there and how the survivors of the mighty conflicts
entered "In new ignorance, the agony of Time" (35), like the
nestlings that are "blind yearning lifeward" (8 and 37). At the other
end of the volume is "VIII. Coda" and its one poem, "Fear and
Trembling" (also the title of the seventh section). The persona thinks
about the end of summer and wants "to meditate on what the season
has meant" (4), but is stymied by the lack of meaningful language
for such meditation. He then asks, "Can one, in fact, meditate in the
heart, rapt and wordless?" (13). Feeling that his life may have been
misspent, the narrator wonders then whether the heart's meditation
can even "wake us from life's long sleep" (17) for such a reckoning.
The very thought turns one of happiness and joy to one of fear and
trembling at life's end.

The section "II. Paradox of Time" zeroes in on the central question of time, but it does not offer definitive answers, only ideas and
images of what constitutes time. "Blessèd Accident," for example, is
another poem in unrhymed couplets. In it the persona raises the tele-

ological question about "how you got where you now are" (6), by
logic or by accident? He leans toward "the awful illogic of / The
tremor, the tremble, of God's palsied hand shaking / The dice-cup?
Ah, blessèd accident!" (35–37). The three-poem sequence, "Paradox
of Time" (same title as the second section of poems) begins with "I.
Gravity of Stone and Ecstasy of Wind." The aging persona cannot
help but imbue nature with an attitude of disdain toward him. He conjectures, however, that the paradox of time instructs him about where
"The fleshy glory may gleam" (12). It resides in the child, who came
closer in youth to communicating with nature than the speaker, who
has struggled to do so. "II. Law of Attrition" evokes images of
nature's existence and evolution, which humanity still does not
understand, and questions man's significance in the larger scheme. In
"III. One I Knew" the poet is thrown back on his memory to recall
what perhaps he does know. He tries to name those past contributors
to an understanding of the human condition and does recall one who
said that "To deny / The self is all" (20–21). This man died of cancer. He was the poet's father.

The counting-of-names exercise helps people reconstruct themselves, the persona contends in "Small Eternity" and hopes selfishly
that someone else will stumble on his name after the he is gone. To be
remembered is perhaps our closest hope for immortality. The poems
follow one another in structured order. "Basic Syllogism" is the persona's reflection on the sun's basic syllogism and the transitory nature
of life that comes and goes in the ever-presence of the sun's blaze. The
persona then reminisces on the stages of life—infancy, youth, and old
age—and on when, or if, one learns wisdom in age.

In the first poem of the third section, "III. Events," the title of which is "Going West," the persona traveling through the mid-West hits a pheasant. "The bloody explosion / On the windshield" (ll.27–28) obscures his vision of the future, the "blue shadow of foothills" which are his destination, but hones his vision of life, for in that bird's death he experiences "the imagined / Vision of snow-caps" (46–47). The poem also gives evidence of another recurrent motif in Warren's work: the place for man to go to make his fortune and to grow is in the West. This motif is apparent, for example, in *All the King's Men,* as Jack Burden goes west to work out some internal conflicts. The last line of "Going West" helps transition into the next poem, "Nameless Thing." The unnamed thing walks the house after midnight and represents the persona's imagination, which cannot rest. The discovery is shocking and leaves the speaker "Rigid abed" (28). The image of horror continues into "Rumor Verified," in which the "terror / Of knowledge" (30–31) of the self must be faced by the poet, who must accept that he is simply a man, nothing more (33–34).

In "Sunset Scrupulously Observed" the persona explores his mortal bond to humanity by observing the contrast between natural birds and a mechanical bird, a military jet high in the sky. The jet seems to blend in as it wings its way out of sight in just ten minutes, while five swifts, "Their twitter / Is a needle-sharp, metallic sound" (35–36), remind the persona of attack planes. The poem's concern with questions of mortality is apparent in the image of the flycatcher seen at the beginning of the poem. The flycatcher has gone "to fulfill his unseeable and lethal / Obligation, alone" (38–39). The ironic play between the artificial and the natural connects the various flying images—the man-made war plane makes clouds (contrails), while nature emits mechanical noises—for the persona at the quiet end of a day. Another event of metaphysical significance for the persona is evident in "Minneapolis Story." In Minneapolis the narrator stumbles on a homeless person covered with snow. Another time, another place he ponders "The mystery of Time and happiness and death" (29) after his friend's recent death. This event might lead naturally to the feeling of loneliness the persona experiences riding horseback on a mountain trail in "Mountain Mystery": "In the world's metaphysical beauty of light," he realizes, "Only alone do you then think of love" (28–29). He worries, too, about the frailty of life. The third section ends with "Convergences," an account of a pleasant hike in the woods. The event is quickly marred by an encounter with a stranger who steals the persona's meal, leaving him to contemplate the meaning of that experience years later. The persona knows he still cannot know what his real self-identity is.

The sense of sound plays an important part in Warren's later poetry, and many poems refer to or end with an acknowledged silence. This silence often comes at a point when the persona has exhausted his inquiry and has again found no resolution or answer. The sounds of his heart, of a metaphysical drip in the world, and of the world's grind and heave are reminders that humanity does not communicate with the world in any satisfactory manner. "IV. A Point North" begins with "Vermont Thaw," a poem full of the sounds of heartbeats as well as of spruces and house eaves dripping. During the night the speaker tries to relate the thaw to some loftier concept and abstract understanding only to realize that, after imagination plays out, the drip is the mundane reality of the moment. He must continue to "try to think of some other answer, by dawn" (40). The thaw is one part of the cycle of seasons ("Cycle"). The narrator watches a porcupine step past during a summer's day in which the air is paralyzed, the sun "Is pasted to the sky" (15). The persona believes that the birds "have no instruction in / Cycles of nature, or astronomy" (16–17), but human beings know nature and history are cyclical. He seems to find solace in this knowledge; however, his comfort is dissipated in "Summer Rain in Mountains," which contains the image of an afternoon shower that is also part of the natural cycle—a normal, expected event. But the speaker is disturbed by the event, which reminds him of "a nameless apprehension" (18). When the shower is over, conversation resumes on the sundeck as the group admires "the glory / Of sunset" (32–33). The persona rationalizes that such a moment of unnamed fear can and does happen to anybody. Not surprisingly, the speaker's cynicism and depression in the last poem of this section, "Vermont Ballad: Change of Season," is apparent in his vision of a God-abandoned world. He seems to associate his mind with the gray sky, an identification that is completely man-made and contrary to the indifference that he has repeatedly found in nature. He checks himself, asking "But who is master here?" (22). He looks out the window and sees "A man with no name" (34), who, like so many men in that region, is "Just a man in his doom" (36).

"Section V. If This Is the Way It Is" starts with "Questions You Must Learn to Live Past," which contains a series of questions that pertain to hanging on in a dangerous situation, seeing a father on his deathbed, remembering the face of a dead friend "drowned and glimmering under / Time's windless wash" (16–17), or calling out to emptiness in the darkness. The speaker's discovery in his garden of a big garter snake's three-foot translucent skin prompts a moment of fear—he feels his heart stop—and a meditation that "this bright emptiness / Is all your own life may be" (28–29). The following poem, "After Restless Night," suggests the persona's recognition of "the noble indifference of Eternity" (3) and the clutter of people's lives. In the end, actions define the self, for we are what we do. "What Was the Thought" is another night poem. The persona philosophizes about a mouse heard scurrying along the baseboard of his bedroom and is consoled by the warmth of his bed and the comfort of his family. At dawn his pussycat proudly presents to him in bed the dead mouse, "Skull crushed, partly eviscerated" (33). "Dead Horse in Field" presents another reflection on life as the narrator thinks about a thoroughbred put down because it has a "left foreleg shattered below knee" (3) that cannot be mended. Warren's persona returns a week later to the spot where the horse was put down, unable to get closer because of the smell of the carcass. A year later he returns to find "That intricate piece of / Modern sculpture" (26–27) covered with green vine, "each leaf / Heart-shaped" (32–33), not unlike the love vine growing up the death marker on the highway to Mason City in the opening paragraph of *All the King's Men*.

This section contains other philosophical speculations about life, such as the failing of fleshly pleasure for pay ("Immanence"), capturing a poem on the oblique, "just beyond the corner of the eye" ("The Corner of the Eye"), and discovering "A new concept of salvation" (29) as well as the idea that life might require more than courage ("If"). Having pondered the way life is, the persona shifts to possible alternatives in the next section, "VI. But Also."

"What Voice at Moth-Hour" portrays the speaker remembering his youth when he was beckoned home by the voice that keeps repeating itself in his mind: *"It's late! Come home"* (20). This voice hearkens us back to an earlier poem in *Promises,* "What Was the Promise That Smiled from the Maples at Evening?" In each poem the persona recalls people from his past, loved ones who gave him a sense of place and identity as a child. "Another Dimension" relies also on sound, the lost song the narrator knows "is there at an altitude where only / God's ear may hear" (5–6). He imagines that at one time he felt redemption in the world and existed only in the present, with "no future or past" (13). He asks, "Who knows that history is the other name for death?" (17), and poses other questions about jealousy and cruelty, yet the lost song he seeks, "that Platonic song" (25), eludes his ears.

If history is synonymous with death, and if history is merely time past, then Time, too, must be another name for death. In a four-poem sequence, "Glimpses of Seasons," the persona weighs time against nature. He challenges the listener to "try to think, at the same moment, / Of the living and the dead" (20–21), of Time and no-Time, and of Self and no-Self in "I. Gasp-Glory of Gold Light." Nature is not absolutely bound by any strict clock and can bring snow "far too early, far out of phase" ("II. Snow out of Season") to catch "zinnias ablaze" and threaten the dogwood berry. The poem terms such pointed anomalies in the natural cycle God's "willed dissolution" (4). The persona remembers that all living things can be caught unprepared by abnormalities in nature. In "III. Redwing Blackbirds" the blackbirds survive the changing seasons and return in April. The world's business proceeds "with the business of Aprils and men" (21). The season of spring is heralded in "IV. Crocus Dawn," which offers an unending promise of life. The poem "Dawn" raises the philosophical questions, "Are you / Real when asleep?" (11–12) and

will the tree cast a shadow in grayness? (29). The narrator, wanting
to be real, ponders whether he should ask God to let the crow, a symbol of another opportunity for life, call once more.

The sixth section concludes with two poems about the persona's past life. "Millpond Lost" is his attempt to recall the setting
and the "names of the boys who there shouted in joy, once" (26). He
tries to imagine this scene in darkness after a long lapse of time. In
"Summer Afternoon and Hypnosis," however, he is mesmerized by
the murmuring of a stream, the sunlight, and the "muted-music of
sheep bells" (4) and wonders: "Was this / The life that all those years
I lived, and did not know?" (14). Snapping out of this hypnotic
trance, he rouses to return to "The mystery of love's redeeming
smile" (24). In the last section of *Rumor Verified,* Warren turns
more explicitly to the idea of love.

"VII. Fear and Trembling" opens with "If Ever." The persona
wonders "can love at the end, have an end / That is absolute?" (4–5).
He invokes a carpe diem attitude, urging: "Seize the nettle of self,
plunge then into / Cold shock of experience, like a mountain lake,
and let / Stroke, after stroke, sustain you. And all else forget"
(19–21). The next poem bears the working title of the entire volume,
"Have You Ever Eaten Stars?" with a subtitle, "A Note on Mycol-
ogy." The scene is a mountain glade in which the persona finds joy
in "A glade-burst of glory" (34) after the drought-breaking rain has
purified air and earth. He offers the following imaginative description of the scene: "Later, I gathered stars into a basket" (35). The
poem then juxtaposes the speaker's imaginative pose with a pragmatic question: "What can you do with stars, or glory?" (36). The
persona's optimism in the face of fear and trembling leads him to
suggest that one should absorb the stars and see life as glory. The

persona's fear is somewhat abated in "Twice Born" when he realizes that a storm of fifteen years ago is merely a metaphor of his past, for what he had undergone long before (37–38). Again, in "The Sea Hates the Land," the persona recognizes that "as a man, / Know that only in loneliness are you defined" (11–12). This definition accumulates meaning in "Afterward," the concluding poem in section 7. After an unsuccessful relationship with "a once-girl, photograph unrecognizable" (8), who is now dead, the ashamed speaker alone tries to communicate with nature, to get in touch with his self, knowing "There must be so much to exchange" (37). At least hope is not lost and love may thereafter be redefined.

Warren's shorter lyric poetry is interrupted temporarily by a longer trek into history in the long narrative poem, *Chief Joseph of the Nez Perce*. Warren is a storyteller supreme—in fiction, in poetry, and in drama. His long poems such as *Chief Joseph* ably demonstrate that fact. In a prefatory note to the volume, Warren provides the historical background concerning the treaties with the Nez Perce broken by the U.S. Government, the corralling of the Nez Perce onto reservations after a three-month war, and Chief Joseph's unending hope that justice would prevail and his people would be returned to their land. Chief Joseph's hopes were not realized in his lifetime. Interspersed throughout this long, nine-section narrative poem are quotations from various documents about the Nez Perce as a people and a culture and about related matters.

Chief Joseph is structured not unlike a three-act play with three scenes in each act. Part 1 of the poem provides background through the voice of old Chief Joseph's son, young Joseph, whose tribal name is Thunder-Traveling-to-Loftier-Mountain-Heights (63). The Great White Father's word "faded like mist in the day's heat" (109).

Part 2 shows old Chief Joseph's death, before which he gives the following admonition to his son: "You must never sell the bones of your fathers— / For selling that, you sell your Heart-Being" (22–23). Warren is not simply interested in an historical event, but focuses on the cultural identity of the Nez Perce as he works to understand their concerns about identity, vision, truth, family, and the land. The narrative shows us Chief Joseph's band as they leave their land, Wallowa, with the young braves swallowing their rage. Chief Joseph himself is torn between keeping his word or else fighting the white man. In the third part the speaker recounts episodes from the Nez Perce Indian War. The battle began after a U.S. soldier fired at the Nez Perce, who had moved forward under a white flag, a symbol of peace. During the fighting the Nez Perce fought successfully as thirty-four U.S. soldiers were killed. Although Chief Joseph was willing to "stand, fight, and die" (115) by continuing the resistance against U.S. troops, "the chiefs / In council said *no*" (116–17). Chief Joseph recognizes his heart's pride, however, and knows "a true chief no self has" (120). The Nez Perce attempt to escape war by traveling eastward out of what is now Montana in order to be free.

Part 4 of the poem opens with an attack by the reinforcements, "the new horse soldiers" (1), and the initial victory of Looking Glass and the Nez Perce as they make their way into the mountains of Yellowstone. Part 5 reveals the U.S. military strategy, according to which Gen. O. O. Howard pursues the Nez Perce through the mountains toward Colonel Sturgis, whose son was killed with Custer. Sturgis awaits the time for his revenge on the plains. Chief Joseph and his half-breed scout, Poker Joe, trick Sturgis and head toward "Clark's Fork and freedom" (63). In keeping with its dramatic form, the sixth part of *Chief Joseph* produces a climax. Howard knows that Colonel Miles, summoned for backup, might be in better position to intercept and capture Chief Joseph. Reluctant to give the glory of victory to another officer, Howard nevertheless sends word to Miles. Sturgis, in the meantime, falls into an ambush set by the Nez Perce and is defeated. Not aware of Miles's movement, Chief Joseph is lulled into a sense of security and freedom because Howard has relaxed the pressure of his pursuit. Chief Joseph fails to send out scouts. Colonel Miles arrives, miscalculates the terrain, yet manages to conduct a siege that catches the Nez Perce off guard. Chief Joseph surrenders. Warren brings into relief the contrast between white culture's shoddy values and the values of Nez Perce culture by pointing up the professional rivalry between Howard and Miles, whose subtly deceptive looks betray their greed for glory and their hypocritical pretense of honor.

Part 7 tells of the Nez Perce plight in captivity and how they endured in spite of Gen. William Tecumseh Sherman's belief that all Native Americans should die. The irony, of course, is heightened in "the name he bore, / That of the greatest Indian chief— / Tecumseh" (29–31). Befriended by Miles, Chief Joseph tells the story of "The fraud of, the suffering of, his people, the lies" of the white man that the government told (63). The action falls in part 8 as the Nez Perce are saved and moved to a reservation—not Wallowa as promised, but one in Washington state where Chief Joseph laments his error and his weakness. He prays. He also ponders the purpose of human existence: "But what is a man? An autumn-tossed aspen, / Pony-fart in the wind, the melting of snow-slush? / Yes, that is all. Unless—unless— / We can learn to live the Great Spirit's meaning" (44–47). In time Chief Joseph gains fame, is an invited guest to the

White House, and has his bust preserved forever in bronze; however, he is still a prisoner at Nespelem in Washington, where he dies. The dénouement takes place in part 9. The poet, who has been telling this story through the voice of Chief Joseph, visits Snake Creek a century later in 1981. Historical markers indicate the spot. The poet imagines the scene with Chief Joseph standing there. He looks into his own heart and longs for a profound sense of contact with those who have gone before him.

Warren's next group of new poems is titled *Altitudes and Extensions, 1980–1984* and further discloses his increased interest in the individual's coming to terms with his past. Even in his moving long narrative poem, Warren examined life, man's heart, and the meaning of being part of the human condition. The volume also exhibits Warren's interest in writing poetry about nature. *Altitudes and Extensions* is structured in nine untitled sections. This collection and twenty-two uncollected poems published between 1943 and 1989 complete Warren's poetic oeuvre.

In *Altitudes and Extensions* Warren's investigation of love, hope, and endurance becomes most apparent, possibly as a result of the more explicit values and loss of values in society as well as his own aging. Although Warren does not designate poems as preliminary and coda in this volume, "Three Darknesses" and "Myth of Mountain Sunrise," respectively, could easily serve in those capacities.

In "Three Darknesses" the persona examines the darkness of wisdom, the darkness of carnal knowledge, and the darkness of death. The darkness of wisdom emerges years later after the persona's visit to the zoo in Rome. A large bear pounds in a one-two rhythm on an iron door that prevents his entering his "cave." The "ineluctable / Rhythm continues" (14–15), reverberates throughout the zoo the entire morning. The child visitor does not know what the world is trying to tell him. The persona then explores the next kind of darkness, an outing up Black Snake River. The host goes out on the lagoon at midnight and upon his return will have wine in the cabin with the hostess. The persona wonders what the host thinks about while drifting on the lagoon, whether the world speaks to the host. Then, in the last section of this poem, the persona lies in darkness in the hospital for a supposedly trivial operation, a prelude perhaps to an impending, more serious encounter. He watches an old-fashioned western on television that "has something to do with vice and virtue" (13), and he admits almost grudgingly: "God / Loves the world. For what it is" (22–23). He has progressed from the endurance of the bear to the unstated love on his outing to the hope that "virtue will triumph" (19) and that God does love the world.

This hope is symbolized by a hawk in "Mortal Limit." The hawk serves as a symbol of the height to which the human imagination and hope can soar. On the other hand, in "Immortality over the Dakotas," the speaker looks out an airplane window and imagines the mortality of a figure "Who must be down there" (20), diagnosed with a fatal illness. So the two are looking at one another, the speaker thinking of the other's mortality and the other, staring at "the blackness of sky. / . . . at lights, green and red, that tread the dark of [the persona's] immortality" (28–29) in a life that both must endure.

Imagery of darkness and questions of one's mortality and place in the natural world dominate the poems of the first section and seem to suggest the uncertainty of the future. The section suggests that the one certainty in life is death. The persona observes in nature the movement of a herd of caribou ("Caribou") moving on instinct without knowledge of their specific errand but with their destiny "as bright as crystal, as pure / As a dream of zero" (27–28). In "The First Time" he sees an elk, "a bull wapiti, wild, before—the / Great head lifted in philosophic / Arrogance against / God's own sky" (39–42). This stance is one the persona might admire but not emulate at his age. Clearly in "Minnesota Reflection" the persona thinks about nature's indifference to humanity amid a ferocious snowstorm. Human beings have a sense of conscious knowledge that puts on them the burden of moral duties and responsibilities, whereas animals function purely according to instinct. The poem suggests that humans do not always survive the force of nature. It reveals the image of a farmer who, while out to feed his cattle, becomes disoriented in the darkness of the storm and freezes to death. Those who brave the storm to look for him use a rope as a lifeline, as a contact with human hope. They discontinue their search at night and find him "Snagged on a barbed-wire fence" (79) the next morning with a calm face and an innocent expression. "Arizona Midnight" stages the persona's response to a coyote's mournful wail, a sound of grief to which he would respond with his own grief were he capable of it. The speaker's obstacle is his inability to understand his grief. His journey out West concludes in "Far West Once," a poem about the vastness of the sky, the darkness of the nights, and the beauty of "redemptive music" at dawn with the Edenic promise symbolized by the "first birdsong" (49). In that promise he finds hope.

The second section starts with "Rumor at Twilight," in which the persona, alone under the sky, reflects on his good life and his early ambition "In a rage of joy, to seize, and squeeze, significance from, / What life is, whatever it is" (23–24). He must, however, return to his responsibilities inside, perhaps not as set or determined as the first bat that "Mathematically zigzags the stars" (26). Hope is anticipation of the fullness of the moon "in white forgiveness" (26) after the darkening of dusk and the visual transformation of light. In "Hope" the persona defines hope as the peace that comes after a hard day, the enabler that gives one the resolve necessary to meet the next day. That resolve is what keeps the persona climbing "up the mountain's heave and clamber" (13) or swimming in the Pacific in "Why You Climbed Up." The hope is to find one's identity, to discover an authentic self, knowing each time it begins again and "you are you" (29).

The setting of these poems takes on autobiographical significance for Warren. "Old Dead Dog" is about the family English cocker spaniel, while "Literal Dream" is about Thomas Hardy's *Tess of the d'Urbervilles*. "After the Dinner Party" concerns friends long since dead and the desire to communicate with one another. The "Doubleness of Time" focuses on "The grind of love" (16) in the present and the past as the persona recalls his mother's illness in the hospital before she died, his feelings of grief, not understood, which are termed the "*Selfishness* and *Precious Guilt*" (83). "Snowfall" then concludes section 2 with the persona's introspection, his feelings about nature, and his lack of self-knowledge. He realizes, standing "in the darkness of whiteness," that this moment "is the perfection of Being" (49–50).

Section 3 stands alone with a fifteen-poem sequence, "New Dawn," about the dropping of the first atomic bomb on Hiroshima on 6 August 1945. The poet details the suspense, dreams, and psychological after-effects on the crew after the mission was completed.

It is a powerful narrative lyric that suggests the end of an era and the beginning of a new one. This new era is perhaps a harbinger of hope for a better day, but the cost of this destructive act is undetermined.

If hope dominates the first three sections of poems, the next three sections might be viewed in the context of love, although none of the sections is exclusively concerned with any one of Warren's three main subjects. The three poems of section 4 deal with love and relationships. The friends in "The Distance Between: Picnic and Old Friends" share old memories and a sudden act of physical love, unwanted but not resisted. "True Love" is a poem about a young boy's infatuation with beauty, a young love that lasts in memory if not in his present feelings. In "Last Walk in Season" two lovers, perhaps married, climb a mountain "To see the last light" (4) of day, to find the meaning of their joy, to exist "as part of that one / Existence" (27–28), to make contact with each other.

Section 5 carries the idea of love over to family. "Old-Time Childhood in Kentucky" involves a recollection of a young boy and his grandfather. The ghosts of his memories rejoin him, and he asks his grandfather what a person does in this world, things being what they are. The grandfather's response is the following simple advice: "Love / Your wife, love your get, keep your word, and / If need arises die for what men die for" (34–36). The persona looks back in wonder about what he might become ages later. He again dwells on this love for his grandfather in "Re-interment: Recollection of a Grandfather" and the thought that at some point no one will remember his stories, his values, or even his face. The symbol of the covered bridge in the poem "Covered Bridge" represents the persona's desire to go somewhere in life, an understanding he has not yet achieved. Without that understanding he perhaps can never know and, therefore, love himself. "Last Meeting" returns the persona to a chance meeting one Saturday night with the black woman who helped rear him. After that meeting, he feels the guilt of not seeing her again before she died and struggles with what her love for him meant.

The theme of love continues in section 6 and is linked to the speaker's efforts to understand reality and truth. The title of "Muted Music" reminds us of earlier references to the music of nature as one form of communication. It focuses on the hum of a fly in a barn on a sultry Sunday afternoon. The fly's hum raises the question in the persona about the past and "the only sound that truth can make" (22). Philosophers have long dealt with these questions and with the inadequacy of language to define and to identify reality, truth, and other abstract concepts. In "The Whole Question," in which the speaker describes birth as "the terrible thing called love" (9), Warren too grapples with finding the "words that make the Truth come true" (28). "Old Photograph of the Future" calls attention to the unreality of a photograph and its impact on memory and psychological guilt. Yet the persona repeats in "Why Boy Came to Lonely Place" that his aloneness allows belief in his reality, in who and what he is. "Platonic Lassitude" follows "Why Boy Came to Lonely Place." In silence and stillness the persona counters "That nothing defines itself in joy or sorrow" (26) and "that history is only the fruit of tomorrow" (28).

The poetic sequence "Seasons" has two parts. "I. Downwardness" is set at the time of spring melting when water is drawn toward downwardness in what the narrator concludes is "a sacred cycle" (24). "II. Interlude of Summer" is the season that interrupts the cycle and brings in the scorching heat, a customary symbol of nature's indifference. The season following, however, creates the beauty of New England foliage. The persona reminds us that "aesthetics is a branch of philosophy" (25) thus adding meaning to nature's changes. The remaining six poems continue to address nature and the seasons in an attempt to understand the natural process. "The Place" starts at "the hour of the unbounded loneliness" (9) "of the self's uncertainty / Of self" (10–11). A mountainous spot of stone and fern represents the physical place that is merely the setting for seeking the self. It is a place where others too have come to seek "the most difficult knowledge" (39). "First Moment of Autumn Recognized" records an image of the "Perfection of crystal" that captures the persona's reflection in it, his "being perfected" (16) there in the fleeting instant between breaths—a moment recognized but not defined, perhaps indefinable. "Paradigm of Seasons" uses the time-honored simile of a snake swallowing its own tail to describe each year. Warren's reference to serpents invokes the image of the betrayer in the Garden of Eden and hearkens back to his deep concern with original sin, but the references become more explicit in his later poetry. The speaker recognizes that "Spring / Brings hope" (5–6), and that the seasons represent archetypes for stages of life, each devouring the other only to start over each spring. "If Snakes Were Blue" describes a condition that literally contradicts factual reality but that offers a metaphorical description of a particular type of day, dream-like, lazy, full of promises and the hope that "such promises may come true" (21). Another poem that reminds one again of Ransom's "Bells for John Whiteside's Daughter" is "Little Girl Wakes Early." The little girl, now grown, remembers her best friend who has died and her inability to explain her anxiety to her mother, who is now also dead. She cannot articulate her experience of the loneliness of loneliness. The last poem in section 6, "Winter Wheat: Oklahoma," is also about loneliness. The old farmer, now a widower, finishes his day's work in the field but is in no rush to go home to an empty house full of memories. He thinks about God and His reason, and has a momentary thought of taking a season off to go "skylarkin'." In this way the poem gives symbolic expression to hope understated. The difficulty in coming to terms with such issues is the basic quandary. For the poet, the task seems endless, a perspective that provides an example of the endurance Warren addresses in the last three sections of *Altitudes and Extensions*.

The thrust of section 7 is life in decline and the lessons learned, or not learned, by the end of one's life. "Youthful Picnic Long Ago: Sad Ballad on Box"—the "box" being a guitar—brings the persona face to face with a moment in Tennessee around a campfire, watching a woman play the guitar and listening to her sing. He perceives in retrospect a truth enacted by her "dancing fingers" (22) but cannot even recall her name. The loss of memory becomes more and more distressing for the persona in later poems when this loss is related to history and time and the aging process. Warren's history poems once more explore questions about time and often about how one's life is affected by or affects time. In "History during Nocturnal Snowfall" the persona touches the wrist of his companion, perhaps his wife, to feel a pulse. The felt pulse, "a watch-tick / Or a century off?" (5–6), might be the connection of their lives "In the synchronized rhythm of heart, and heart, with no sound?" (16). At that moment, they are perhaps outside of, or at one with time and, therefore, in position to intuit the pulse's truth. The call of "no sound" (silence) informs the reader that the persona has no definitive answer. In "Whistle of the 3 A.M." the train whistle lingers in the speaker's mind even though times have changed and "The schedule's gone dead of the 3 A.M." (25). In "Last Night Train" the persona's imagination is caught up with another passenger, "a hundred and eighty pounds of / Flesh, black, female, middle-aged" (5–6). The sound of the train's departure after he gets off prompts his thoughts of loneliness. The other passenger is now on her way to some other destination, while the green station light, the starlight, the sounds and the smell of the ocean, and the nostalgic moment offer him a sense of freedom, as he imagines himself "swimming, naked and seaward, / In starlight forever" (30–31). In this way the poem offers another form of endurance.

The last section before what serves as a kind of coda for the volume continues the idea of endurance as a virtue. The imagery of darkness and light remains in play, signifying the irony of life in death and death in life. A tribute to John Milton's endurance, "Milton: A Sonnet" praises the poet's knowledge and ability to handle life in his blindness and to leap repeatedly "like a gleaming fish" from "the medium of deep wisdom" (12) to "joy-flashed curve" (11). The persona in "Whatever You Now Are" is dreaming of a definition of Self and raises a question similar to Yeats's dancer/dance question at the end of "Among School Children": How can one define the difference between dreamer and dream? In "Wind and Gibbon" the narrator, who cannot sleep, likens the wind to "a dream of History" (12), which is not truth. Once awake, he randomly selects a volume of Gibbon from the shelf, "more comforting / Than the morning newspaper" (15–16). Asleep at dawn, he cannot see the single beam of sunlight lighting "The mountain to dazzlement" (38). Snow-capped mountain peaks perhaps symbolize enlightenment, a sense of transcendence from the ordinary world of day-to-day living and dying. The image of mountains as an emblem of transcendence here and elsewhere in Warren's canon may represent a subtle allusion to Eliot's line from *The Waste Land,* "In the mountains, there you feel free." The last point from "Wind and Gibbon" is clarified somewhat in the next poem, "Delusion?—No!" The persona imagines standing in the "divine osmosis" and feeling "the momentous, muscular thrust / Skyward of peak" (14–15). At this point he is "part of all" (17) and knows the "Glorious light of inner darkness" (18). The sense that his imagination is "the power creating all" (24) exhilarates him and offers perhaps a moment of truth. In "Question at Cliff-Thrust" the speaker is again elevated geographically and contemplates the dive into the green depths of the ocean. At least in his imagination, he takes the dive into "the nothingness of sound" (26). The puzzle in "It Is Not Dead" hinges on the survivability and endurance of the "it" over the ages. What "it" seems to be is a large stone, on which the persona can now lay and contemplate its weighty wisdom under "the immensity of the night sky" (35). In the eighth and final section "Sunset" may symbolize the end of life. The poem reiterates Warren's career-long exploration of the question of identity as the persona wants to know the name of his soul so that he can speak to his naked self "never / Before seen, nor known" (24–25). It may be his last request.

Warren leaves readers on the brink of discovery; however, he does not explicitly articulate the meaning of the potential discovery. One might conclude that meaning is found in the questions asked and that it is the responsibility of our imagination to answer these quintessential questions for ourselves. The twenty-two uncollected poems written between 1943 and 1989, which John Burt has included in *The Collected Poems of Robert Penn Warren,* do not

provide a more concise, ready answer to Warren's probing existential questions. The uncollected poems were not inserted into Warren's various volumes of poetry, although their subjects of concern
clearly augment the poems included in the earlier volumes. Some of
his uncollected poems re-emphasize Warren's sense of timing.
"Bicentennial," for example, clearly shows a talent for occasional
poetry required of a poet laureate, which he would indeed become a
decade later, in spite of his claim that he would not write an ode for
anyone's damn cat. Warren's tireless interest in history in general
and his commemoration of specific historical events in particular
permeate his poetry. "Bicentennial" characterizes a cross-section of
the U.S.A. that does not exclude the darker side of rape, burglary,
suicide, drug addiction. The other uncollected poems are also about
love, hope, and endurance, about accepting the world as it is, and
about discovering one's own true identity. The difficulty of discovering what self made the image in "Problem of Autobiography:
Vague Recollection or Dream?" is a major obstacle in knowing Self.
The last uncollected poem, "John's Birches," comes closest to
expressing a sense of closure for the poet: "If boyhood is lonely
enough, the moss-bearded stone / Communicates wisdom" (19–20).
The persona realizes in this peaceful, reassuring poem that perhaps
now he has found a way to communicate with the world and ultimately with his authentic self.

Reading through Warren's entire poetic corpus brings into
focus a sense of the relationship between the poems and the lifelong
concerns Warren had with family, love, nature, and the self. The
quest, which begins in youthful innocence and wonder, ends after an
agonizingly demanding self-analysis with the peace and assurance
that old age can bring if one knows himself and gains wisdom from

that knowledge. The leaf stands as the single most recurring image of that journey of life, comparable to the cycle of seasons. A. L. Clements's view of Warren's sacramental vision serves as a summary of Warren's poetic journey in these terms: "Warren's poetry, like much poetry of great or important poets, begins in pain, makes its progress through darkness to death, and then, perfectly aware of the often inexplicable violence and suffering that human flesh is heir to, through its earned and integrated vision ends in rebirth, truth, selfhood, even joy,"[9] though this joy may be a raging joy. Warren's profound vision, his articulate mastery of language, and his metaphysical questions continue in his dramatic works as well.

CHAPTER SIX

Drama

> the special virtue of the dramatic method is that it
> allows the author to throw conflict into very sharp
> focus.
>
> *An Approach to Literature* (1939)

Although Warren is best known as the author of *All the King's Men*
and as the first poet laureate of the United States, he seemed to want
to be a dramatist all along. Readers would be remiss if they did not
at least consider three of his plays: *All the King's Men (A Play)*, *Listen to the Mockingbird,* and *Brother to Dragons.* He consulted with
Francis Fergusson, Eric Bentley, Aaron Frankel, Erwin Piscator, and
Adrian Hall, among others, about his scripts and adaptations from
book to stage. He was, after all, professor of playwriting at Yale University and long before he joined the Yale faculty he had written the
senior play for his high school class in Clarksville. Warren was
meticulous in his revisions, but especially painstaking in revising his
dramatic works. He worked and reworked his scripts, reshaping and
redefining his dramas. They seemed to be a constant source of frustration and raging joy to him. His unrelenting enthusiasm for drama
also reminds one of his strong interest in Shakespeare's works, an
interest that manifests itself throughout his writing.

All the King's Men (A Play)

Before the 1959 off-Broadway dramatic production of *All the
King's Men,* Warren had worked with the Willie Stark story in its
original dramatic conception as *Proud Flesh* (1937) and in its

revised form as *Willie Stark: His Rise and Fall* (1958). In the interim, the play had become a novel (1946) and then a movie (1949); it would later become an opera as well (1981).[1] *Proud Flesh* includes five acts and a series of choruses that function like Sophoclean choruses. Its focus is the political career of Willie Stark and his exceptional ability to manipulate the external needs of the people around him to his benefit. The price of his success, always high, is the devastation of his family life and is ultimately paid in blood. In *Proud Flesh* Jack Burden is a reporter who does not appear until the last scene in a very minor part. Warren later developed this reporter into the narrator of the two stories that form the plot of the novel *All the King's Men,* the Willie Stark story and the Jack Burden story. In the dramatic versions, however, Burden's role is definitely subordinated to Willie Stark's.

After the success of the novel, Warren returned to the stage version with alterations in form, cutting the play down from five acts to three, while making changes in the use of the chorus as well as in the line of action. Francis Fergusson and Eric Bentley had been particularly helpful in their readings of earlier versions of the script. When Erwin Piscator produced the revised play in 1958, it was closer to the off-Broadway production and the 1960 publication of the play.

All the King's Men (A Play) is set in the deep South in the 1930s. Divided into a prologue and three acts, the play uses the essence of the Willie Stark story as the point of action around which several of the subplots turn. Because of the restrictions of the medium, Warren's descriptions of place, character, and time are left to the talents of the director and actors to represent them for the audience. The key points and lines from the novel are somewhat abbreviated and are thus magnified in significance on stage. An added character, the Professor, serves as an interlocutor, a man of science who questions and challenges Burden's idealistic view of Stark. During these exchanges between characters emerge the concerns that manifest themselves in Warren's later poetry: the search for truth, self, love, hope, endurance, and a way to live in the world.

Stark's view of the truth, for example, is made evident in the prologue: "You live in the world and you try to know the truth of the world. You live, and you try to know the truth that is in you. . . . The truth is there. But you walk in the darkness of the world. You walk in the darkness of yourself. The darkness whirls. And in the sick hour before dawn, you are sick of the world. You are sick of yourself."[2] The images of darkness, the sleepless nights, and the unresolved inner conflict are common motifs in a variety of contexts in Warren's poetry. Stark expounds on the "law" (22) and on "dirt" (24) using the same language Warren employs in the novel. When Burden defends Stark against the Professor's attacks, he mentions the hope that Stark instills in people (30). This short revelation carries considerable meaning with respect to understanding Stark's character, who has the ability to perceive the needs of people and to answer those needs in a way that gains their support of his cause.

Stark wins Sadie Burke's loyalty as his personal assistant and mistress. He uses Tiny Duffy as his scapegoat, his alter ego whom Stark can insult as a tribute to what he wants to be (52). He attracts Anne Stanton's love with his pragmatism as a man of action. He persuades Adam Stanton, the idealistic physician, to direct his new memorial hospital. And he turns Burden's life of inactivity into a life that is deeply involved in the world. To counter some of these conceptions about Stark, the Professor is given lines of opposition. For example, he explains to Adam about the hard realities of the world and self, harshly dubbing Adam's idealism as a "self-indulgent dream" (75). As a realist, the Professor tells Burden that "Nature prescribes her own values" (82) and explains to him in utilitarian terms that "the morality of an act, the means to an end, must not be confused with the end result" (132), which, as he states in the prologue, is what counts.

The idea of love is addressed explicitly three times in the play, in relation to Anne and Burden (80), Burden's mother and Burden (105), and Lucy Stark to Willie (118). Each of these episodes expresses the same idea about love: namely, that it should be unconditional, not selfish, and should be active. As Anne says, love "is trying to live, Jack" (80). Part of this mature ideal of love has to do with endurance. Although Willie Stark is a man of endurance, this quality alone will not guarantee unconditional love. The interplay of power politics, idealism, love, and endurance is crystallized in this stage version of the Willie Stark story.

By the late 1950s, however, a third story from the novel had captured Warren's dramatic imagination, the Cass Mastern story, which appears in chapter 4 of the novel and which Adrian Hall adapted for the stage in 1990 as *A Prologue to All the King's Men.*

Listen to the Mockingbird

Listen to the Mockingbird, the title of the 1959 version that does not represent the last revision, centers on the tryst between the young Cass Mastern and his host's wife, Bella Trice.[3] The play as written seems to be more concerned with Bella, though Cass is clearly a central figure. The idea of betrayal is a major theme in the play. Bella betrays her husband by having an affair with Cass. She betrays

Phebe, her personal servant since childhood, by selling her to a slave trader. She betrays Cass when he decides to leave. Cass, of course, also betrays Duncan Trice, who has generously opened his home to him while Cass attends Transylvania College in Lexington, Kentucky. Cass also betrays his older brother Gilbert, who has reared him after their parents died and who has plans for his brother's future. Most of all, Cass betrays himself and what he stood for prior to meeting Bella Trice and her corrupt brother, Abbott Coleman.

In preparing *Listen to the Mockingbird,* Warren again adapted fiction into drama, compressed longer sections of description and background into brief statements delivered by a character in conversation, and highlighted significant portions of the action. The time of the play goes from 1859 to the start of the Civil War in 1861, the point at which Cass leaves the Trice plantation to join in the fight. His reason is altruistic but also self-serving in that he wants to right the wrong done to Phebe and at the same time set himself free from that guilt. Mark Trice, a character added to the story as Duncan Trice's cousin and a professor of philosophy at Transylvania University, remarks to Gilbert that he can see Cass marching into battle in the ranks with his rifle "but never firing a bullet, waiting until some bullet finds him" (3.2.50). Thus, while Cass's "darkness and trouble" does not literally end as it does in the novel, Mark's vision prophesies the same end. Gilbert, however, has the last word when Bella accuses Mark of being a coward in not standing up for her. Gilbert responds that Mark is not a coward, and he argues that "It's just that he knows the truth," though "he never knows what to do about it" (3.2.53). Gilbert, like Stark, is a pragmatist who believes he knows how the world works.[4]

In a note on the chronology of an earlier version of this story titled *The Wedding Ring,* Warren writes: "This play, then, is a historical play, but I hope that if it means anything it means that history is never over. For history is only the image of our present anguish and of the hope—the only hope we have—for our future victory."[5]

Brother to Dragons

History is a fundamental backdrop to *Brother to Dragons* as well. The work assumed several forms, first as a narrative poem (1953) that was later published in a revised edition (1979), then as an adaptation for television (PBS) by Adrian Hall (1975), in which Warren has a cameo role as the writer's father, and finally as a published two-act play in the *Georgia Review* (1976).[6] In his foreword to this two-act play, Warren writes: "what I am concerned with is the symbolic interpretation of the event for the Jeffersonian notion of the perfectibility of man and the good American notion of our inevitable righteousness in action and purity in motive."[7] The event to which Warren refers is the brutal meat-axe murder of a slave named George (John in the play) by two of Thomas Jefferson's nephews, Lilburn and Isham Lewis. They murdered the slave because he broke a favorite water pitcher of their deceased mother. As Warren tells us in the foreword, the event "occurred at their home, Rocky Hill, on the night of December 15, 1811, the night when the New Madrid Earthquake struck its first blow at the Mississippi Valley" (295). The crime was discovered a few weeks later. The Lewis brothers were arrested and released on bail. They agreed to commit suicide, each brother shooting the other simultaneously; however, Isham, the younger fired first, killing Lilburn, who with his Last Will and Testament in his pocket had no intention of firing his pistol. Isham

evaded the law again, and the last report of him was his death in the
Battle of New Orleans. Although Jefferson's papers do not mention
this event at Rocky Hill, Boynton Merrill, Jr., has documented the
event in his book *Jefferson's Nephews: A Frontier Tragedy*.

Drawing on this historical event for his drama, Warren once
again has created a powerful story that looks at the moral implications of love, hope, and endurance and at modern humanity's relation to this gruesome event. To his verse drama, the narrative poem,
he added the character of a poet," R. P. W.," as "a kind of interlocutor."[8] In the play he is referred to as "Writer." Two other characters, Aunt Cat and Billy Rutter, were added to the play. The Slaves
and Frontier People serve as a chorus that interrupts the play's action
to provide background and interpretations.

The Jeffersonian ideal is represented by the Louisiana Pur-
chase, which is "the new land / Worthy of gleaming distance for
the New Man to come," a new Eden (71). The Writer serves as an
antagonist to Jefferson, or to the ghost of Jefferson, with whom
the Writer has his dialogue. The Writer is aware of Jefferson's
struggle to come to terms with what life means and is also aware
of the burden of ordinary men who have less hope. With respect
to Lilburn's act, the Writer says to Laetitia, who is Lilburn's wife,
and to Jefferson:

> Forgiveness—forgiveness—that's what he wanted again!
> How sweet is forgiveness and restoration—yes, that
> Is the sweetness you can whet the sharp edge of self in,
> Like a blade in oil. It's the way, you might say,
> To put a razor edge on reality.

(85)

Charles Lewis is the patriarch of the Lewis family, a family that seems starved for love, for the capacity to love. He has married Jefferson's sister and moved to the West to seek his personal destiny (95). Charles's moving his wife Lucy to Kentucky from Virginia destroys the family and, consequently, destroys her. Aunt Cat, Lilburn's wet-nurse, fights for emotional possession of Lilburn and assumes this maternal role after Lucy dies. She is also the one who sees bones in the air when the Sheriff asks the Slaves if they know where the bones of the murdered slave are buried. Aunt Cat does not tell him where the remains are; in this way, she does not betray Lilburn and Isham directly. Her love of Lilburn is not diminished by his bloody act. Lilburn claims that he butchered John out of his love for his mother Lucy. The water pitcher symbolized Lilburn's love for his mother since it was given to her by her brother Thomas Jefferson. His act, which clearly confirms human imperfectability, is an act of betrayal; death must be his redemption, his hope. This hope may represent a reduction in Warren's allowance for hope as "a valid response to the human condition." It suggests a change in his attitude between the 1953 and the 1979 versions of *Brother to Dragons* and may result, as Lewis Simpson has noted, from his intensified attention "to his lifelong search for the meaning of the self," a search that "culminates in the compelling realization that the meaning of the self is to be discovered in the self's isolation in history," or "in the isolation of history in the self." [9]

On a thematic level Warren's later drama parallels his later poetry, since the plays grapple with the same fundamental questions of individual identity and purpose. Though his output in the genre of

drama is relatively small, the fact that he put each play through multiple revisions suggests his intensity and dedication to playwriting.

By the end of his career Robert Penn Warren received every
major literary award that the U.S. bestows on authors. His work has
been translated and published in thirty-one foreign countries.
Despite his exemplary contributions to literature, he did not receive
the Nobel Prize for literature, an omission probably dictated by politics and his own intellectual independence. The awards, however,
were not the central focus of his literary life. His writing was. Yet,
as Victor Strandberg has shown, Warren's works are not widely
anthologized today, largely as a result of the politics that underlie
contemporary canon formation. However, Warren's genius can be
readily observed not only in his fiction and poetry, but also in his
interviews. He was a master teacher who could make even insignificant questions seem meaningful. His breadth and depth of reading
and his ability to deal with the larger issues of life provide the firm
foundation of his own writing, writing that became clearly the voice
of his imagination in his later years. Readers who have not read at
least *All the King's Men, Brother to Dragons, Chief Joseph of the
Nez Perce,* "Blackberry Winter," and a healthy selection of his
essays have not completed their education in American letters.

Warren's legacy in the realm of letters is extensive, and his work
was recognized, along with that of Cleanth Brooks, at the London
conference, "Cleanth Brooks, Robert Penn Warren, and the Southern
Literary Tradition" in March 1997. Through their textbooks, their
own critical works, their editing of *The Southern Review,* and their
teaching, as well as Warren's own creative work, they laid the

groundwork for that legacy in the late 1930s. Their literary movement became a predominant mode for critical and creative writing in
the following two decades. The critical part of their legacy was
dubbed the New Criticism and has been challenged and even
denounced in recent years. Nearly sixty years later, however,
Christopher Clausen reports "that certain core elements of the New
Criticism . . . may be coming around" again.[10] Ample evidence is
available to suggest that their legacy remains visible and viable
today.

Warren's legacy in American literature remains firm and intact
because through his writing Warren addresses the universal concerns of a society, concerns that are as much a part of the arts today
as they were a century ago. Warren displays depth, breadth, versatility, and imagination in his writings. Readers will discover these
qualities if they read his interviews; they will certainly discover
them if they read the texts of his work. At the beginning of the
twenty-first century, Robert Penn Warren remains a leader in American letters.

Chapter One—Understanding Robert Penn Warren

1. The *Collected Poems of Robert Penn Warren*, edited by John Burt (New York: Random House, 1998), 266. Unless otherwise noted, quotations from Warren's poetry will be from this edition and will be cited parenthetically by page number in the text.

2. Joseph Blotner, *Robert Penn Warren: A Biography* (New York: Random House, 1997), 47–51.

3. Donald Davidson, "Introduction," *The Fugitive: April, 1922–December 1925* (reprint, Gloucester, Mass.: Peter Smith, 1967), iii.

4. Robert B. Heilman, "RPW at LSU: Some Reminiscences," *Kentucky Review* 2, no.3 (1981): 31–46.

5. Richard B. Sale, "An Interview in New Haven with Robert Penn Warren," in *Talking with Robert Penn Warren*, edited by Floyd C. Watkins, John T. Hiers, and Mary Louise Weeks (Athens: University of Georgia Press, 1990), 129–30.

6. David H. Richter, ed., *The Critical Tradition: Classic Texts and Contemporary Trends* (New York: Bedford Book of St. Martin's Press, 1989), 726; Alvin Kernan, *In Plato's Cave* (New Haven: Yale University Press, 1999), 59. In Greek mythology Castor and Polydeuces (Pollux) were twin brothers whose sister was Helen and whose father was Zeus. They were associated with the cult of the Dioscuri and were deified for their heroism in battle. Because of their textbooks, Brooks and Warren were considered leaders in the New Critical approach to literature. A convenient overview of this school of criticism is found in William Harmon and C. Hugh Holman, *A Handbook of Literature*, 7th ed. (Upper Saddle River, N.J.: Prentice Hall, 1996), 345–46.

7. Robert Penn Warren, *Democracy and Poetry* (Cambridge: Harvard University Press, 1975), 31.

8. Cleanth Brooks, *The Hidden God: Studies in Hemingway, Faulkner, Yeats, Eliot, and Warren* (New Haven: Yale University Press, 1963), 98.

9. Warren, *All the King's Men* (1946; reprint, San Diego: Harcourt Brace and Company, 1996), 49.

10. In *Robert Penn Warren's All the King's Men: A Critical Handbook,* edited by Maurice Beebe and Leslie A. Field (Belmont, Calif.: Wadsworth Publishing Company, 1966), 59.

11. Bill McCarron and James Grimshaw, "Cicero's *De Senectute* and Warren's *Night Rider,"* *Mississippi Quarterly* 50, no.1 (Winter 1996–1997): 115–16.

12. All three reviews are reprinted in *Critical Essays on Robert Penn Warren,* edited by William Bedford Clark (Boston: G. K. Hall and Co., 1981), 38, 43, 64.

13. "Knowledge and the Image of Man," 61.

14. For more on Bergsonian time, see F. L. Pogson, trans., *Time and Free Will,* by Henri Bergson (London: George Allen and Unwin Ltd., 1910).

15. Harold Bloom, Foreword, *The Collected Poems of Robert Penn Warren,* xxiii.

16. Paul Hoover, ed., *Postmodern American Poetry* (New York: W. W. Norton and Company, 1994), xxv.

17. "Pure and Impure Poetry," in *New and Selected Essays* (New York: Random House, 1989), 21, 15. Subsequent references to essays from this edition will be included parenthetically in the text.

18. Alvin B. Kernan, *The Imaginary Library: An Essay on Literature and Society* (Princeton: Princeton University Press, 1982), 11, 18, 36.

19. *A Plea in Mitigation: Modern Poetry and the End of an Era* (Macon, Ga.: Wesleyan College, 1966), 2.

20. James A. Grimshaw, Jr., ed., *Cleanth Brooks and Robert Penn Warren: A Literary Correspondence* (Columbia: University of Missouri Press, 1998), 276.

21. Robert Penn Warren, *Listen to the Mockingbird,* YCAL MSS 51, Box 158, F.2852 (Draft P [marked "version D"], typescript, carbon corrected), Beinecke Rare Book and Manuscript Library, New Haven, Conn., June 1959.

22. *Brother to Dragons: A Tale in Verse and Voices* (New York: Random House, 1953), 214–15.

23. Warren, *New and Selected Essays,* 55.

Chapter Two—Early Fiction (1939–1955)

1. Both vignettes are reprinted in *Southern Quarterly* 31, no.4 (Summer 1993): 113–18.

2. For identification and description of manuscripts and particular editions of books, see James A. Grimshaw, Jr., *Robert Penn Warren: A Descriptive Bibliography, 1922–1979* (Charlottesville: University Press of Virginia, 1981). Entries for these manuscripts are located in section I2–I4.

3. Leonard Casper, *Robert Penn Warren: The Dark and Bloody Ground* (Seattle: University of Washington Press, 1960), 106.

4. James H. Justus, *The Achievement of Robert Penn Warren* (Baton Rouge: Louisiana State University Press, 1981), 165.

5. Alasdair MacIntyre, "Tradition and the Virtues," in *Vice and Virtue in Everyday Life,* edited by Christina Sommers and Fred Sommers, 4th ed. (Fort Worth: Harcourt Brace College Publishers, 1997), 323.

6. Textual citations of this novel are from *Night Rider* (1939; reprint, Nashville: J. S. Sanders and Company, 1992), 16. In my citations of reprints of Warren's books, pagination is identical to the first edition unless otherwise noted.

7. For a discussion of nihilism and the isolated temperament, see Alvan S. Ryan's analysis of *Night Rider* in *Robert Penn Warren:*

A Collection of Critical Essays, edited by Richard Gray (Englewood Cliffs, N.J.: Prentice-Hall, 1980), 32–39.

8. For more on Longley's reading of *At Heaven's Gate,* see his essay in *Modern Fiction Studies* 6, no. 1 (Spring 1960): 13–24. A revised version of the essay appears as "Self-Knowledge, the Pearl of Pus, and the Seventh Circle: The Major Themes in *At Heaven's Gate,*" in *Robert Penn Warren: A Collection of Critical Essays,* edited by John L. Longley, Jr. (New York: New York University Press, 1965), 60–74.

9. *At Heaven's Gate* (1943; reprint, New York: New Directions Publishing Company, 1985), 56. Other references to this edition are cited parenthetically within the text.

10. For further details about Warren's use of this allusion to Shakespeare's sonnet, see Casper's *Robert Penn Warren: The Dark and Bloody Ground,* 187, n.10.

11. For more on Ladell Payne's discussion of parallels between Willie Stark and Huey Long, see Payne's article in *American Quarterly* 20 (Fall 1968): 580–95.

12. *All the King's Men* (New York: Harcourt Brace and Company, 1946), 167. Other references to this edition of the novel are cited parenthetically in the text.

13. Loren J. Kallsen has edited a useful and informative casebook about the events surrounding this murder and about the fictional accounts inspired by the killing. Kallsen's casebook comes complete with a bibliography listing five plays, six other novels, two folk songs, and one magazine story based on this Kentucky tragedy. *The Kentucky Tragedy: A Problem in Romantic Attitudes* (Indianapolis: Bobbs-Merrill Company, 1963).

14. *World Enough and Time* (New York: Random House, 1950; reprint, Baton Rouge: Louisiana State University Press, 1999), 512. Other references to the 1950 edition of the novel are cited parenthetically in the text.

15. Untitled essay, n.d., 78M1, Robert Penn Warren Papers, King Library, University of Kentucky, Lexington. This untitled essay stops at the third page, though the last line suggests additional pages may be missing. It reads like an author's introduction to an edition of the novel, although Warren may have written it for the director of the movie version of *Band of Angels,* which starred Clark Gable and Yvonne DeCarlo.

16. *Band of Angels* (New York: Random House, 1955; reprint, Baton Rouge: Louisiana State University Press, 1994), 62. Other references to the 1955 edition of the novel are cited parenthetically in the text.

17. Philip Hallie, "From Cruelty to Goodness," in *Vice and Virtue in Everyday Life,* edited by Christina Sommers and Fred Sommers, 3d ed. (Fort Worth: Harcourt Brace College Publishers, 1993), 15.

18. References to the short stories are from *The Circus in the Attic and Other Stories* (New York: Harcourt, Brace and Company, 1947; reprint, San Diego: Harcourt Brace Jovanovich, 1983), 17.

19. Warren talks at great length about Kent Greenfield in an interview with William Ferris in West Wardsboro, Vermont, titled "A Conversation with Robert Penn Warren," videocassette, University, Miss., Center of the Study of Southern Culture, August 1987. For more on Kent Greenfield and Warren's friendship, see Joseph Blotner, *Robert Penn Warren: A Biography* (New York: Random House, 1997).

Chapter Three—Late Fiction (1955–1977)

1. For an interesting account of this real-life drama, see Jack Fincher, "Dreams of Riches Led Floyd Collins to a Nightmarish End," *Smithsonian,* May 1990, 137–38, 140–42, 144–50.

2. John Burt. *Robert Penn Warren and American Idealism* (New York: Yale University Press, 1988), 190.

3. *The Cave* (New York: Random House, 1955), 387. Further references to this novel are cited parenthetically in the text.

4. In *Robert Penn Warren Talking: Interviews 1950–1978,* edited by Floyd C. Watkins and John T. Hiers (New York: Random House, 1980), 187.

5. *Wilderness: A Tale of the Civil War* (New York: Random House, 1961), 310. Further references to this novel are made parenthetically in the text.

6. From a 1971 program with Edwin Newman, included in *Robert Penn Warren Talking,* ed. Watkins and Hiers, 163.

7. For an account of an actual flood, see Donald Dale Jackson, "When 20 Million Tons of Water Flooded Johnstown," *Smithsonian,* May 1989, 50–54, 56, 58–60. Warren, of course, may have in mind more than one of the floods in the TVA system in Tennessee.

8. From a 1969 interview with Richard B. Sale, included in Watkins and Hiers, *Robert Penn Warren Talking,* 103.

9. Robert Penn Warren, "Faulkner: Past and Future," in *Faulkner: A Collection of Critical Essays,* edited by Robert Penn Warren (Englewood Cliffs, N.J.: Prentice-Hall, Inc., 1966), 17.

10. *Flood: A Romance of Our Time* (New York: Random House, 1964), 4. Further references to this novel are cited parenthetically within the text.

11. Robert Penn Warren, "Louisiana Politics and *All the King's Men,*" in *All the King's Men: A Critical Handbook,* edited by Maurice Beebe and Leslie A. Field (Belmont, Calif.: Wadsworth, 1966), 27.

12. *Meet Me in the Green Glen* (New York: Random House, 1971), 46. Further references to this novel are cited parenthetically within the text.

13. Lucy Ferriss, *Sleeping with the Boss: Female Subjectivity and Narrative Pattern in Robert Penn Warren* (Baton Rouge: Louisiana State University Press, 1997), 129.

14. These lines are from the poem "Moral Assessment," contained in the sequence "Homage to Theodore Dreiser," in *The Collected Poems of Robert Penn Warren,* 297.

15. Beebe and Field, *All the King's Men: A Critical Handbook,* 60.

16. This analysis of *Meet Me in the Green Glen* appeared in slightly different form in my essay-review "Robert Penn Warren's *Annus Mirabilis*" in *Southern Review* 10, no. 2 (Spring 1974): 509–16.

17. *A Place to Come To* (New York: Random House, 1977), 3. Further references to this novel are cited parenthetically within the text.

18. Robert S. Koppelman, *Robert Penn Warren's Modernist Spirituality* (Columbia: University of Missouri Press, 1995), 123–45.

Chapter Four—Early and Middle Poetry (1922–1966)

1. Unless otherwise noted, all quotations from Warren's poems in this chapter are taken from *The Collected Poems of Robert Penn Warren,* edited by John Burt (Baton Rouge: Louisiana State University Press, 1998). Parenthetical citations refer to the line numbers of the poems.

2. *New York Times Book Review,* 12 May 1985, 9–10.

3. Harold Bloom, *The Western Canon: The Books and School of the Ages* (New York: Harcourt Brace, 1994), 17–18.

4. Neither John Burt nor I have found the published version of this poem. In his textual notes to *The Collected Poems of Robert Penn Warren,* Burt speculates with just reason that this poem might have been published by the Poetry Society of South Carolina.

5. Vachel Lindsay, "The Congo," in *American Poetry and Prose,* edited by Norman Foerster, 4th ed. (Boston: Houghton-Mifflin Company, 1957), 2:1331.

6. The translation of the Latin is taken from Floyd C. Watkins's discussion of the poem in *Then and Now: The Personal Past in the*

Poetry of Robert Penn Warren (Lexington: University Press of Kentucky, 1982), 70–75. Watkins provides the details of the lynching of Primus Kirby in Gutherie.

7. Bill McCarron and James Grimshaw, "Robert Penn Warren and William Dunbar: *Timor Mortis Conturbat Me," Robert Penn Warren Circle Newsletter,* no. 18 (January 2000): 4–5.

8. For their more detailed discussions of naturalism in Warren's poetry, see Victor H. Strandberg, *A Colder Fire: The Poetry of Robert Penn Warren* (Lexington: University of Kentucky Press, 1965), 9–73: Justus, *The Achievement of Robert Penn Warren,* 4–6 *et passim;* and Casper, *The Dark and Bloody Ground,* 72.

9. In *The Grotesque in Art and Literature: Theological Reflections,* edited by James Luther Adams and Wilson Yates (Grand Rapids, Mich.: William B. Eerdmans Publishing Company, 1997), 245. The title of the poem sequence in *Promises* is "Ballad of a Sweet Dream of Peace" without the subtitle.

10. R. W. B. Lewis, *Literary Reflections: A Shoring of Images, 1960–1993* (Boston: Northeastern University Press, 1993), 261.

11. Casper, *Robert Penn Warren: The Dark and Bloody Ground,* 80.

12. Warren, *A Plea in Mitigation,* 12.

13. David Perkins, *A History of Modern Poetry,* vol. 2 (Cambridge: Belknap Press of Harvard University Press, 1987), 490.

14. Warren, *A Plea in Mitigation,* 13–14.

15. G. W. Mackail, *Lectures on Poetry,* quoted in I. A. Richards, *Principles of Literary Criticism,* (1925; reprint, New York: Harcourt, Brace and World, Inc., 1965), 19; Harold Bloom repeats this idea in *The Western Canon,* 11: "The anxiety of influence cripples weaker talents but stimulates canonical genius."

16. Cleanth Brooks, *Modern Poetry and the Tradition* (1939; reprint, Chapel Hill: University of North Carolina Press, 1965), xiv.

17. Lewis, *Literary Reflections,* 261; the quoted phrase Lewis attributes to Monroe K. Spears, 269.

18. Richards, *Principles of Literary Criticism,* 2–7.

19. John Crowe Ransom, *The World's Body* (1938; reprint, Baton Rouge: Louisiana State University Press, 1968), 329, 342–45.

20. Robert S. Koppelman, *Robert Penn Warren's Modernist Spirituality* (Columbia: University of Missouri Press, 1995), 52.

21. Cleanth Brooks and Robert Penn Warren, *Understanding Poetry: An Anthology for College Students* (New York: Henry Holt and Company, 1938), 27.

22. Blotner, *Robert Penn Warren: A Biography,* 311.

23. In *Democracy and Poetry* Warren defines his concept of the self by invoking the psychological process of "individuation, the felt principle of significant unity"; by *felt,* individual experience; and by *significant,* continuity—"the self as a development in time" and responsibility, "the self as a moral identity." *Democracy and Poetry,* xii.

24. Brooks and Warren, *Understanding Poetry,* 119.

25. Strandberg, *A Colder Fire,* 220–21.

26. Calvin Bedient, *"In the Hearts' Last Kingdom": Robert Penn Warren's Major Poetry* (Cambridge: Harvard University Press, 1984), 9.

27. Brooks and Warren, *Understanding Poetry,* 24–25.

28. Brooks, *Modern Poetry and the Tradition,* 85–86.

29. Frank Kermode, *Poetry, Narrative, History,* Bucknell Lectures in Literary Theory (Oxford: Basil Blackwell, 1990), 67.

30. Norman Fruman, "Reconstructing English," *ALSC Newsletter* 3.1 (Winter 1997): 9–10.

31. Warren, preface to *Selected Poems: New and Old, 1923–1966* (New York: Random House, 1966), vii.

Chapter Five—Late Poetry (1966–1985)

1. Harold Bloom, "Sunset Hawk: Warren's Poetry and Tradition," in *Robert Penn Warren,* edited by Harold Bloom (New York: Chelsea House Publications, 1986), 196.

2. These definitions are adapted from the *American Heritage Dictionary,* 2d college edition, and *Webster's Third New International Dictionary.*

3. Unless otherwise noted, all quotations from Warren's poems in this chapter are taken from *The Collected Poems of Robert Penn Warren.* Parenthetical citations refer to the line numbers of the poems.

4. John Burt, *Robert Penn Warren and American Idealism* (New Haven: Yale University Press, 1988), 92–93.

5. In *Cleanth Brooks and Robert Penn Warren: A Literary Correspondence,* edited by James A. Grimshaw, Jr. (Columbia: University of Missouri Press, 1998), 377.

6. Leonard Casper, *The Blood-Marriage of Earth and Sky: Robert Penn Warren's Later Novels* (Baton Rouge: Louisiana State University Press, 1997), xii.

7. Randolph Paul Runyon traces many of the images of Warren's later poetry in *The Braided Dream: Robert Penn Warren's Late Poetry* (Lexington: University Press of Kentucky, 1990).

8. In *American Poetry: The Nineteenth Century* (New York: Library of America, 1993), 1:122–24 and 125–26.

9. A. L. Clements, "Sacramental Vision: The Poetry of Robert Penn Warren," in *Critical Essays on Robert Penn Warren,* edited by William Bedford Clark (Boston: G. K. Hall, 1981), 233.

Chapter Six—Drama

1. The two early versions, *Proud Flesh* and *Willie Stark: His Rise and Fall,* previously unpublished, have recently been made available in *Robert Penn Warren's "All the King's Men": Three Stage Versions,* edited by James A. Grimshaw, Jr., and James A. Perkins (Athens: University of Georgia Press, 2000).

2. Robert Penn Warren, *All the King's Men (A Play)* (New

York: Random House, 1960), 6–7. References to this edition are hereafter cited parenthetically by page number within the text.

3. Robert Penn Warren, *Listen to the Mockingbird,* YCAL MSS 51, Box 158, F.2852, Beinecke Rare Book and Manuscript Library, Yale University, 1959. The parenthetical references are to act, scene, and page of manuscript.

4. Parts of this discussion are adapted from Kay Coughenour and James A. Grimshaw, Jr., "*Listen to the Mockingbird:* Some Production Notes," in *Robert Penn Warren's Cass Mastern Story,* edited by James A. Perkins (Baton Rouge: Louisiana State University Press, forthcoming).

5. Robert Penn Warren, *The Wedding Ring,* Robert Penn Warren Collection, 78M1, #58, King Library, University of Kentucky, Lexington, KY, 1951.

6. Robert Penn Warren, *Brother to Dragons: A Play in Two Acts, Georgia Review* 30 (Spring 1976): 65–138. Quotations from this play are cited parenthetically by page number in the text.

7. In *Robert Penn Warren's "Brother to Dragons": A Discussion,* edited by James A. Grimshaw, Jr. (Baton Rouge: Louisiana State University Press, 1983), 296.

8. Robert Penn Warren, "The Way It Was Written," *New York Times Book Review,* 23 August 1953, 25; also quoted in Grimshaw, *Robert Penn Warren's "Brother to Dragons,"* 2.

9. Lewis Simpson, "The Concept of the Historical Self in *Brother to Dragons,*" in Grimshaw, *Robert Penn Warren's "Brother to Dragons,"* 245.

10. Christopher Clausen, "Reading Closely Again," *Commentary,* February 1997, 56.

BIBLIOGRAPHY

Works by Robert Penn Warren

Listed in order of publication

Books

John Brown: The Making of a Martyr. New York: Payson and Clarke Ltd, 1929. Reprint, with an introduction by C. Vann Woodward, Nashville: J. S. Sanders and Company, 1993.

Thirty-Six Poems. New York: Alcestis Press, 1935.

Night Rider. Boston: Houghton Mifflin Company, 1939. Reprint, with a foreword by George Core, Nashville: J. S. Sanders and Company, 1992.

Eleven Poems on the Same Theme. Norfolk, Conn.: New Directions, 1942.

At Heaven's Gate. New York: Harcourt, Brace and Company, 1943. Reprint, New York: New Directions, 1985.

Selected Poems, 1923–1943. New York: Harcourt, Brace and Company, 1944.

All the King's Men. New York: Harcourt, Brace and Company, 1946. Fiftieth Anniversary Edition, with a foreword by Joseph Blotner, San Diego: Harcourt Brace and Company, 1996.

The Circus in the Attic and Other Stories. New York: Harcourt, Brace and Company, 1947. San Diego: Harcourt Brace Jovanovich, Publishers, 1983.

World Enough and Time: A Romantic Novel. New York: Random House, 1950. Reprint, Baton Rouge: Louisiana State University Press, 1999.

Brother to Dragons: A Tale in Verse and Voices. New York: Random House, 1953.

BIBLIOGRAPHY

Band of Angels. New York: Random House, 1955. Reprint, Baton Rouge: Louisiana State University Press, 1994.

Segregation: The Inner Conflict in the South. New York: Random House, 1956. Reissue, with an introduction by William Bedford Clark, Athens: University of Georgia Press, 1994.

Promises: Poems, 1954–1956. New York: Random House, 1957.

Remember the Alamo! Illustrated by William Moyers. New York: Random House, 1958.

Selected Essays. New York: Random House, 1958.

The Cave. New York: Random House, 1959.

The Gods of Mount Olympus. Illustrated by William Moyers. New York: Random House, 1959.

You, Emperors, and Others: Poems, 1957–1960. New York: Random House, 1960.

The Legacy of the Civil War. New York: Random House, 1961. Reprint, Cambridge: Harvard University Press, 1983.

Wilderness: A Tale of the Civil War. New York: Random House, 1961.

Flood: A Romance of Our Time. New York: Random House, 1964.

Who Speaks for the Negro? New York: Random House, 1965.

Selected Poems: New and Old, 1923–1966. New York: Random House, 1966.

Incarnations: Poems, 1966–1968. New York: Random House, 1968.

Audubon: A Vision. New York: Random House, 1969.

Homage to Theodore Dreiser, August 27, 1871–December 28, 1945, on the Centennial of His Birth. New York: Random House, 1971.

Meet Me in the Green Glen. New York: Random House, 1971.

Or Else—Poem/Poems, 1968–1974. New York: Random House, 1974.

Democracy and Poetry. The 1974 Jefferson Lecture in the Humanities. Cambridge: Harvard University Press, 1975.

Selected Poems, 1923–1975. New York: Random House, 1976.

A Place to Come To. New York: Random House, 1977.

Now and Then: Poems, 1976–1978. New York: Random House, 1978.

BIBLIOGRAPHY

Brother to Dragons: A Tale in Verse and Voices (A New Version).
New York: Random House, 1979. Reprint, Baton Rouge:
Louisiana State University Press, 1996.

Being Here: Poetry, 1977–1980. New York: Random House, 1980.

Jefferson Davis Gets His Citizenship Back. Lexington: University
Press of Kentucky, 1980.

Rumor Verified: Poems, 1979–1980. New York: Random House, 1981.

Chief Joseph of the Nez Perce. New York: Random House, 1983.

New and Selected Poems, 1923–1985. New York: Random House, 1985.

A Robert Penn Warren Reader. New York: Random House, 1987.

Portrait of a Father. Lexington: University Press of Kentucky, 1988.

New and Selected Essays. New York: Random House, 1989.

The Collected Poems of Robert Penn Warren. Edited by John Burt.
Baton Rouge: Louisiana State University Press, 1998.

Books as Coauthor and Editor

Brooks, Cleanth, Jr., John Thibaut Purser, and Robert Penn Warren,
eds. *An Approach to Literature: A Collection of Prose and Verse
with Analyses and Discussions*. 1936. Rev. ed., New York: F. S.
Crofts and Company, 1939.

Warren, Robert Penn, ed. *A Southern Harvest: Short Stories by Southern Writers*. Boston: Houghton Mifflin Company, 1937.

Brooks, Cleanth, and Robert Penn Warren, eds. *Understanding
Poetry: An Anthology for College Students*. New York: Henry Holt
and Company, 1938.

———. *Understanding Fiction*. New York: F. S. Crofts and Company, 1943.

———. *Modern Rhetoric*. New York: Harcourt, Brace and Company,
1949.

———. *An Anthology of Stories from the "Southern Review."* Baton
Rouge: Louisiana State University Press, 1953.

220

BIBLIOGRAPHY

Warren, Robert Penn, and Albert Erskine, eds. *Short Story Masterpieces*. New York: Dell Books, 1954.

———. *Six Centuries of Great Poetry*. New York: Dell Books, 1955.

———. *A New Southern Harvest: An Anthology*. New York: Bantam Books, 1957.

Warren, Robert Penn, ed. *Faulkner: A Collection of Critical Essays*. Twentieth Century Views. Englewood Cliffs, N.J.: Prentice-Hall, 1966.

———. *Selected Poems of Herman Melville: A Reader's Edition*. New York: Random House, 1970.

———. *John Greenleaf Whittier's Poetry: An Appraisal and a Selection*. Minneapolis: University of Minnesota Press, 1971.

Brooks, Cleanth, R. W. B. Lewis, and Robert Penn Warren, eds. *American Literature: The Makers and the Making*. 2 vols. New York: St. Martin's Press, 1973.

Warren, Robert Penn, ed. *Katherine Anne Porter: A Collection of Critical Essays*. Twentieth Century Views. Englewood Cliffs, N.J.: Prentice-Hall, 1979.

Cleanth Brooks and Robert Penn Warren: A Literary Correspondence. Edited by James A. Grimshaw, Jr. Columbia: University of Missouri Press, 1998.

Selected Articles and Essays

"The Briar Patch." In *I'll Take My Stand: The South and the Agrarian Tradition, by Twelve Southerners,* 246–64. 1930. Reprint, with an introduction by Louis D. Rubin, Jr., Baton Rouge: Louisiana State University Press, 1977.

"A Poem of Pure Imagination: An Experiment in Reading." In *The Rime of the Ancient Mariner,* by Samuel Taylor Coleridge. New York: Reynal and Hitchcock, 1946.

BIBLIOGRAPHY

"Knowledge and the Image of Man." *Sewanee Review* 62 (Spring 1955): 182–92.

"Why Do We Read Fiction?" *Saturday Evening Post,* 20 October 1960, 82–84; reprinted in *New and Selected Essays,* 55–66.

"The Use of the Past." In *A Time to Hear and Answer: Essays for the Bicentennial Season,* edited by Taylor Littleton, 3–35. Tuscaloosa: University of Alabama Press for Auburn University, 1977.

"Poetry Is a Kind of Unconscious Autobiography." *New York Times Book Review,* 12 May 1985, 9–10.

"The Episode in the Dime Store." *Southern Review* 30.4 (Autumn 1994): 650–57.

Miscellaneous

How Texas Won Her Freedom: The Story of Sam Houston and the Battle of San Jacinto. San Jacinto Monument, Tex.: San Jacinto Museum of History, 1959.

"Listen to the Mockingbird: A Drama of the American Civil War." Robert Penn Warren Papers. Yale Collection of American Literature (MSS 51). New Haven: Beinecke Rare Book and Manuscript Library, 1959.

A Plea in Mitigation: Modern Poetry and the End of an Era. Eugenia Dorothy Blount Lamar Lecture. Macon, Ga.: Wesleyan College, 1966.

Brother to Dragons: A Play in Two Acts. Georgia Review 30 (Spring 1976): 65–138.

"The Dramatic Version of *Ballad of a Sweet Dream of Peace: A Charade for Easter.*" In *The Grotesque in Art and Literature: Theological Reflections,* edited by James Luther Adams and Wilson Yates, 243–74. Grand Rapids, Mich.: William B. Eerdmans Publishing Company, 1997.

Robert Penn Warren's "All the King's Men": Three Stage Versions. Edited by James A. Grimshaw, Jr., and James Perkins. Athens: University of Georgia Press, 2000. Contains *Proud Flesh, Willie Stark: His Rise and Fall,* and *All the King's Men (A Play).*

Interviews

Ferris, William. "A Conversation with Robert Penn Warren." University, Miss.: Center for the Study of Southern Culture, August 1987. Video.

Kennedy, William. "Robert Penn Warren: Willie Stark, Politics, and the Novel." In *Riding the Yellow Trolley Car,* 165–73. New York: Viking Penguin, 1993.

Watkins, Floyd C., and John T. Hiers, eds. *Robert Penn Warren Talking: Interviews 1950–1978.* New York: Random House, 1980.

Watkins, Floyd C., John T. Hiers, and Mary Louise Weaks, ed. *Talking with Robert Penn Warren.* Athens: University of Georgia Press, 1990.

Books about Robert Penn Warren

Listed in alphabetical order by author

Bedient, Calvin. *"In the Heart's Last Kingdom": Robert Penn Warren's Major Poetry.* Cambridge: Harvard University Press, 1984.

Beebe, Maurice, and Leslie A. Field, eds. *Robert Penn Warren's "All the King's Men": A Critical Handbook.* Belmont, Calif.: Wadsworth Publishing Company, 1966.

Bloom, Harold, ed. *Robert Penn Warren.* Modern Critical Views. New York: Chelsea House Publishers, 1986.

————. *Robert Penn Warren's "All the King's Men."* Modern Critical Interpretations. New York: Chelsea House Publishers, 1987.

Blotner, Joseph. *Robert Penn Warren: A Biography.* New York: Random House, 1997.

Bohner, Charles. *Robert Penn Warren.* Twayne's United States Authors Series, no. 69. Rev. ed. Boston: Twayne Publishers, 1981.

Burt, John. *Robert Penn Warren and American Idealism.* New Haven: Yale University Press, 1988.

Casper, Leonard. *The Blood-Marriage of Earth and Sky: Robert Penn Warren's Later Novels.* Baton Rouge: Louisiana State University Press, 1997.

————. *Robert Penn Warren: The Dark and Bloody Ground.* Seattle: University of Washington Press, 1960.

Chambers, Robert H., ed. *"All the King's Men": A Collection of Critical Essays.* Twentieth Century Interpretations. Englewood Cliffs, N.J.: Prentice-Hall, 1977.

Clark, William Bedford. *The American Vision of Robert Penn Warren.* Lexington: University Press of Kentucky, 1991.

————, ed. *Critical Essays on Robert Penn Warren.* Boston: G. K. Hall and Co., 1981.

Cleopatra, Sr. *The Novels of Robert Penn Warren.* New Delhi: Associated Publishing House, 1985.

Corrigan, Lesa Carnes. *Poems of Pure Imagination: Robert Penn Warren and the Romantic Tradition.* Baton Rouge: Louisiana State University Press, 1999.

Cullick, Jonathan S. *Making History: The Biographical Narratives of Robert Penn Warren.* Baton Rouge: Louisiana State University Press, 2000.

Donohue, Cecilia S. *Robert Penn Warren's Novels: Feminine and Feminist Discourse.* New York: Peter Lang Publishing, 1999.

Edgar, Walter B., ed. *A Southern Renascence Man: Views of Robert*

Penn Warren. Baton Rouge: Louisiana State University Press, 1984.

Ferriss, Lucy. *Sleeping with the Boss: Female Subjectivity and Narrative Pattern in Robert Penn Warren.* Baton Rouge: Louisiana State University Press, 1997.

Gray, Richard, ed. *Robert Penn Warren: A Collection of Critical Essays.* Twentieth Century Views Series. Englewood Cliffs, N.J.: Prentice-Hall, 1980.

Graziano, Frank, ed. *Homage to Robert Penn Warren: A Collection of Critical Essays.* Durango, Col.: Logbridge-Rhodes, 1981.

Grimshaw, James A., Jr., ed. *Robert Penn Warren's "Brother to Dragons": A Discussion.* Baton Rouge: Louisiana State University Press, 1983.

———. *" Time's Glory": Original Essays on Robert Penn Warren.* Conway: University of Central Arkansas Press, 1986.

Guttenberg, Barnett. *Web of Being: The Novels of Robert Penn Warren.* Nashville: Vanderbilt University Press, 1975.

Hart, John A., chm. *"All the King's Men": A Symposium.* Carnegie Series in English, no. 3. Pittsburgh: Carnegie Institute of Technology, 1957.

Hendricks, Randy. *Lonelier Than God: Robert Penn Warren and the Southern Exile.* Athens: University of Georgia Press, 2000.

Justus, James H. *The Achievement of Robert Penn Warren.* Baton Rouge: Louisiana State University Press, 1981.

Koppelman, Robert S. *Robert Penn Warren's Modernist Spirituality.* Columbia: University of Missouri Press, 1995.

Light, James F., comp. *Studies in "All the King's Men."* Columbus, Ohio: Charles E. Merrill Publishing Company, 1971.

Longley, John L., Jr., ed. *Robert Penn Warren: A Collection of Critical Essays.* New York: New York University Press, 1965.

Millichap, Joseph R., ed. *Robert Penn Warren: A Study of the Short Fic-*

tion. Twayne Studies in Short Fiction, no. 39. New York: Twayne Publishers, 1992.

Moore, L. Hugh, Jr. *Robert Penn Warren and History.* The Hague, Netherlands: Mouton, 1970.

Nakadate, Neil, ed. *Robert Penn Warren: Critical Perspectives.* Lexington: University Press of Kentucky, 1981.

Runyon, Randolph Paul. *The Braided Dream: Robert Penn Warren's Late Poetry.* Lexington: University Press of Kentucky, 1990.

————. *The Taciturn Text: The Fiction of Robert Penn Warren.* Columbus: Ohio State University Press, 1990.

Ruppersburg, Hugh. *Robert Penn Warren and the American Imagination.* Athens: University of Georgia Press, 1990.

Strandberg, Victor H. *A Colder Fire: The Poetry of Robert Penn Warren.* Lexington: University of Kentucky Press, 1965.

————. *The Poetic Vision of Robert Penn Warren.* Lexington: University Press of Kentucky, 1977.

Walker, Marshall. *Robert Penn Warren: A Vision Earned.* Edinburgh, Scotland: Paul Harris Publishing, 1979.

Watkins, Floyd C. *Then and Now: The Personal Past in the Poetry of Robert Penn Warren.* Lexington: University Press of Kentucky, 1982.

Weeks, Dennis L., ed. *"To Love So Well the World": A Festschrift in Honor of Robert Penn Warren.* New York: Peter Lang Publishing, 1992.

Books Related to Robert Penn Warren

Cowan, Louise. *The Fugitive Group: A Literary History.* Baton Rouge: Louisiana State University Press, 1959.

Kallsen, Loren J., ed. *The Kentucky Tragedy: A Problem in Romantic Attitudes.* Indianapolis: Bobbs-Merrill Company, 1963. Background to *World Enough and Time.*

BIBLIOGRAPHY

Kington, Donald M. *Forgotten Summers: The Story of the Citizens' Military Training Camps, 1921–1940.* San Francisco: Two Decades Publishing, 1995. Background to the setting in which Warren published his first poem.

Merrill, Boynton, Jr. *Jefferson's Nephews: A Frontier Tragedy.* Princeton, N.J.: Princeton University Press, 1976. Background to *Brother to Dragons.*

Simpson, Lewis P. *The Brazen Face of History: Studies in the Literary Consciousness in America.* Baton Rouge: Louisiana State University Press, 1980.

———. *The Fable of the Southern Writer.* Baton Rouge: Louisiana State University Press, 1994.

———. *Mind and the American Civil War: A Meditation in Lost Causes.* Baton Rouge: Louisiana State University Press, 1989.

———, ed. *The Possibilities of Order: Cleanth Brooks and His Work.* Baton Rouge: Louisiana State University Press, 1976. Contains Warren's interview with Brooks.

Stewart, John L. *The Burden of Time: The Fugitives and Agrarians.* Princeton, N.J.: Princeton University Press, 1965.

Vanderwood, Paul J. *Night Riders of Reelfoot Lake.* Memphis: Memphis State University Press, 1969. Background for *Night Riders.*

Winchell, Mark Royden. *Cleanth Brooks and the Rise of Modern Criticism.* Charlottesville: University Press of Virginia, 1996. Provides insights into Warren's relationship with Brooks.

Woodward, C. Vann. *The Burden of Southern History.* Rev. ed. Baton Rouge: Louisiana State University Press, 1968.

Essays about Robert Penn Warren

Brooks, Cleanth. "Episode and Anecdote in the Poetry of Robert Penn Warren." *Yale Review* 70, no. 4 (Summer 1981): 551–67.

————. "R. P. Warren: Experience Redeemed in Knowledge." In *The Hidden God: Studies in Hemingway, Faulkner, Yeats, Eliot, and Warren,* 98–127. New Haven: Yale University Press, 1963.

Drake, Robert. "Robert Penn Warren's Enormous Spider Web." *Mississippi Quarterly* 48, no. 1 (Winter 1994–1995): 11–16.

Empson, William. "'The Ancient Mariner': An Answer to Warren." *Kenyon Review* 15, no. 1 (Winter 1993): 155–77.

Garrett, George. "Warren's Poetry: Some Things We Ought to Be Thinking About." *South Carolina Review* 23 (1990): 49–57.

Grimshaw, James A. "Robert Penn Warren's *Annus Mirabilis*." *Southern Review* 10, no. 2 (Spring 1974): 504–16.

————. "Strong to Stark: Deceiver, Demagogue, Dictator." *Texas College English* 23, no. 1 (Fall 1990): 17–22.

Hollander, John. "Modes and Ranges of a Long Dawn: Robert Penn Warren's Poetry." In *The Work of Poetry,* 271–79. New York: Columbia University Press, 1997.

Justus, James H. "The Power of Filiation in *All the King's Men*." In *Modern American Fiction: Form and Function,* edited by Thomas Daniel Young, 156–69. Baton Rouge: Louisiana State University Press, 1989.

————. "Warren's Later Poetry: Unverified Rumors of Wisdom." *Mississippi Quarterly* 37, no. 2 (Spring 1984): 161–71.

————. "Warren's *Terra*." *Mississippi Quarterly* 48, no. 1 (Winter 1994–1995): 133–46.

Law, Richard G. "*At Heaven's Gate*: The Fires of Irony." *American Literature* 53, no. 1 (March 1981):87–104.

Lewis, R. W. B. "The Great Dragon Country of Robert Penn Warren." *Southern Quarterly* 31, no. 4 (Summer 1993): 13–36.

————. "Robert Penn Warren's Canon of Precursors." In *Literary Reflections: A Shoring of Images, 1960–1993,* 259–91. Boston: Northeastern University Press, 1993.

BIBLIOGRAPHY

McCarron, Bill, and James Grimshaw. "Cicero's *De Senectute* and Warren's *Night Rider*." *Mississippi Quarterly* 50, no. 1 (Winter 1996–1997): 115–16.

Metress, Christopher. "Fighting Battles One by One: Robert Penn Warren's *Segregation*." *Southern Review* 32, no. 1 (Winter 1996): 166–71.

Miller, Mark Daniel. "Robert Penn Warren: On the Dark Side of Creation." *The Mind's Eye: A Liberal Arts Journal* (Massachusetts College of Liberal Arts) (Fall 1998): 5–23.

Newton, Thomas A. "A Character Index of Robert Penn Warren's Long Works of Fiction." *Emporia State Research Studies* 26, no. 3 (Winter 1978): 3–104.

Olney, James. "Parents and Children in Robert Penn Warren's Autobiography." In *Home Ground: Southern Autobiography,* edited by J. Bill Berry, 31–47. Columbia: University of Missouri Press, 1991.

Payne, Ladell. "Willie Stark and Huey Long: Atmosphere, Myth, or Suggestion?" *American Quarterly* 20 (Fall 1968): 580–95.

Perkins, James A. "Notes on an Unpublished Robert Penn Warren Essay." *Southern Review* 30, no. 4 (Autumn 1994): 650–57.

———. "Racism and the Personal Past in Robert Penn Warren." *Mississippi Quarterly* 48, no. 1 (Winter 1994–95): 73–82.

Quinn, Sister Bernetta, O.S.F. "Robert Penn Warren's Promised Land." *Southern Review* 8, no. 2 (Spring 1972): 329–58.

Shepherd, Allen. "Chief Joseph, General Howard, Colonel Miles: The Context of Characterization in Warren's *Chief Joseph of the Nez Perce*." *Mississippi Quarterly* 39, no. 1 (Winter 1985–1986): 21–30.

———. "The Craft of Salvage: Robert Penn Warren's 'God's Own Time' and Three Stories." *Kentucky Review* 2, no. 1 (1980): 11–19.

Simpson, Lewis P. "The Loneliness Artist: Robert Penn Warren." In *The Fable of the Southern Writer,* 132–54. Baton Rouge: Louisiana State University Press, 1980.

Smith, Dave. "Robert Penn Warren: The Use of a Word Like Honor." *Yale Review* 74, no. 4 (Summer 1985): 574–80.

BIBLIOGRAPHY

Spears, Monroe K. "The Critics Who Made Us: Robert Penn Warren." *Sewanee Review* 94, no. 1 (Winter 1986): 99–111.

Strandberg, Victor. "Warren's 'Worst' Book." *South Carolina Review* 23 (1990): 74–83.

Suarez, Ernest. "Toward a New Southern Poetry: Southern Poetry in Contemporary American Literary History." *Southern Review* 33, no. 1 (Winter 1997): 181–96. Focuses on the poetry of Warren and James Dickey.

Watkins, Floyd C. "Following the Tramp in Warren's 'Blackberry Winter.'" *Studies in Short Fiction* 22, no. 3 (Summer 1985): 343–45.

———. "Robert Penn Warren's Roman Poems: You and the Emperors." *Essays in Literature* (Macomb, Ill.) 10, no. 2 (Fall 1983): 255–62.

———. "The Ungodly in Robert Penn Warren's Biblical Poems." *Southern Literary Journal* 15, no. 3 (Fall 1983): 34–46.

Weaks, Mary Louise. "The Search for a 'Terra' in *A Place to Come To*." *Mississippi Quarterly* 37, no. 4 (Fall 1984): 455–68.

Winchell, Mark Royden. "A Place to Come From: The Nashville Agrarians and Robert Penn Warren." *Canadian Review of American Studies* 15, no. 2 (Summer 1984): 229–39.

———. "Renaissance Men: Shakespeare's Influence on Robert Penn Warren." In *Shakespeare and Southern Writers: A Study in Influence,* edited by Philip C. Kolin, 137–58. Jackson: University Press of Mississippi, 1985.

Young, Thomas Daniel. "*Brother to Dragons:* A Meditation on the Basic Nature of Man." *Mississippi Quarterly* 37, no. 2 (Spring 1984): 149–59.

Essays Related to Robert Penn Warren

Cobb, Len. "Night Riders Terrorized Tobacco Counties." *Winchester Sun,* Tobacco Harvest [19]80, pp.15–16.

Fincher, Jack. "Dreams of Riches Led Floyd Collins to a Nightmarish

End." *Smithsonian,* May 1990, 137–38, 140–42, 144–50. Background for *The Cave.*

Heilman, Robert B. "Baton Rouge and LSU Faculty Forty Years After." *Sewanee Review* 88 (Winter 1980): 126–43.

Jackson, Donald Dale. "When 20 Million Tons of Water Flooded Johnstown." *Smithsonian,* May 1989, 50–54, 56, 58–60. Background for *Flood.*

Lytle, Andrew. "Reflections of a Ghost: An Agrarian View after Fifty Years." *Southern Partisan* 4, no. 4 (Fall 1984): 16–17, 23–27.

MacIntyre, Alasdair. "Tradition and the Virtues." In *Vice and Virtue in Everyday Life: Introductory Readings in Ethics,* edited by Christina Sommers and Fred Sommers, 316–37. 4th ed. Fort Worth: Harcourt Brace College Publisher, 1997. A historical perspective on virtue and our "particular social identity."

Park, Edwards. "John Brown's Picture." *Smithsonian,* August 1997, 18, 20.

Rubin, Louis D., Jr. "The Gathering of the Fugitives: A Recollection." *Southern Review* 30, no. 4 (Autumn 1994): 658–73.

Wood, Ralph C. "Flannery O'Connor, H. L. Mencken, and the Southern Agrarians: A Dispute over Religion More Than Region." *Flannery O'Connor Bulletin* 20 (1991): 1–21.

Bibliographies

Eller, Jonathan R., and C. Jason Smith. "Robert Penn Warren: A Bibliographical Survey, 1986–1993." *Mississippi Quarterly* 48, no. 1 (Winter 1994–1995): 169–94.

Grimshaw, James A., Jr. "Bibliographical Trends in Warren Criticism: The 1980s." *Southern Quarterly* 31, no. 4 (Summer 1993): 51–67.

———. "Robert Penn Warren." In *Bibliography of United States Literature, 1919–1988.* Edited by Judith G. Haig et al., 522–26. Columbia, S.C.: Bruccoli Clark Layman, Gale, 1991.

BIBLIOGRAPHY

————. "Robert Penn Warren." In *First Printings of American Authors.* Edited by Matthew J. Bruccoli and C. E. Frazer Clark I, 401–6. Detroit: Bruccoli Clark Gale Research, 1977.

————. *Robert Penn Warren: A Descriptive Bibliography, 1922–1979.* Charlottesville: University Press of Virginia, 1981.

Huff, Mary Nance. *Robert Penn Warren: A Bibliography.* New York: David Lewis, 1968.

Nakadate, Neil. *Robert Penn Warren: A Reference Guide.* Boston: G. K. Hall, 1977.

INDEX

Page numbers in bold type denote extended discussion.

INDEX

INDEX